THAT FAVOURITE RESORT

THAT FAVOURITE RESORT

The story of Bray, Co. Wicklow

Mary Davies

Mary Davies

Word*well*

First published in 2007
Wordwell Ltd
PO Box 69, Bray, Co. Wicklow

Cover design: Wordwell Ltd

ISBN-10: 1-86985785-2
ISBN-13: 978-1-86985785-1

British Library Cataloguing-in-Publication Data.
A catalogue record for this book is available from the British Library.

This publication has been funded under the Heritage Council's 2006 Publication Grant Scheme.
Thanks are also due to Bray Town Council for its support.

Editor: Mary Davies.

Book design: Alicia McAuley, Nick Maxwell.

Modern photographs by the author.

Text maps by Sarah Gearty.

Printed by Graficas Castuera, Pamplona.

LANCASHIRE & YORKSHIRE RAILWAY
Via Liverpool & Northwall; Via Holyhead & Northwall
BEAUTIFUL·BRAY
QUEEN OF IRISH WATERING PLACES
GATE OF COUNTY WICKLOW
"THE LOVELY GARDEN OF IRELAND"
12 MILES SOUTH OF DUBLIN OPPOSITE HOLYHEAD
BRAY
BREEZY & BRACING
CLIMATE PERFECT · SCENERY UNRIVALLED
GRAND MARINE PROMENADE A MILE LONG
FREE BATHING·GOLF·CRICKET·GAMES·FISHING
YACHTING·BOATING·MILITARY BANDS·CONCERTS
FREE GUIDE ETC FROM TOWN CLERK

To the dedicated local historians, past and present,
who keep the story of Bray alive.
And for Kelvin and Lyell.

Contents

Preface 9
Introduction: Liam Clare 11

Prologue: The scene is set 14

PART I: MANOR VILLAGE AND BUDDING TOWN
1. 'Our manor of Bree': Bray 1173–1311 29
2. 'In continual fear of like mischief': Bray 1311–1666 41
3. More settled times: Bray 1666–1760 54
4. 'A very small town': Bray in 1760 64

PART II: THAT FAVOURITE RESORT
5. 'Sea bathing and goat's whey': Bray 1760–1850 79
6. 'A favourable bathing place': Bray in 1850 110
7. 'The Brighton of Ireland': Bray 1850–70 140
8. 'All the advantages': Bray in 1870 184
9. 'This delightful locality': Bray 1870–1910 210
10. 'Bray, beautiful Bray': Bray in 1910 253
11. Buckets and spades: Bray 1910–1970 274

Postscript: Bray reinvented 1970–2006 305

Bibliography 315
Index 325

Bray from Bray Head.

Preface

For over a hundred years, starting in the 1850s, Bray attracted holiday makers both from all parts of Ireland and from across the Irish Sea. During this same period enjoyment of the seaside gradually changed from prim bathing, sedate walks and genteel attendance at band performances to the altogether freer pleasures of the mid twentieth century. But although Bray is often thought of as a creation of the Victorian age, this is only one part of the lengthy story of the town. For long centuries it was a small village centred on a church, castle and mill, uncomfortably sited on the dangerous margin of the area of English influence in Ireland. In the late eighteenth and early nineteenth centuries it blossomed into a successful resort, catering for invalids and for those seeking fresh air away from grimy Dublin, and forming a base for visitors to the beauty spots of Wicklow. This existing resort role was a factor in the deliberate choice of the town for development when the railway was built in the 1850s. As a planned town — albeit one planned by businessmen rather than by a great landowner — Bray is one of a small distinctive group of Irish towns; as a major Irish holiday resort on the British pattern it has a character all its own. Although the general decline of the traditional seaside holiday after 1970 has changed Bray's role yet again, the lengthy Esplanade, the long straight roads and the grand late-nineteenth-century terraces and houses survive as a reminder of the town's special history.

This study is intended for all those who value this special history, including the many who have fond memories of holidays in Bray. The prologue and part I cover the early history up to 1760; the development of the resort from 1760 to 1970 is covered in part II, with a short postscript bringing the story up to the present. Digressions from the main narrative describe the appearance of Bray in 1760, 1850, 1870 and 1910. Numerous original text extracts have been included to convey the flavour of the times and as a source for further studies; these are fully referenced and there is an extensive bibliography.

For its size, Bray has a large number of enthusiastic local historians, and my thanks go to all those who have published books and articles over the years and who for reasons of space have not had their work individually cited here. Part of the material used in this study was originally collected for *Irish historic towns atlas no. 9 Bray*, published by the Royal Irish Academy in 1998, and those who gave freely of their expertise then again deserve credit. Special thanks are due to Andrew Bonar Law, Anne Denard, John Doyle, Cathal Duddy, Patrick Early, Michael Kelleher, Kathleen Kinsella, Brendan Martin, Jim Scannell and Brian White, and also to Rosemary Brown, Robert Butler, Norman Colin, Saive Coffey, Ray Cranley, Rachel Dunne, John and Elinor Medlycott, Canon Richard Rountree and Janet Sheehy.

Much use was made of the records at Killruddery House, and my grateful thanks go to the late earl of Meath, the present earl and the family. The late Joe Loughman was for many years an encouraging presence, while Henry Cairns has given freely of his extensive photographic archive and made many helpful comments on the modern chapters.

Outside of Bray, I have to thank the Irish Historic Towns Atlas editors Anngret Simms, H.B. Clarke and Raymond Gillespie, and former colleagues in the Royal Irish Academy, particularly Siobhán Fitzpatrick, Anthony Harvey, Richard Hawkins, Angela Malthouse and Christopher Woods.

The following also deserve warm thanks: Terry Barry for comment on the medieval section, James Fairley for Bray items in *The World's Fair*, the Knight of Glin for a reference to goat's whey, Irene Furlong for information on twentieth-century tourism, Peter Harbison for the Beranger and Jones views, Patricia Kelly for help with seventeenth-century Irish, Donal Kivlehan for material from the Garda Museum, Bob Montgomery for a photograph of an early omnibus and Henry Peel, O.P., for access to the *Irish Ecclesiastical Record*; Malcolm Walker, Royal Meteorological Society, also gave assistance. Roisín Berry and Mary Sweeney transcribed newspaper entries in the National Library. In Britain Malcolm R. Shifrin was generous with information on Turkish baths and Alastair Durie and J.K. Walton provided useful pointers on the history of resorts. Thanks are also due to the Heritage Council for its interest in the publication.

Above all particular thanks go to J.H. Andrews for support and for many helpful comments, to Liam Clare for his introduction and for valuable comments based on his considerable local knowledge, to John O'Keefe for a meticulous reading of the text and not least to Sarah Gearty for finding time to draw the maps. Alicia McAuley has applied her particular skills to the page make-up. Finally, Nick Maxwell and the staff of Wordwell, themselves local to the Bray area, have been immensely supportive.

Introduction

by Liam Clare

Most inhabitants of Bray who have passed their fiftieth birthday, as well as former day-trippers from the city and holiday-makers from around the country, will have nostalgic memories of the days when Bray was still Ireland's premier seaside resort.

I have my own memories ...

... the buzz of activity heard when emerging onto the Strand Road from Albert Avenue, the 'times-of-the-tides' notice at the baths — would the waves be reaching the sea-wall, or would there be a strip of sand on which to play?, the big jump down from the broken steps to the sand below, the waves to be dodged on windy days, the warm sandy pools at low tide on calmer days, the stringy seaweed, crabs near Bray Head, an unexpected shoal of jelly fish as terrifying as sharks, hastily-constructed dams of wet sand to hold back the incoming tide, sandy socks, sunburnt skin, trunks wrapped in a towel on the journey home up Albert Avenue, ice-cold drips falling on your head from the railway bridge above ...

... the Fun Palace with the punch ball outside being battered by big men, the distorting mirror inside, Barry's deafening jukebox repeating over and over the hit of the day, Tofts' — later Gordon Hunt's amusements, the dodgems, the hobby-horses, the swing-boats, Jean, Claud and Nadine in the Globe of Death, rolling a penny, the rifle ranges, the ghost train, bucking-bronco bikes, pongo, later bingo — yellow seventeen — blue sixty nine — check!, the fruit machines, the crane hovering tantalisingly over watches and other goodies — give the machine a thump ...

... Albert Walk, buckets and spades hanging above the shop doors, cartoon postcards, bog oak souvenirs, boiling water for sale, deck chairs, candy floss, soft whipped ice-cream cones, 'tuti-fruity north poles', Kennymore's honey-bee bars, manually-rolled Bray rock, Candelli's chips ...

... the Railway Buffet, the Sunshine Café's customers eating ice-cream out of 'silver' dessert dishes in the open air, the Venetian Café, 'Little Mezzas' on Albert Avenue, the kiosks, the putting green, the decrepit Victorian shelters, the purple-flowered hebe hedging, coloured lights along the Prom on late August evenings, the Ace of Clubs, the cliff walk, the Eagle's Nest, the chair lift, the Royal, the Roxy and Mac's cinemas ...

... Naylor's cove, Bray Cove Swimming Club, the rival Bray Swimming Club, the swimming galas, the Kilmartin Cup, Eddie Heron the high diver, water polo ...

... donkey rides, motor boats Congress and Erin, amphibious DUKWs rolling down the beach and into the sea, rowing boats, pedal boats ...

... the boat house, the photograph shop, tourists around the window scanning the photographs taken the day before, the photographer outside snapping the crowds and handing out cards, "prints ready within twenty-four hours" ...

... the baths, the promenade behind it privatised during each day, old people sitting on the benches along its wall, hundreds crowded in under the glass awning when it rained, the water fountain out in front, Scraggs' buses lining up for trips to Glendalough and the Vale of Avoca, vis-à-vis open horse-drawn carriages for sightseers, closed cabs for the more inhibited, the jaunting cars at the railway station ...

... Punch and Judy on the esplanade, George Daniel's Road Show, céilís for tourists in Fatima House, Duffy's Circus ...

... day-trippers ten deep behind the closed railway gates waiting to surge down to the Esplanade, others pouring out of the station by the door under the bridge on Albert Avenue, picnic parties all over the grass, long queues for the toilets, longer bus queues at the boat house for the journey home, children crying, piles of litter every Monday morning ... .

My concept of a holiday resort in those days was superficial and sketchy; I never thought about the geographic, economic, social and cultural pressures and processes which resulted in the physical features, the structures, the services, the personalities that combined to create a modern seaside resort. Neither did I anticipate the imminent demise of the tourist-centre role for the town.

Mary Davies in this work has combined her expertise as a geographer and as an historian to produce a valuable and comprehensive chronicle of the development of Bray through its successive roles as manor town, market town, seaside town and commuter town. She has capitalised on her unique knowledge of the town, previously demonstrated when she was author of *Bray* in the *Irish historic towns atlas* series. In her current work she gives life to the various documents, maps and statistics which form the raw materials of local history.

General readers, as well as amateur historians, who are interested in the town of Bray in particular, or in the social phenomenon of holidays-by-the-sea in general, will find her images and descriptive passages of the town during its various creations and its successive physical developments, both immeasurably intriguing and immensely interesting. Research students, seeking to push back the frontiers of knowledge about Bray even further, can confidently work on the basis of using a combination of her Bray atlas and this book.

It is truly a comprehensive well-researched resource, which will stand the test of time. Indeed it will survive as a source book for students of Bray's history, geography, architecture, physical planning and development, for as long a period as Canon Scott's classic work *The stones of Bray* did throughout the twentieth century.

Prologue

The scene is set

'This highly-favoured seaside resort was half a century ago the habitation of a few fishermen; but now the site where their huts once stood is crowded with handsome villas, and the lonely beach of those times has been transformed into a magnificent esplanade, where in the summer evenings numbers of fashionably-dressed people are to be seen sitting and walking about enjoying the bracing sea breeze. A band plays several evenings during the week, adding much to the pleasure of a stroll or quiet sit-down on the esplanade. The town is pretty, and contains some fine shops, where everything needful can be purchased, and the shore is all that can be desired for boating & bathing purposes.'
(*Irish Tourist*, vol. i, no. 3, 1894, p. 68)

Two hundred years ago as sailing ships made their way into Dublin, their passengers had little reason to rest their gaze on Bray. When they looked at the shore beside the rocky landmark of Bray Head there was only a long, shingly beach with a few thatched cottages scattered along its length. They might just have picked out the insignificant shapes of a few bathing huts clustered at the north end, not far from the masts of the small schooners moored in the mouth of the Dargle River. Behind, barely visible across the fields, were the irregular roofs of Bray's main street.

Some fifty years later, after the railway was opened in 1854, the passengers on the new steamships would have found the view more intriguing as they contemplated an expanse of new houses, some completed, some half-built, spreading along the shoreline. Puffs of smoke from waiting steam trains marked the whereabouts of the railway station just behind the substantial bulk of Bray's first sea-front hotel. A few years more, and they would have seen a fine sea wall catching the light and an esplanade thronged with holiday-makers, and perhaps heard the distant sound of band music.

Bray thus underwent an amazing transformation in the middle years of the nineteenth century, one that has left it to this day with an ambience all

0.1. Postcard showing Bray from Bray Head in the 1930s — virtually all the buildings visible were built after 1854.

its own. Having grown from its small beginnings as a medieval village to become an eighteenth-century watering place, the town blossomed over the space of a few years into Ireland's most important seaside resort — a role it was to fulfil for a hundred and twenty years. But the path was not a smooth one, and at the start of the twenty-first century Bray's prosperity is probably more secure than it ever was in the days when it boasted of being 'the Brighton of Ireland'.

Climatically Bray lies just within one of the most-favoured parts of Ireland, the south-eastern area with lowest rainfall and warmest summers — advantageous for a holiday resort. Its setting in north-eastern County Wicklow, twelve miles south of Dublin, offers all the benefits of attractive mountain and coastal scenery, with the rounded granite summits of the Dublin and Wicklow mountains forming a backdrop to low hills nearer the Irish Sea. The smoothly-curved upland landscapes are made dramatic by ice-age features such as the deeply-gouged mountain valleys with their waterfalls and the abrupt V-shaped gorges of the Scalp and the Glen of the Downs. Resistant quartzite rocks help to form the crenellated crest of Bray Head, sometimes evocatively likened to a cock's comb. The same shining quartzites form the two imposing peaks of the Great Sugar Loaf and Little Sugar Loaf to the south of Bray, once picturesquely known as the Giltspurs.

From the mid-eighteenth century the spectacular mountain scenery of Wicklow attracted visitors, many of whom stayed in Bray's much-praised Quin's Hotel, forerunner of the Royal Hotel. But proximity to the mountains had not always been an advantage — in the medieval period they were feared

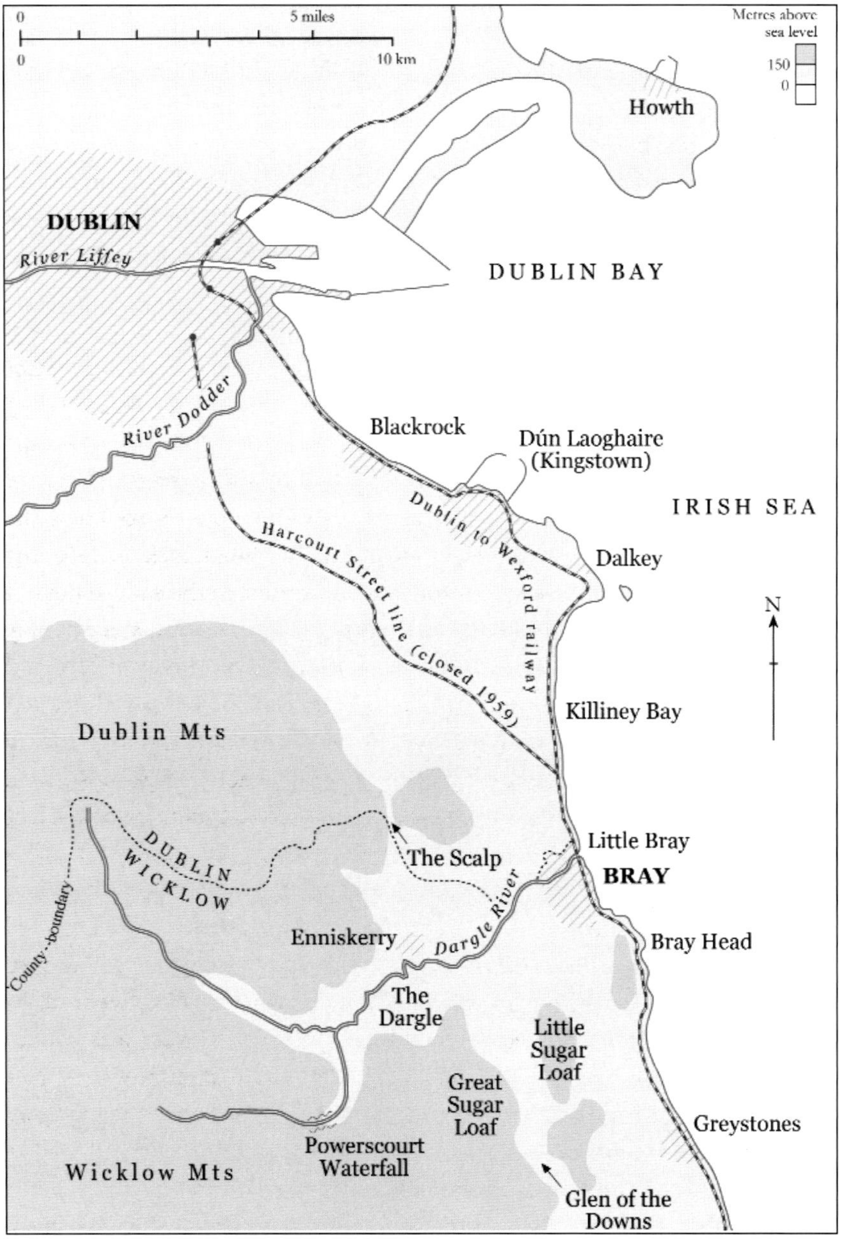

0.2. *Bray in its setting — near to Dublin and with all the benefits of attractive mountain and coastal scenery.*

for sheltering rebel groups, peoples displaced from the lowlands, who survived by making periodic raids on the settled lands near the sea. Bray lost crops and animals many times and its houses were burnt at least once.

Along the coast a thick layer of glacial boulder clays mantles the underlying rock, a spread that extends from Killiney Hill in the north to Bray Head, and again on the south side of the Head to Greystones and beyond. In addition to the boulder clays, the shore just north of the Dargle estuary retains one unusual reminder of the last Ice Age — the remnant of a forest that lies submerged close to low water mark. Its ancient pine trunks, visible at lowest tides and dating from some 7,000 years ago, bear witness to an era when sea levels were lower than today.

The boulder clay cliffs along the shore are soft and yielding, a prey to coastal erosion. After many attempts to stabilise the cliffs, the railway track north of Bray had to be moved inland in 1917 and recently the coastal walk between Bray Head and Greystones has been threatened — one estimate before the newly-completed restoration work was that ground was being lost at a rate of four metres a year. Raked by easterly gales, Bray Head is subject to rock falls; the railway line here, built with much effort through solid rock to skirt the headland, also required diversion through a new tunnel in the early 1900s.

The ravages of the sea have played a large part in the recent story of Bray itself, with waves washing over the sea front in stormy weather and inundating houses and gardens. Once this affected only poor fishermen families in their cottages along the strand, and warranted no more than a charitable collection on their behalf; when expensive houses bordered Strand Road the town commissioners were eventually forced to build the sea wall at considerable cost, placing a serious burden upon the ratepayers. Today, a hundred years on, extensive new coastal protection measures have again been necessary. At the same time the attitude to the sea, like the attitude to the mountains, has changed from fear to enjoyment. The sea, too, was once seen as a hostile, unpredictable place, infested with monsters, where lives were regularly lost in shipwrecks and where fishermen made a hard and precarious living. It was also lawless, the realm of pirates and smugglers. This view was replaced in the eighteenth century by the belief that sea bathing strengthened the body and, as time went on, by the view that the shore is a place for healthy pleasures — swimming, boating, sunbathing.

Bray's link between the mountains and the sea is the Dargle River, formerly in its lower reaches called the Bray River or Bray Water. The Dargle rises at a height of 650 metres above sea level, tumbles spectacularly over the Powerscourt Waterfall and forces its way past massive boulders down the

0.3. *Bray Head, Little Sugar Loaf and Great Sugar Loaf dominate the skyline beyond Bray in this bird's eye view of 1848; Killiney Hill is in the foreground (part of T.R. Harvey's* Panoramic view of the county of Wicklow ...*).*

Dargle Glen, once a much-prized beauty spot, to reach lower ground. The river waters mingle with the salt waters of the Irish Sea near Bray Bridge, and the bridge marks the high point of medium tides.

Over its last miles to the sea the Dargle has carved out a low-lying flood plain, shifting its course over the centuries from the north side of its valley to the south. The cliffs along the Upper Dargle Road mark the limits of its northern swing; those below the old St Paul's Church in Bray and the gardens of Herbert Road its southern one. On the northern bank the flood plain remained common land until enclosed in the 1860s, but on the south Bray's medieval corn mill and its successors used the strip of land beneath St Paul's, today's site of The Maltings housing estate.

Inevitably the Dargle valley has been subject to floods, worst when cloudbursts in the mountains coincide with high tides driven onshore by easterly winds. The river itself has been both an advantage and a disadvantage to Bray. On the one hand, for eight hundred years it supplied water power for the mill, while the harbour in its shallow estuary was shelter for small trading ships and coastal fishing boats. On the other hand, the river formed a barrier for many centuries between Bray and the Dublin area, and after County Wicklow was created in 1606 the Dublin/Wicklow boundary followed part of its course. Indeed it created a division between the two parts of Bray itself: 'Great Bray', 'Much Bray' or 'Big Bray' (the last still a familiar term) south of the river and Little Bray to the north. Until the first bridge was built in the 1660s Bray and Little Bray were linked only by a ford, which was never easy to cross and could be positively dangerous at high tide or after heavy rain. And thanks to the line of demarcation created by the Dargle, Little Bray has always had a distinct personality, evident even after its incorporation into Bray Townshp in 1866.

Bray's immediate setting is a combination of the various elements — ancient resistant rocks, flat coastal deposits and, not least, the Dargle and its

0.4. *The Dargle River has always formed a line of demarcation between 'Great' Bray and Little Bray, and until the 1660s the two were linked only by a dangerous ford. The present bridge, shown in this postcard view of* c. *1900, is the third on the site.*

cliffs. Main Street, representing the older part of the town, curves gently uphill from Bray Bridge towards the south-west, to reach the 'Rock of Bray' on which Christ Church and the Loreto Convent stand forty metres or so above sea level. Victorian Bray lies mainly below the ten-metre contour on the flat boulder clays near the sea that made its development so easy. And it was the riverside cliffs overlooking the lowest fording point of the Dargle that were chosen in about the year 1173 as the site of the first settlement that can be given the name Bray — the manor village established by the newly-arrived Anglo-Normans.

The Anglo-Normans were not, of course, the first settlers in the Bray area — the region had been lived in for many thousands of years. But only tantalising traces survive of these early lives, with a scattering of earthworks, burial sites and standing stones in the wider area. Remains dating back at least to the Bronze Age (2300 to 600 B.C.) have been found during recent archaeological work on the western side of Bray Head and the lower slopes of the Little Sugar Loaf.

These farming peoples began the first clearances in the landscape and left behind burnt mounds, which may be cooking sites, and scatters of flint from the manufacture and use of stone tools. They would have fished in the Dargle and gathered shellfish along the strand. And they could raise their eyes to the distinctive peak of the Great Sugar Loaf, which provided an important religious focal point for a wide area.

Gazing from a height, on clear days these early residents could see across the Irish Sea to the distant mountain peaks on the far shore, a reminder that there was another land to the east, inhabited by other peoples with whom to communicate and trade. In the mid first century B.C. word must have filtered across of the arrival of Julius Caesar in Britain and within a few generations the people of the Bray area were to meet Romans — or at least Romano-Britons, born in Britain but living in Roman style — in the flesh. At one time there was a firm belief that the Romans never set foot in Ireland; today it is recognised that Ireland had links with Roman Britain, possibly even with the wider Roman Empire. And Bray is one of the places where evidence of this link has been found.

In 1835 several skeletons — the exact number is not recorded — were unearthed on Bray sea front, roughly on the site of the two most northerly houses of the present Esplanade Terrace, between Victoria Avenue and Convent Avenue. The bodies had been interred in neat Roman-style graves accompanied by coins of the emperors Trajan (A.D. 97–117) and Hadrian (A.D. 117–138). The graves were found when foundations were being prepared for new gateposts at the strand entrance to Sans Souci, today's Loreto Convent, which then belonged to George Putland and had grounds extending right down to the shore — the sea front was not yet built up and there was only a stony storm beach between the fields and the water. (The approach of Putland's drive to the beach is clear on the 1870 Ordnance Survey map and can still be traced; when the railway embankment was built the path was provided with a pedestrian tunnel, now closed off but still visible.) When the burials were discovered the site lay some 85 metres west of the high-water mark, but the coastline would have been different in Roman times and they may originally have been further from the sea.

0.5. *Part of Esplanade Terrace — built on the site of the Roman-style burials unearthed in 1835.*

DISCOVERY OF ROMAN ARTEFACTS ON GEORGE PUTLAND'S ESTATE

> *'A few years ago G. Putland, Esq., of Bray, had occasion to build piers for a gate contiguous to the sea beach, on the north side of Bray Head. His workmen, on digging for a foundation, were surprised to meet with the skeletons of several human bodies, which on further examination, they found to be placed, not confusedly heaped together, as the slain on a battlefield, but in graves placed regularly side by side, and separated each from its neighbour, by thin partitions of flag or stone. On the exposure to the air, the bones crumbled to atoms; the teeth alone were more durable, and in tolerable preservation. The most remarkable circumstance connected with these skeletons was a number of Roman copper coins, one or two of which lay on or beside the breast of each. Of these coins, which were about the size of our penny pieces, some bore the image and superscription of Adrian, and others those of Trajan, in clear and distinct relief.'*
> (W.H. Drummond, note in *Proceedings of the Royal Irish Academy*, vol. ii, 1841, pp 186–7)

Perhaps Romano-British traders landed briefly on the shore at Bray in the second century A.D. and buried their dead; perhaps, as Canon G.D. Scott surmised in his classic *The stones of Bray*, the graves were those of shipwrecked sailors. Or it may be that the graves were those of voyagers from Britain who settled for a while, and that other graves have either been destroyed or still lie buried beneath the houses and gardens of Strand Road. The fate of the Roman coins found in 1835 is unknown; there is no record that George Putland did other than keep them for himself.

Any effect Roman customs and beliefs may conceivably have had on the peoples of the Bray area did not last, but a few centuries later a far more powerful influence was to arrive across the Irish Sea with the coming of Christianity. Glendalough, tucked into its deep mountain valley sixteen miles (26 km) south-west of Bray, was to become one of Ireland's premier early-Christian monastic sites after its foundation in about 575 A.D. Two hundred years later it was to become a prime target for Viking raiders when their longboats reached the seas around Ireland at the end of the eighth century. By this time the Uí Briúin Chualann were the Leinster people who ruled the coast and the mountain foothills around Bray in what is now south Dublin and north-east Wicklow.

The territory of the Uí Briúin Chualann was not an important one, cut off by the backbone of the mountains from the centres of power that had

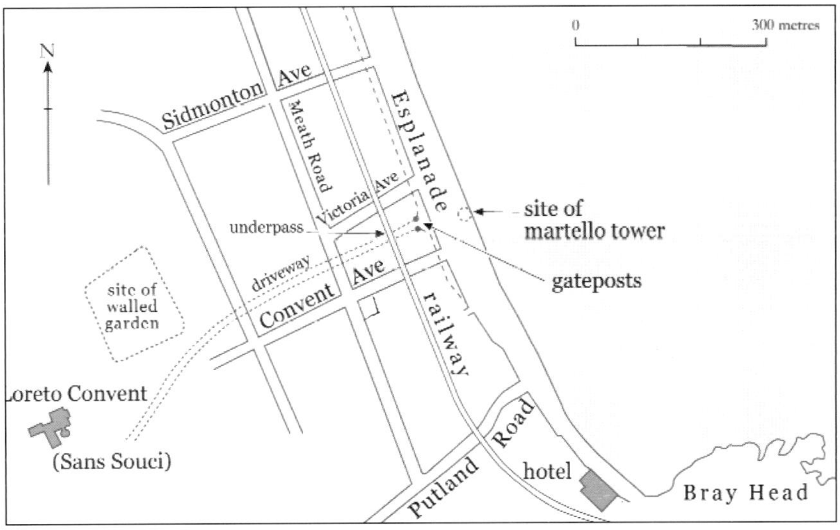

0.6. Location of George Putland's gateposts; the Roman graves were found when foundations were being dug.

developed in the rich farming areas of the present Counties Carlow and Kildare. The region was still heavily forested, there were extensive marshes and the rivers acted as barriers rather than as easy routes to be followed. It may be, though, that one of the abiding features of Bray, the line of the main road through the town, dates at least to this far back in time. The coastal way from the growing Liffey-side settlements of Gaelic Dublin to south-eastern Ireland may well have passed through Little Bray and crossed a ford near the present Bray Bridge — in the twentieth century Dublin Road in Little Bray was given the ancient road name Slí Chualann to commemorate this route. The curve of today's Main Street may reflect the road's course south of the Dargle.

Although Bray Head would have been a familiar navigation point, the Vikings seem to have taken little interest in the estuary of the Dargle River, probably already choked by a long sandspit not very different from the one shown on maps in the eighteenth century. The Vikings found good harbours at Arklow and Wicklow and penetrated far into east Wicklow. Under their control Dublin grew over the centuries into an important trading centre and they and their descendants settled as farmers in the surrounding region including the territory of the Uí Briúin Chualann. Viking influence and prosperity must surely have extended into the Bray area.

Bray's most substantial memorial to the period before the arrival of the Anglo-Normans, though, is the early-medieval church on the northern slopes of Bray Head just above Raheen Park. Raheenacluig (Ráithín an Chloig), the 'little rath of the bell', is a simple rectangular building, 38 feet long by 16 feet wide; the gable ends and some of the walls survive. There were once two smaller buildings close by, and slightly further away an enclosure that was probably a graveyard — this may have been quietly used over the centuries as a cillín, a burial ground for unbaptised infants.

Although its church bell must have sounded far across the Dargle, little is known of Raheenacluig's history, nor when it fell into disuse (although there is a suggestion that it may have been used during the time of the penal laws). Today it remains in a tranquil position, set in a wide expanse of gently sloping meadow and looking out over Bray towards magnificent views. The

***0.7.** Raheenacluig, the 'little rath of the bell', on the slopes of Bray Head.*

THE CHURCH AT RAHEENACLUIG

'The sites of two smaller buildings, close together, may be traced near it [Raheenacluig] on the east side, with a nearly choked trench running north and south between them and the church. The whole appears to have been enclosed by a moate, parts of which remain on the east and north east. Twenty eight yards south east of the church is a piece of ground enclosed by a trench and low mound, sixty yards long by twelve broad; two stones at the south east angle would seem to point to the place of a gate or entrance. Probably this was a graveyard … .

About a quarter of a mile south east of the church, in a hollow on the brink of the cliff and under the very nose of Bray Head, they shew a well called by some the Church Well, but by the older people Patrick's Well. It is still resorted to, but not much by invalids.'

(Eugene Curry, 27 December 1838, Ordnance Survey letters, County Wicklow)

Church Well, some distance to the south-east close to the cliff edge, was traditionally associated with St Patrick. The base of a cross with sculpted figures, found on the roadside south of Newtown Vevay and today in the grounds of Oldcourt House, may possibly also have some connection with Raheenacluig. In addition to Raheenacluig, there was probably already a similar church on the site of St Paul's. This may have been the 'church of Derdach' mentioned with various spellings in early documents together with 'the cottages of Derdach'. This church stood on a commanding cliff position overlooking the ford and the road to Dublin and there may already have been some settlement — perhaps even a ringfort — nearby. When the Anglo-Norman settlers arrived in the late twelfth century it was to be at the heart of the manor of Bray. The territory that was to become the manor was part of the lands of Uí Briúin Chualann granted in about the year 1173 to one of the knights of the conquering Richard de Clare, better known as Strongbow. The grant was a reward for distinguished service in the capture of Dublin in September 1170 and the knight was Sir Walter de Ridelesford.

Bray from martello tower no. 3.

PART I

Manor village and budding town

Chapter 1

'Our manor of Bree': Bray 1173–1311

'12 November 1207. Grant and confirmation to the convent of St. Mary of Grane and the nuns there ... [from] Walter de Ridelesford, namely ... all benefices of churches and chapels in his barony of Bre, namely the churches of Derdac, Kilmohud, and Kilescosather; the tithes of his mill of Bre ... .' (*Calendar of documents relating to Ireland, 1171–1251*, London, 1875, p. 53)

Bray was almost a blank canvas when the Anglo-Normans arrived. Sir Walter de Ridelesford or his agent must have stood on the cliff top some twelve metres above the level of the river, perhaps close to the old early-medieval church, and just possibly on the site of an older defensive site, and surveyed the scene through 360 degrees, looking for a suitable spot to establish a manorial village in his new territory. The most dramatic — and perhaps threatening — view lay to the west, the source of the river that winded its

***1.1.** The cliffs alongside the Dargle are largely obscured today by vegetation and new housing on the flood plain. St Paul's Church on the high ground is probably on the site of the first church in Bray.*

way at the viewer's feet, where low wooded hills merged gradually into the forbidding shapes of the mountains. To the north were more low hills and the route to Dublin. To the east was the sparkling sea, perhaps giving the comfort of knowing that beyond lay the settled lands from which the incomers had set out. The long shingle beach would have been out of sight, but Bray Head and the two Sugar Loaf peaks closed the views over rising ground to the south.

WALTER DE RIDELESFORD

Walter de Ridelesford came to Ireland from England in 1171 as one of Strongbow's supporters. He was well-connected, having married Amicia, granddaughter of King Henry I; they had three children, Walter, Basilia and Hakut. The original grant made to him by Strongbow on behalf of the crown seems to have encompassed a wide area in the lands of the Úi Bruíun Cualann, but the grant was more narrowly interpreted by King John, who confirmed a much smaller area around Bray to Walter junior when he inherited his father's lands in about 1200. The name de Ridelesford was to have only a short connection with Bray. It ended in 1239 when the second Walter died without a son and his properties were inherited by his infant granddaughter, Christiana de Marisco. The name was only revived in the last part of the twentieth century, when a new housing estate off the Southern Cross route was called 'Riddlesford'.

Under its accretions of fields and buildings, the bones of the landscape are basically still the same today. The course of the Dargle River, though, has changed over the centuries, probably a number of times, and we cannot know exactly where the river flowed in the twelfth century. The first Anglo-Normans would have looked down at low-lying marshy ground, perhaps with the river flowing close below the cliff. The river estuary, too, was very different. Downstream the newcomer would have seen a wide, shallow tidal stretch with an irregular outline and with gravel banks in midstream breaking the flow. The view out to sea was probably already blocked by a gravelly spit that turned the river waters southwards and made entry for boats difficult.

The choice of a site for the focal point of the new manor may have been swayed by the proximity of the church, but the main factor would have been the practicality of crossing the river. The site of the present Bray bridge is also presumably the site of the earlier ford, at the lowest crossing point of the

1.2. *The site of Bray's original mill and its later successors, now occupied by modern housing, as seen from Bray Bridge.*

Dargle. It was not ideal, for it must have been impassable at high tide even then, as it was later, and the road sloped steeply upwards away from the river on the south side. But the combination of what seemed a good defensive site above the cliffs with the need to protect a ford on what was already an established route were decisive. Bray had its first beginnings on the cliff-top looking down over the river, centred on the area now bounded by Main Street, Herbert Road, the Dargle, and, to the west, roughly the vicinity of the present Herbert Road car-park.

Bray came into being in the last decades of the twelfth century, soon after de Ridelesford took possession of the manor in about 1173 and the name 'Bre' (brí, a hill), apparently applied to the settlement rather than to Bray Head, appears for the first time in about 1180. This was when Walter de Ridelesford granted property in Bray to the newly-founded St Thomas's Abbey, south of the River Liffey in Dublin city; he also made grants to the Convent of St Mary's, Graney, County Kildare. Bray would have been a typical manorial village, one of many similar small settlements scattered over the newly-acquired parts of Ireland. The manor was the basic land division of the Anglo-Normans, a relatively self-sufficient unit with farmland, common land and wood; its owner, the 'lord of the manor', had an administrative centre, a village where the three key buildings were usually the church, the castle and the corn mill. This was the case in Bray.

We know nothing of the appearance of Bray's Anglo-Norman church. Perhaps the pre-Norman church was extended to serve as a parish church, as happened elsewhere; perhaps a new more substantial church was built to satisfy the aspirations of the new settlement. At any rate the building was probably still a simple stone rectangle with a bell tower on the east end. On the whole it can be assumed, though not proven, that it lay on the site of the present St Paul's Church.

The mill, too, has to be imagined. Mentioned in a grant of 1207, it lay at the bottom of the cliffs, slightly upstream of the church and where it could be protected by the castle. The position of the mill-wheel, the mill-race and the weir probably did not change much over the centuries, so we know its location. The mill building would have been sturdy, probably built of wood and with a thatched roof, and the miller would have had his house nearby. A steep path west of the churchyard, known from much later, probably already linked the mill with the top of the cliffs.

The third key building was the castle, one of very many built in Ireland at this time, just as a century before the invading Normans had built similar strongholds across England. Although it is known that Bray's Anglo-Norman castle must have been built soon after de Ridelesford took possession of the manor, there is no direct evidence as to its appearance; this has to be guessed at from comparable castles elsewhere. Unlike the great stone castles built by powerful lords at strongholds such as Trim and Kilkenny, or Dublin Castle itself, this first castle in Bray was almost certainly a modest affair of earth and timber — a motte, or motte-and-bailey.

The motte typically had a wooden tower, the residence of the lord, on top of a flat-topped mound, surrounded by an earthern rampart and a deep ditch. A second enclosure, the bailey, with its own rampart and ditch, protected the other buildings necessary to the heart of the manor such as stables, storehouses and barns. We have to assume that Bray's first castle was something along these lines. It may well have stood upon a rocky protuberance; certainly it commanded fine views and must have been a prominent feature in the landscape — a fitting reminder to the local populace of the power of Sir Walter de Ridelesford and his entourage.

There is no certainty as to exactly where this castle stood. But there are pieces of useful evidence. It is possible to work backwards from Jonathan Barker's map of 1762, discussed in Chapter 4, which shows the later stone castle, Great Bray Castle, itself destroyed before the first accurate maps, and make the reasonable assumption that the first castle stood on much the same site. This places the castle south-west of St Paul's Church, close to the much

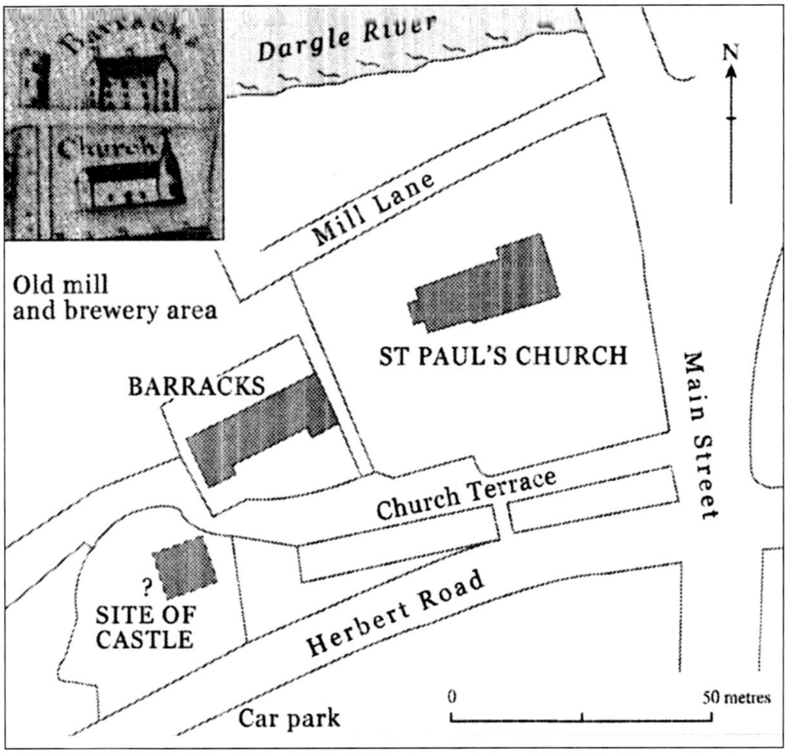

1.3. Probable site of Great Bray Castle. Inset: part of Barker's map of 1762 (see Chapter 4).

later barracks. As it happens, just across from the barracks is one of the most distinctive property boundaries in Bray, a curving wall built upon an outcropping rock foundation and rising from Church Terrace to the level of the present Herbert Road gardens. Using Barker's map as a guide, the Ordnance Survey placed its antiquity symbol for the castle within this property boundary, and this seems as good a guess as any as to the location. A map attached to a mid-nineteenth-century rental shows the same curved boundary to a plot that is in every way unusually shaped, but this unit of land lost much of its identity when Herbert Road was laid out in 1858–9. Some of the masonry at the bottom of the curving wall has the appearance of great age — perhaps the very last trace in Bray of the town's Anglo-Norman origins.

Clustered around the church, mill and castle were the homes and workshops of the people of Bray. Here again, imagining how these looked and what daily life was like in medieval Bray is partly a matter of guesswork. But there are also flashes of illumination, some of them in legal documents, and in particular in two 'extents' of 1284 and 1311 which list the names and occupations of some of the inhabitants. The most important point is that Bray was more than just a village at this time; seen from present-day perspectives, it was what is now known as a 'rural borough'.

The grant of borough status meant that the residents had certain privileges. Under a Norman law, the law of Breteuil, each landholder or 'burgess' was granted a 'burgage holding' at a rent of one shilling a year, and also a share in the manor's common fields. The burgesses also had a right to a borough court to deal with local matters. On the debit side, they were liable to pay taxes to the state or the lord from time to time. A rural borough was the centre for the administration of the manor, but it was usually too small to have defensive walls and too unimportant to attract a religious order to its vicinity: Bray, indeed, had neither walls nor a religious house of any kind. Boroughs were established for various reasons, including the need to attract settlers from Britain. The larger ones — though perhaps not Bray — attracted craftsmen and tradesmen as well as the basic occupations of miller, baker and brewer.

South of Dublin, these new settlements established by the Anglo-Normans were mainly strung out along the coastal lowlands. There were boroughs at Shankill and Dalkey, while some dozen boroughs were established in what is now County Wicklow, of which the nearest to Bray would have been Newcastle Mackinegan, adjacent to the present village of Newcastle, and Wicklow town; there may also have been a borough at Powerscourt. Walter de Ridelesford's grant to St Thomas's Abbey in 1180 mentions a burgage, which shows that Bray had been granted borough status by that date.

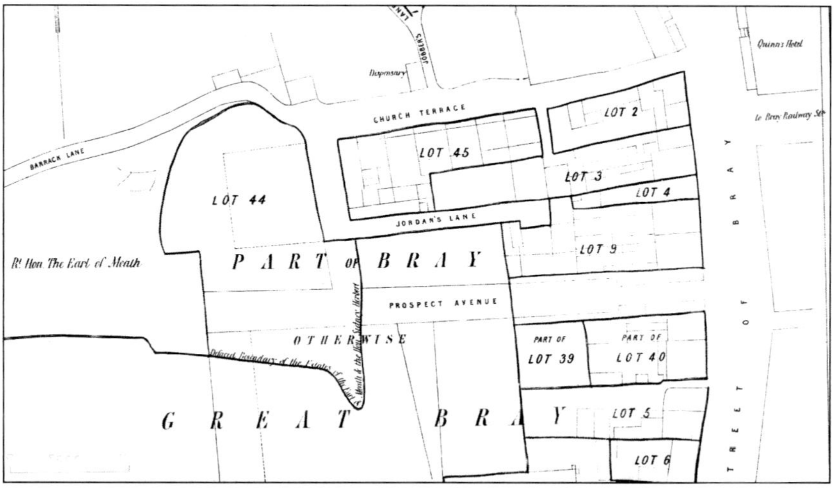

1.4. A rental of 1858 shows lot 44 as a strangely-shaped piece of land, which may represent the last traces of the castle's enclosure.

Another vital role associated with a borough was formally allocated to Bray on 26 July 1213, when King John granted de Ridelesford a weekly market on Thursdays 'in his vill of Bre'. A market day was essential if the infant settlement was to prosper as a local centre, and market tolls were a valuable additional source of income for the landowner. This regular market, although the day of the week varied over time, was to be held for eight hundred years, right through until the twentieth century. Much later it was based on the south side of the Dargle, roughly where the Heritage Centre is today, and this may well be its original location. It would have made the village a lively place, with farmers and their wives drawn in from a large area, and no doubt hucksters from Dublin supplying items not produced in Bray itself.

While the legal grants build up an impression of the framework within which Bray functioned, it is the two surviving documents of 1284 and 1311 that add life to the picture of these early years. By 1284 ownership had passed through several hands. Bray had been owned by the two Walter de Ridelesfords, father and son, and then by Christiana de Marisco; Christiana much later exchanged her Irish estates for land in England and in 1280–81 Bray became the property of the English Crown. The rents of Bray were listed in 1284 on behalf of Edward I. By 1290 the manor had been granted to Theobald le Botiller or Boteler of the Butler family of Kilkenny, soon to be earls of Ormond, and the 1311 survey is one of the accounts of Butler properties set out in *The Red Book of Ormond.* Both surveys were originally written in medieval Latin; although sometimes difficult to interpret, they are full of information about Bray a hundred or so years after its birth.

THEOBOLD BUTLER HOLDS BRAY

1290 *'Whereas Theobald [Boteler] holds of the King land* in capite *named Bree, in the county of Dublin, by the service of finding an armoured horse at the gate of the castle of Dublin when the King's service is summoned, the treasurer of Ireland converted this service into money, that is to say, 40s. where no money was ever given, no demand of money made, and his ancestors had rendered the service in the form aforesaid. Prays that he may render the service as his ancestors were wont to render it.'*
(*Calendar of documents relating to Ireland, 1285–92*, London, 1879, p. 315)

The castle is mentioned in 1284, while in 1311 there is a 'stone house' (*domus lapidea*), which may mean that the original timber motte had been rebuilt as a stone tower house — possibly the one that survived into the

1700s. 'Robert the baker' (or miller) has a holding 'under the castle' in 1284 for which he pays a rent of two shillings and four pence a year; in 1311 the mill itself is mentioned at a rent of forty shillings. A pound of pepper was paid as rent by Eustace Carrich in 1284, and the same by 'John the cook' in 1311.

RENTS OF BRAY, 1284

From the Master of the Templars, for 1/2 carucate of land, which he claims to hold by charter, 1 mark; from the same, for a tenement which John Lissebon held, 1 mark; from the same, for the tenement of J. de Howth, 11s. 3d.;
Adam Galbaynach and Elias his brother, 19s. 2d.;
Eustace Carrich, 1 lb of pepper or 12d.;
The burgage of Bray, 31s.
Cottages and autumnal works, 4s. 8d.;
The cottages of Derdach, 2s. 3d.;
1/2 carucate of land held by William le Deveneys, 60s.;
John Clement, for land held to farm, as is said, 17s. 10d.;
Nicholas Andrew for 1/2 carucate of land, 60s.; from the same, for 3 1/2 acres, 2s. 4d.;
Robert the baker, for 20 acres, 20s.; from the same, for a tenement under the castle, 28d.;
Walter de Belinges, for 149 acres of arable land, £7. 9s.; from the same, for a park, 6s. 8d.;
Sir John, the father, for a fishery, 1/2 mark;
For 7 acres of meadow, 8s. 2d.; from John Clement, for 1/2 carucate of land, 1/2 mark.
Total, £21. 15s. 8d.
(*Calendar of documents of Ireland, 1252–84*, p. 560)

There were thirty-one burgage plots in 1284 and one more in 1311 — these holdings and their dwellings would have been the core of the village. This was a highly respectable number, showing that Bray was a settlement of some size, much larger than many of its contemporary boroughs. There were also the 'cottages of Derdach' listed in 1284, perhaps the same as the eight cottages listed in 1311. There were other cottages in 1284 linked with 'autumnal works', probably a form of annual harvest duties.

Another very long-lasting feature of Bray now mentioned for the first time was the salmon and sea trout fishery in the Dargle and its estuary; in

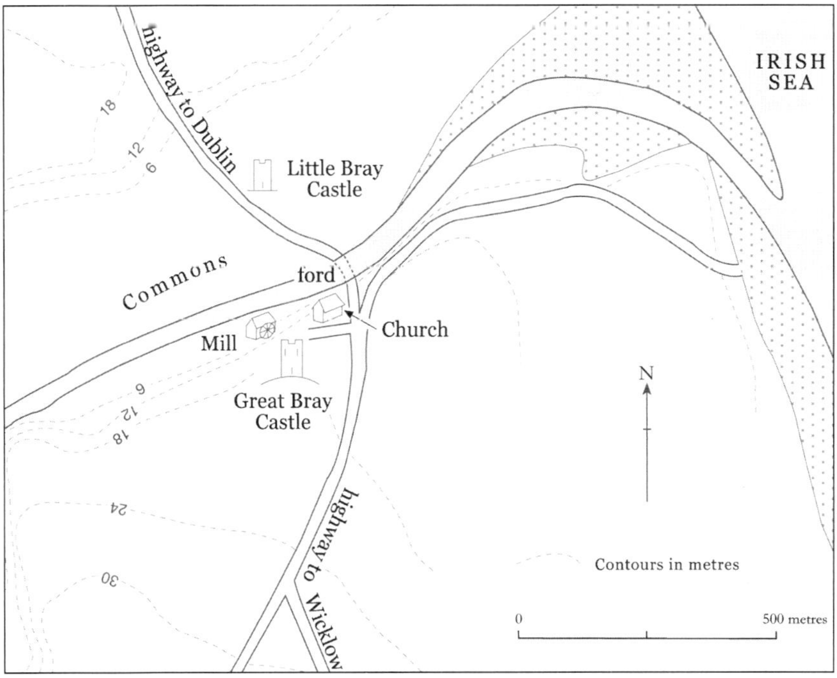

1.5. Bray in medieval times (contours from Irish Historic Towns Atlas no. 9, Bray, *fig. 1).*

later years it was to be closely associated with the mill. In 1284 the fishery was held by 'Sir John, the father', Bray's priest (the second for whom we have a name — his predecessor in 1272 was Philip Mackagan). Beyond the houses lay areas of arable and meadow; there was a sixty-acre deer park enclosed with a ditch and common land with grazing rights for one hundred sheep. As for the people of Bray in 1284, some of the landholders' names are recorded, all of them male. The rental list is brief: John Lissebon, J. de Howth, Adam and Elia Galbaynach, Eustace Carrich, William le Deveneys, John Clement, Nicholas Andrew, Robert the baker, Walter de Belinges, Sir John the father.

The survey of 1311 is set out differently. It begins by listing the names of twelve persons who swore that the information for the manor was correct — presumably these reputable gentlemen would have been burgage holders. Two of these — Nicholas Andrew (*Nicholaum Andree*) and Robert the miller/baker (*Robertum pistorem*) — are the same as twenty-seven years previously. In the main part of the survey the same Nicholas Andrew and John the cook are listed as free tenants, Robert son of Radulf and Richard McEthenard are 'firmarii', that is farmers who leased land for a fixed term. Three men with native Irish surnames — Robert McKerny, Gilcrist McGylmoy and John McGylmoy — are of the lowest ranking 'betagii', who were essentially serfs, tied to the land and its owner. There were nearly fifty households altogether, which would give a population of perhaps two hundred or more.

The surveys provide the bare bones of our knowledge of Bray in the thirteenth and early fourteenth centuries; the rest is guesswork. It is an obvious guess that the village of Bray, the heart of the manor, was focussed on the church, castle and mill, concentrated near to the ford and the 'king's highway', that is, modern Main Street. There was probably a track running westwards along the present Church Terrace and past the castle to continue along the cliffs high above the river; this was in use until Herbert Road was built in the 1850s. Another track, the distant ancestor of Seapoint Road, must already have run eastwards down to the sea. The road leading to the south may already have divided into two, as it does today, at the Y-junction by the present Town Hall. Much later, the courthouse stood here and both this junction and the gently-curving extent of Main Street that leads to it seem long-standing features.

Houses probably lined both sides of Main Street close to the Dargle. These would have been single-storey, rectangular buildings perhaps post-and-wattle, perhaps of stone and earth, thatched, and with their long sides parallel to the street front. The homes of the thirty or so landholders, they would have made an impressive sight as they came into the view of travellers arriving over the ford from Dublin. The tiny thatched mud cabins of the poorest labourers would have been scattered here and there. There is no trace in Bray, though, of the typical patterns of long, thin gardens that in other towns still represent the medieval burgage plots. If they ever existed, they were obliterated long ago.

Around Bray village there would have been extensive areas where crops were grown on the open-field system. Typically part of the land of a manor was divided into three large 'fields', subdivided into strips. Each tenant held one or more strips in each field, and a three-year crop rotation — winter wheat, spring oats, fallow — was used to maintain fertility. The common grazing land, then as later, was probably on the Dargle flood plain and also close to the strand. The sea provided fish, cockles and mussels, and no doubt useful pieces of driftwood and other wreckage. The local woods were a source of plentiful timber, some of which was sent by boats or carts to Dublin, for instance to St Thomas's Abbey which had been granted the right to a supply by de Ridelesford. (Irish oak exported via Dublin was used in major English building projects, notably the roof of Salisbury Cathedral; it would be good to think the source was Bray.)

'The extent of the manor of Bree, done in that place, openly &c on the next Saturday after the feast of St Luke the Evangelist, in the year as above [23 October 1311] *by the following:*

Nicholaum Andree	Robertum Portraham
Ricardum Faille	Laurencium Blund
Ricardum Conyntre	Petrum Roland
Henricum Godfrey	Adam de Carrig
Robertum pistorem	Willelmum Nocistayn
Adam carpenter	Philippum Malyn

THE SURVEY OF 1311

And these jurors say upon their oath that there is in that place a certain stone house and a certain courtyard which are valued at 3 shillings a year.

And there are in that place 160 acres of arable land in the demesne of which each acre is valued at 12 pence a year.

And there are in that place 12 acres of meadow of which each acre is valued at 12 pence a year.

And there is there a certain outside pasture indeed it is [one] in which others have rights in common, from which the lord can take nothing unless he have beasts on the same on which 100 sheep and no more may be kept.

And there is one park which is surrounded by a ditch, which contains 60 acres and is valued at 20 shillings a year.

And there is a certain wood outside from which the lord can take nothing on account of robbers and war.

And there is a certain mill which is valued at 40 shillings a year.

The fishing of the waters is valued at 5 shillings a year. ... .'

(translation, from the Latin in N.B. White (ed.), *The Red Book of Ormond*, Dublin, 1932, p. 24)

Although in many respects a self-contained community, Bray would also have been affected by the presence of Dublin only twelve miles to the north. At this period Bray was in any case within the administrative area of County Dublin — County Wicklow was not to be permanently created, among the last of the Irish counties, until 1606. Dublin was flourishing under English rule; it had substantial dwellings, churches and great monastic houses. There were craftsmen — leather workers, wood turners, coopers, iron workers — and flourishing provision markets. Everyday goods would have found their way to Bray, together with luxury items such as bronze pins, brooches and buckles. The people of Bray, as settlers, would also have shared a common language with their neighbours up the road. Their everyday speech was probably based on the English and French of the time, with some Irish and Norse mixed in.

But daily life in Anglo-Norman Bray remains elusive and can only be imagined. Cloudy, moonless nights would have had a blackness now totally alien to us. The sounds of everyday activities would have carried through the air: the church bell, the turning of the mill wheel, the cries of carters urging their beasts across the difficult ford. There would have been the smell of baking bread and of wood smoke as it curled upwards out of the cottages. And no doubt the people of Bray looked anxiously up towards the mountains for signs of smoke rising from the fires of the 'Irish of the mountains' who lurked there — raiders poised to raid the lowlands. For life in the medieval manor of Bray was often far from peaceful.

Chapter 2

'In continual fear of like mischief': Bray 1311–1666

'... the rebels ... in natural malice destroying the labours of other men ... the inhabitants take less pleasure to till their grounds or plant trees, content to live for the day in continual fear of like mischief.'
(Fynes Moryson, Itinerary, 1617, in C.L. Falkiner (ed.), *Illustrations of Irish history and topography*, London, 1904)

Although the coastal areas had been settled by the Anglo-Normans, the same was not true of the backbone of mountains extending southwards from Dublin. English settlement with its intensive farming was largely confined to land below 600 feet (180 metres). The higher mountain land and the deep upland valleys remained in the hands of the Irish, a lowland/highland division that was to be crucial for many centuries. Indeed matters had been made worse than they might otherwise have been by the displacement of two important Irish families, the Ó Broin (O'Byrnes) and Ó Tuathail (O'Tooles), from their traditional bases in south and north-east County Kildare. Pushed out by the allocation of their lands to powerful Anglo-Normans, ironically one of whom was Walter de Ridelesford, both families became established in the mountains and foothills, in areas difficult of access to the forces of the English crown, where they were joined by other fugitives from English rule. Secure in their territories, they were to be a thorn in the flesh of their settled neighbours.

East Wicklow was 'in the march', the edge of 'the land of war' formed by the mountains, rather than being included in 'the land of peace' under the control of the royal forces based in Dublin. For much of the period Dalkey with its many tower houses marked the southern boundary of English control — the edge of the 'The Pale' — as did the Walshes' great castle at Carrickmines, controlling the main route south from Dublin. Bray was too far from Dublin for safety, and, as it turned out, on the wrong side of the river.

The first hundred years of Anglo-Norman settlement were peaceful enough, but from about 1270 onwards the O'Byrnes and O'Tooles, faced with severe winters and occasional famines, rose up in anger and increasingly supported themselves by attacks on the settled communities, taking cattle and raiding crops at harvest time. Some of the forays were relatively small and localised, but they created havoc nonetheless. Lands not far from Bray were laid waste again and again. *Archbishop Alen's Register* for March 1326, for instance, makes sorry reading; at Rathmichael the land was untilled 'through war', at Shankill 'the burgagers have fled from that country on account of the Irish', at Dalkey 'nothing can be levied'.

Larger battles raged from time to time, with major attacks on the coastlands and attempts to drive out the settlers. In 1315, at a time of severe snowstorms and famine, the O'Byrnes and O'Tooles 'invaded, burned, and totally destroyed' Bray, as well as burning Arklow and Newcastle. The effect of this event can only be imagined. Many of Bray's inhabitants probably fled in terror to the safer environs of Dublin city; certainly the manor became poverty-stricken. Sir Hugh Lawless, descendant of one of the original Anglo-Norman families and leader of the Wicklow settlers, was granted the manor of Bray by the English Crown in 1314, just before the Bruce invasion of 1315 caused severe unrest throughout Ireland. He chose to surrender it again in 1320, saying that his profit during five years of tenancy had amounted to two salmon. His tenants must have been too poor to pay their rents. This was certainly true in the 1330s, when Bray was described as being 'in the march that scarcely anything can be therefore received'.

A MAJOR ATTACK ON BRAY

1315. 'Item, eodem tempore, Hibernici australes, Otothiles et Obrynnes cremaverunt totam patriam australem, scilicet, Arclowe, Novum Castrum, Bree et omnes villas adjacentes...'
(J.T Gilbert (ed.), *Chartularies of St Mary's Abbey, Dublin*, London, 1884, vol. ii, p. 348)
('Also at this time, the southern Irishmen, as the O'Tooles and O'Byrnes, did burn all the south country; this is to say Arklow, Newcastle, Bray and all the towns thereabout.')

In the hope of improvement, Geoffrey Crump or Crampe, a prominent Dublin citizen, was granted the manor of Bray in 1334 for a twenty-year term, to be held without rent for the first two years on condition that he repaired 'a certain castle which is called Rokelscourt'; the grant was renewed in 1360. The identity of Rokelscourt Castle is not certain, but it is likely that the name is a corruption of 'Ridelesford', and so refers to the castle at Bray. Strengthened, Bray's castle would have been able to play a greater military role and in 1356, at another time of pressure from the Irish, it was apparently chosen as the base for twenty horsemen and forty archers defending the approach to the Pale. But in general matters did not improve for the settlers over the following two centuries. Even when left in comparative peace, the inhabitants of the marginal areas were often subject to 'black rents' levied as protection money by the Irish chiefs.

MANOR OF BRAY GRANTED TO GEOFFREY CRAMPE OR CRUMP

> Letters patent given to Geoffrey Crampe or Crump giving him [in 1334?] *'all the lands and tenements in our manor of Bree to be held for the term of twenty years … [at] seven pounds twenty pence and one halfpenny … and for that the aforesaid lands and tenements are in the March that scarcely anything can be received, we pardoned him by our letters patent the rent of the said lands and tenements for two years after the aforesaid sixth day in aid of the repair of a certain castle which is called Rokelscourt … .'*
> (19th-century translation in Meath deeds, from Edward Tresham (ed.). *Rotulorum patentium et clausorum …* , Dublin, 1828, p. 39)

Besides the effects of the bad weather, another natural force added to the general misery of the fourteenth century — the Black Death. This terrible disease which ravaged Europe arrived in Ireland via the harbour at Howth in the late summer of 1348. It spread particularly through the densely peopled area around Dublin, killing over the next two years, it is estimated, perhaps a third of the population. Wherever it raged the Black Death caused serious depopulation and a decline in farming because of fewer people available to work the land. Bray can hardly have escaped.

By the end of the fourteenth century, the people of Bray had spent over a hundred years intermittently fearful of attack and hearing of the counter attacks, some successful, some not so, launched by government forces. In 1401 they were to have a ringside view of a major battle — one that is indirectly commemorated in a Bray place name to this day. In July/August of that year the mayor, John Drake, of Dublin led a force of Dublin citizens and the Walshes of Carrickmines Castle against the O'Byrnes and defeated them, killing some five hundred according to the chroniclers, in a battle just to the north of Bray. The name 'Bloody Bank', applied to the steep cliffs along the Upper Dargle Road behind Rathmore Terrace, traditionally dates back to this

***2.1.** Little Bray Castle in 1913, from* The stones of Bray.

battle, which is still commemorated indirectly in the sanitised version, 'Sunnybank'.

The O'Byrnes kept up their pressure on the coastal lowlands and fifty years later Little Bray Castle was built — a structure that lasted into modern times as a tangible link with medieval Bray. Unlike the older Great Bray Castle in the heart of Bray town, this modest building survived long enough to be mapped by the Ordnance Survey and to appear in drawings and photographs. The defensive site that Walter de Ridelesford had chosen on the south side of the Dargle more than two centuries before would have been an excellent one had danger come from the direction of Dublin. But, of course, it did not; the Irish strongholds lay to the west and south-west and it seemed necessary to the Dublin administration to position another castle on the north side of the ford to defend the main road.

> *'That whereas the Boher of Bray is the most common road for the Obirnes, the Irish enemies of our sovereign lord the King, in coming from day to day into the marches of the said county [Dublin], whereby the said march is likely to suffer great injury ... It is ordained and established that whatsoever person or persons will build or cause to be built a castle or fortalice on the land of Cork adjoining to the said Boher of Bray, containing forty of Paul's feet in height under the entablement, and twenty-four feet in length, and sixteenth feet in breadth within the walls of the said castle or fortilice, that then the said person or persons shall have ten pounds to aid the said work to be levied upon all manner of possessions within the said county, in manner of a subsidy; ...'*
> (H.F. Berry, *Statute rolls of the parliament of Ireland, reign of King Henry the Sixth*, Dublin, 1910, p. 633)

A'TEN POUND' CASTLE FOR LITTLE BRAY

According to a statute of 1459, a proposal was made for the erection of a small castle in Little Bray, which would receive a grant of ten pounds provided it was built within three years. These modest 'ten pound' castles were built at various places in the wider Dublin area from Louth to Kildare following from an act of Henry VI in 1429. In modern times Little Bray Castle stood on the west side of Castle Street, almost opposite Dwyer Park, at the edge of what is now the shopping centre car park. When it was built, however, Castle Street did not exist, and the Dublin road followed the route that later became Back Street. The line of this old road followed the front gardens of the present houses in St Columcille's Terrace, and on in a slight curve close to the shopping centre buildings towards Bray Bridge. The castle was on the east side and its grounds would have extended over part of Castle Street and the shopping centre car park.

Whether Little Bray Castle served its purpose in deterring attack we do not know — it was too small to be a formidable obstacle — and it seems to have been derelict by the seventeenth century, although it later had a second period of occupancy and survived until the 1930s. A photograph of *c.* 1900 shows the castle clearly. Fake battlements had been added at some stage, but the basic structure is visible and the height of the tower seems to be 35 to 40 feet (about 12 metres). The original building is very narrow and at right angles to Castle Street.

Although it had strategic importance, as far as size went Little Bray Castle was still of lesser importance than its older counterpart in the centre of Bray. The original wooden motte buildings of Great Bray Castle may have been

2.2. Little Bray Castle from W.H. Bartlett's view of Bray, 1842 (see fig. 6.1).

replaced by a stone tower house as early as *c.* 1300 or perhaps the stone building dates only from Geoffrey Crump's time — the fourteenth century was the period at which tower houses proliferated in the Irish landscape. This stone tower, as described in a seventeenth-century arbitration mentioned below, was a sturdy 40-feet square with three wooden-floored rooms — considerably more impressive than the slender tower in Little Bray. Great Bray Castle is sketched, with a door at ground level and windows on two levels above, on Jonathan Barker's map of Bray in 1762. It is shown rather more elaborately with a substantial turret at a south corner on an earlier map fragment. It also appears, apparently standing on a mound, on the Down Survey map of 1657.

The details of its appearance have to be guessed at, but presumably it was built of roughly-dressed stones of various sizes, the gaps filled with smaller stones and mortar. The interior would have been simple. Typically the ground floor, often vaulted in stone, was used for storage or for the housing of animals. The first floor was the common room for running the business of the manor; above was the 'lord's hall' used as living quarters by the lord and his family. There might be another room at top level, or simply a low space under a high-pitched roof of slates, wooden shingles or thatch. The castle was surrounded by a bawn or courtyard; this would have had thick, high walls and access would have been under an arched gateway or perhaps even through a gate tower.

> *'At the north end of Castle-street is a small Tower rising conspicuously above the surrounding houses. It is oblong, and topped with modern brick battlements, but it has a projecting dripstone ledge on its southern and eastern sides, about 4 ft. below these brick battlements. The outer faces of the four walls have been rough plastered, but where this plaster has in some places fallen away, the stones of which the walls are formed can be seen, and seem old and of the locality, as in the cases of Puck and Shanganagh Castles. In the very angle of the south and east walls, rather high up, is a slit or loophole as at Robswall Castle, but it is cut across by a short groove, so as to give the resemblance of a small cross. Near this slit on the east side is a face or head standing out in high relief, but disfigured partly by plaster. ... Two loopholes or tiny windows also occur in the east wall, — one very high up. In the opposite or west wall very near the top, but close to the south side, is a small square window. ... The door in the street is somewhat old looking, and studded with big-headed nails. The buildings surrounding and leaning against this old tower, are chiefly modern, I should say, though an attempt has been made to give them a castellated appearance so clearly of recent time as possibly to divert attention from the really ancient tower.'*
> (E.R.McC. Dix, *The Irish Builder*, 1.9.1898.)

LITTLE BRAY CASTLE IN 1898

The clearest account of Great Bray Castle comes from a near hundred years later, when the castle was close to being in ruins — presumably it had been unoccupied for some time. In 1625 a dispute over responsibility for repairs to the castle arose between Lord Brabazon (soon to be the first earl of Meath) who was the owner and Edward Walsh who had acted as guarantor when his brother William had taken out a repairing lease eleven years before. The three 'ancient floors' needed replacing and the stairs were partly non existent ('there are no strong or convenient stairs') and partly in bad shape ('not ... sufficiently repaired as they ought to be'). A certificate was provided by three carpenters that the necessary repairs would cost '£300 English' — a considerable sum at that time and judgement was given for this amount. But there is no evidence that the repairs were carried out, and it is likely that Great Bray Castle was never used again. It was to vanish without trace at some unknown date after 1762.

2.3. *Castle Street today; Little Bray Castle stood at the edge of the shopping centre car park close to the site of the bus shelter. It was demolished during road widening in the 1930s.*

2.4. *The tower of Oldcourt Castle today; traces of the pitched roofline of the hall are still visible half-way up.*

By the end of the fifteenth century there was another castle, or, at least, a tower house, within the area covered by Bray today — one that has survived as a ruin. Oldcourt Castle, like Little Bray Castle, probably dates from the mid 1400s, but unlike the other two was not built on a site of any particular strategic importance. It was simply a small fortified dwelling, measuring 25 feet by 16 feet and some 50 feet high, situated out in the dangerous countryside south of Bray and close to the Swan River, a small north-flowing tributary of the Dargle. As was fairly typical of a tower used mainly as a dwelling, Oldcourt Castle had a stone-built hall 54 feet long attached, and this still survived, thatched, in 1799; the high-pitched inverted 'v' of its original roofline can today be traced on the west wall of the tower. The entrance to the tower was apparently from the upper floor of the hall, and the top floor of the tower held the main room, with lesser rooms on three levels below. A gateway to the castle courtyard, 64 feet to the south of the building itself, is today flanked by two small 'round towers', though these are probably all nineteenth-century additions, as are some of the battlements on the tower.

Oldcourt, though not specifically the castle, is mentioned in 1432 and Oldcourt Castle may perhaps be the 'stonehouse' mentioned in 1464. But its origins are unknown. (One much later account, now discredited, has the castle built by an English knight, Sir Thomas Mulso.) What is certain is that by the mid 1500s Oldcourt Castle was in the hands of the Walsh family of Carrickmines, who held various lands both north and south of Bray. The Walshes also owned a tower house at Old Connaught. The massive granite-built tower house at Fassaroe, of which little now remains, was not built until 1535; tradition records that it was destroyed by Cromwell's artillery. There was probably also a tower at Killruddery, perhaps incorporated into the fabric of the present Killruddery House.

Oldcourt was used for military purposes once, at least, when in September 1597 during a time of great unrest Sir William Russell, the lord deputy, camped there on the way to attack the rebels in Glenmalure. This was not the first time Russell had broken his journey in the Bray area. A page of his journal for 1595 was endorsed 'the camp at the Braye', perhaps a site near the river or else close to Bray Head.

STONE HOUSES ON MAIN STREET

> *'Thomas son & heir of William son of Richard of Corkagh, to Sir Adam de Mareys vicar of Bree. Release and quit claim of one burgage and a half in the town of Bree,viz: in the lordship of James le Boteler earl of Ormond, on which holding a stone house has been commenced, lying in length from the cellar door of said Thomas's stone house on the north to the tenement of William son of William son of Richard of Corkagh on the south, and extends in length from the king's highway on the west, to the land of the house of S. John of Tristildermot on the east ...'*
> (*Calendar of ancient deeds and muniments preserved in the Pembroke estate office, Dublin*, Dublin, 1891. Deed 45, dated 1352)

There are very occasional glimpses of daily life in Bray during these centuries. Surviving deeds show that by the fourteenth century some of the houses on what is now Main Street were substantial enough to be built of stone. Among the landholders were Sir Adam de Mareys, 'vicar of Bree' for some forty years, who in 1352 acquired a partly-built stone house on the east side of the street (probably in the vicinity of today's Royal Hotel); later he also acquired a stone house on the west side from William Fox. This last was already a familiar name in Bray — a hundred years previously another William Fox, perhaps his great-grandfather, had rented lands in the manor. The two sons of 'Richard of Corkagh', Thomas and William, also held properties, as at different times did John Couyntre, and Patrick Hygdon and Philip Higdon (perhaps father and son). In 1394 Sir Adam, who must by now have been an old man, transferred all his properties in Bray to John Mareys, presumably a close relation.

Sir Adam de Mareys is only the fourth vicar of Bray whose name survives, and there are only fleeting mentions of some of those who succeeded him. Donald Olanagam (O'Lanagan or Flanagan?) and William Went belong to the first half of the fifteenth century; Patrick Longe, Neall Gaffney, Moris or Morgan Burne and Simon Swayne come after the Reformation. Patrick Longe in 1548 and Neall Gaffney in 1578 both figure in the records for the same reason — for failing to keep schools in which to teach English, presumably defying an act of Henry VIII for the establishment of protestant, English-speaking schools. Church services were still conducted in Irish by Moris Burne in 1615, using the Irish book of common prayer, *Leabhar na nUrnaithe gComhchoiteann*. According to later tradition Bray church, by now protestant, was rebuilt in 1609. The church must have been underused, however, for the

2.5. Bray's protestant church, later St Paul's, as rebuilt in 1609, from Letitia Bushe's painting of 1736 (see fig. 3.6).

number of protestants in Bray was apparently very small, as few as sixteen were recorded in 1630. It was to be well over a hundred years before the first Catholic church opened for worship.

Among the surviving fragments of information about medieval Bray is one very human snippet. Maurice Lawless, the king's farmer, when he died on Tuesday the feast of the apostles Peter and Paul 1374–5, had in the manor of Bray nine acres of wheat, seven acres of oats, a horse and a sow with sixteen piglets, total value £3 15s 10d. There is also one mystifying reference. According to the *Calendar of Inquisitions*, King Edward IV, having held parliament at Drogheda on 27 January 1469, travelled first to Dublin and then to Bray. If he held a meeting of the Irish parliament in Bray, or even just stayed briefly, then accommodation would have been necessary for a large assembly — perhaps a hundred or so persons. There is no way of knowing whether Bray was able to cater for such a number.

PROPERTIES OF MAURICE LAWLESS

1374–5 *'Maurice Laweles late farmer of the lord the king of the manor of Bree … had on the said day on which he died in the Bree nine acres of wheat growing in the fields, each acre of the price of 4s, seven acres of oats each acre of the price of 40d and that on the said day he had a horse of the price of one mark [13s 4d] and one sow with sixteen little pigs of the price of 3s …'*
('Inrolment relating to the manor of Bree, 1375–6', Meath deed 5).

Bray changed ownership many times during the first five centuries of its existence and stability was only to come in the mid 1600s. The earls of Ormond received grants of the manor from the crown at various times, but in one instance, at least, only half of the manor was specified. In about 1480 the crown granted the abbot of St Mary's Abbey, Dublin, custody of the castles and manors of Bray and Killruddery for ten years. Later the FitzWilliams became principal players in the question of ownership rights, together with members of the Archbold family — the latter spelt in a wide range of ways over the years from Ashpoll to Archebolde. The FitzWilliams held property in Bray at least from the beginning of the fifteenth century, while the Archbolds held large parts of coastal north-east Wicklow and figured prominently in Bray deeds.

VICARS OF BRAY

1284	Sir John the father	1426	William Went
1294–6	William	1548	Patrick Longe
1352	Sir Adam de Mareys	1578	Neall Gaffney
1391	Sir Adam de Mareys	1610	Moris Burne
1394	Sir Adam de Mareys	1615	Moris Burne
1401	Donald Olanagam	1630–47	Simon Swayne

(Based on *The stones of Bray* and other sources)

BRAY FROM THE DOWN SURVEY, 1657

'… in the north east point of this barony the Bray water disgorgeth itself into the sea. The wares [weirs] on which water are very profitable for salmon fishing … there is at Oldcourt a castle repairable. This barony is not very well inhabited occasioned partly by the roughness of the country and partly by the destruction of the ancient Irish inhabitants during the late wars.'
(Down Survey, 1657)

Grants to the Archbolds continued into the beginning of the seventeenth century, and the creation of County Wicklow in 1606. By 1609, however, their position had become precarious — attempts, soon to be successful, were underway to deprive them of their lands. The records of their ownership were considered to be insufficient and they lost their north-east Wicklow properties. Meanwhile a new family had come onto the scene — the Brabazons. This family, descended from one of William the Conqueror's knights and long settled in England, had arrived in Ireland in 1534 when Sir William Brabazon was appointed vice-treasurer and general receiver of Ireland (he was to serve three times as lord justice). In 1544 Henry VIII granted Sir William the lands of the suppressed St Thomas's Abbey at Thomas Court in Dublin — the same abbey that Walter de Ridelesford had long before supported through grants of land in Bray. The Abbey had also held Killruddery in the early 1500s, which provided the Brabazons with a claim on Archbold territory. Sir William Brabazon died in 1552 and his young son Edward inherited the estates; as Baron Ardee he was formally granted Killruddery by James I in 1619. It was his son, William, who was created earl of Meath in 1627.

The first Lord Meath's interest in the manor of Bray dates from 1636, when the 'manor and castle of Bray alias Bree' were conveyed to him by George Kirke, who had himself been granted the manor by Charles I in 1629. But the ownership of Bray was not finally settled until thirty years later, when to satisfy conflicting claims the manor was divided in 1666 between two great landlords, the second earl of Meath and the earl of Tyrconnell. The Anglo-Norman 'manor of Bree' was finally dismembered, and from this time Bray was to have two landlord families, both influential in their different ways. The earls of Meath, however, were to retain the title of 'lord of the manor' — together with its responsibilities and privileges — on through the centuries to come.

Chapter 3

More settled times: Bray 1666–1760

> *'To end all disputes concerning the lands of Great Bray alias Bree, County Wicklow, part of which lie in common and undivided, it is agreed as follows. ... The earl of Meath shall have the castle of Bray and the ground about it and before it, and ... Thomas Ellinsworth' s house and garden to the highway at the west end of the churchyard, awnd all other houses and garden plots lying between the highway that leads towards Kilruddery from the hollow of [the hill] by the stone piers of the bridge, and the sea; and also all those the mills of Bray ... .'*
>
> (Partition of the manor of Great Bray, 1 April 1666)

The partition of 1666 settled the primary land ownership in Bray once and for all. Its echoes reverberate faintly even today, for it was to have some bearing on the shape into which Bray grew, particularly in the great expansion of the second half of the nineteenth century. It can even be said that the road names 'Meath Road' and 'Herbert Road', both dating from two hundred years after the partition, still bear witness to the decisions of 1666.

The division was between Edward, second earl of Meath, and Oliver, earl of Tyrconnell and, the matter settled, the latter leased his share to Lord Meath for fifty-one years at a rent of £40 and six salmon. Lord Tyrconnell died childless soon afterwards and his interest in Bray was inherited by Thomas Lord FitzWilliam. Later the eldest daughter of the fifth Viscount FitzWilliam was to marry the ninth Earl of Pembroke, and the Bray property passed down through that line, with a notable member of the family, the British statesman Sidney, 1st Lord Herbert of Lea, playing a conspicuous role in the nineteenth century.

A few of Bray's long-lasting landmarks feature in the partition deed: the castle, St Paul's Church and churchyard (not, in fact, named St Paul's until the late nineteenth century), the mill and mill weir, and the 'stream in the glen', the present Swan River. The bridge over the Dargle with its 'stone piers' is mentioned for the first time — it must have been newly built since it did not appear nine years earlier on the Down Survey map. There was also a ford upstream near the weir that diverted water for the mill, perhaps on the same site as one shown on a view of about 1800 (see fig. 5.1).

Given that there is no map with the partition, some of the points of reference are hard to identify. But later estate maps show the same divisions, and so it is known that Lord Meath received all the land south of the Dargle between what is now the line of Main Street/Vevay Road and the sea. On the inland side of Main Street he kept the heart of the town around St Paul's Church, the castle and the mill, and a large field called the Mill Park or Night Park, where Parnell Road, Davitt Road, St Kevin's Square and Kilmaintain Place are today. In Bray itself Lord Tyrconnell had to be satisfied with three small parcels of land and their houses west of Main Street, roughly between the present Church Terrace and St Kevin's Terrace. He also received four fields, two of them very large, running from the Dargle to Killarney Road, two more large fields in the triangle between Killarney Road and Vevay Road and, most extensive of all, the lands of Kilbride and Killarney further along Killarney Road amounting to 150 acres.

The Bray lands were, of course, only a fraction of the holdings of both Lord Meath and Lord Tyrconnell. Meath properties included the nearby

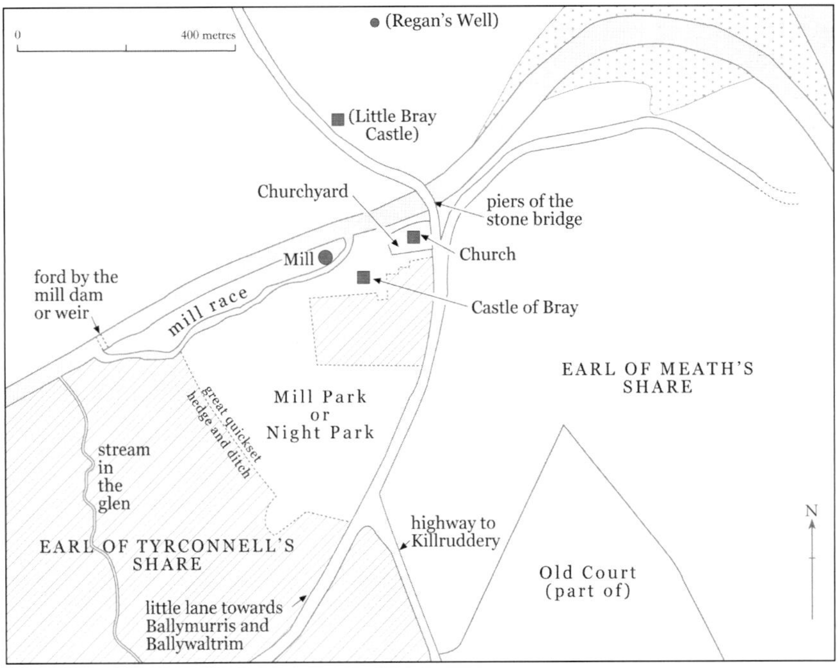

3.1. *Bray in 1666, based on the deed of partition between the earl of Meath and the earl of Tyrconnell.*

3.2. The Y-junction at the top of Main Street leading to the Killarney and Vevay Roads. The courthouse and pound once occupied the site of the late-nineteenth-century Town Hall.

3.3. The area just south of Bray Bridge was once the market place, where the only road to the sea (now Seapoint Road) joined the main street. The courthouse (heritage centre) at the left was built on the site of an earlier market house in 1841.

lands of the manors of Killruddery, Kindlestown, Ballywaltrim, Ballymorris, Templedelgany and Coolegad in County Wicklow, and the valuable properties of Thomas Court and Donore in Dublin. Lord Tyrconnell and his wife Elinor owned extensive lands mainly in Counties Dublin and Meath amounting to a total estate of almost five thousand statute acres. But the Meaths, with a main residence at Killruddery, were always to be far more intimately involved in Bray than were Lord Tyrconnell's succcessors.

The partition deed, together with other documents of the time such as the Down Survey of 1657 and the hearth money rolls of the 1660s, provides a snapshot of the Bray of the middle of the seventeenth century. Although they would not acquire their modern names for another two hundred years, Main Street ('the great road in Bray'), Vevay Road as the 'highway' to Killruddery, and Killarney Road ('the little lane') were all in place. There were fourteen houses and cabins altogether in Great Bray — a very small number which would give a population of less than a hundred. Two of these were apparently cabins with no chimney, probably only one room with a hole for the smoke to escape, nine had one hearth, and there were three larger houses belonging to Robert Gregory, George Atherley and — largest of all with eight chimneys — Richard Wichell. Robert Gregory was a farmer living on the west side of the main street, where he leased the twelve acres of the Mill Park. Richard Wichell or Whicholl's house was somewhere on the east side not far from the bridge. George Atherley remains elusive.

Of the cottages, seven were crowded together on Lord Tyrconnell's land. Thomas Ellinsworth or Ellingsworth, weaver, had a good house with a garden not far from the castle and church; his name crops up frequently in deeds of the time. There were two houses further out at Oldcourt, of which Mr Edwards's house had two chimneys, with a derelict house nearby. Ballywaltrim had six houses, three of them very poor. In Newtown Vevay Mr Fitzwilliams had a house with three chimneys — this may be the same Fitzwilliams who owned a brew house in Bray in the 1680s. The Archbolds had not totally disappeared from the scene, for James Archbold held fifty-eight acres of arable and pasture at Raheenacluig.

Bray now had twice-yearly fair days selling horses, cattle and sheep, as well as the weekly market. The market was held on Tuesdays, with fairs on St Martin's Day (11 November) and St Philip and St James (1 May). In 1674 the market day was changed to Friday and the fairs to the first Tuesdays in May and September. Both the market and the fairs would have been held close to the bridge, in an open space where the Heritage Centre is now, spilling across the river into Little Bray. The regular market days would have given a commercial rhythm to life in Bray, with the shops and inns crowded with farmers and their wives. The fairs were the highlights of the year, drawing in dealers, cattle drovers and hawkers as well as the people of the area.

Little Bray was not part of the 1666 partition. It was granted by Charles I to Jeremy Donovan in 1636, in a document that gives almost as full a description as the partition document does for Great Bray. This shows that Little Bray had its castle, with a house, orchard and garden next to it. There were five other houses and gardens. The names of a number of parcels of land are given, apparently mostly Irish in origin, and there is a mention of Regans Well, a name later to be transmuted into Ravenswell. By the 1660s there seem to have been ten or so houses in all.

The earl of Meath held various pieces of land in Little Bray, as did two landlords 'William Woulferston of Stillorgan' and 'Lord of Merrion' who were specified as Catholics. Woulferston's property in 1654 included Little Bray Castle, described as an old castle valued at £5. A figure for the number of residents in Little Bray at this time has survived; the total in 1659, probably adults only, was twenty-six, of whom fifteen, more than half, had Irish surnames.

From the settlement of 1666, Bray moved into more stable times. Now that ownership had been confirmed, it was possible to develop the lands. In 1676 members of the Brabazon family made an agreement between themselves that leases could be made for 61 years or three lives — the latter, though it seems quaint to us, was a usual if somewhat nerve-wracking way of holding property for the duration of the lives of three named individuals. The Brabazon agreement was drawn up because offers were being made 'by divers persons of valuable estate and substance to erect or build ... several houses, streets, market places and other improvements', provided they could have long leases. Bray was beginning to be a good place to settle and invest in.

During the following century the lands around Bray were leased out, often with the stipulation that a 'good' house was to be built. For instance one major grant, made by the earl of Meath to the prosperous farmer Edward Keatley or Keatly in May 1675, was of forty-nine acres of the coastal strip, where the railway and Meath Road are now, from the Dargle River southwards to the vicinity of the present Convent Avenue. This included 'the Mount or Higher Park', later to be the site of martello tower no. 2 which still stands at the north end of Strand Road. Keatley agreed to build 'one good house after the English fashion with a good chimney of brick or stone' and to 'ditch and quickset all the fences betwixt him and his neighbours' — i.e. to build boundary banks planted with hawthorn. The whereabouts of this house is unknown, although there may be a connection with Seapoint House, overlooking the mouth of the Dargle at Seapoint Road.

Keatley's land was subdivided some twenty years later and the larger portion of thirty-one acres, named in later deeds as 'two-thirds Keatley's holding' was in the early nineteenth century to become one of the most desirable parcels of land in Bray. The most southerly third, quaintly named the Cock Wake or Walk, became a separate eighteen acres leased at the end of the seventeenth century by the weaver Thomas Ellingsworth. He also held the Green Park, twelve acres just south of the present Novara Avenue, another piece of land that figures in later documents.

'And also a castle, several houses and parcels of land in the Town of Little Bray called by the several names or denominations of one castle with the appurtenances, also one house, orchard, and garden with the appurtenances joining to the said castle of Bray and piece of ground without the wall of the said orchard. Also four houses or messuages and four gardens in the holding of Thos Edge, Phelim Redmond, Hugh Maguire, and Thady Doyle. Also one garden in the holding of John Ringrose. Also one house, orchard and garden in the tenancy of John Gossidge. Also the lands and meadows of Cronemore, Gortnisky, High Park called the Acreboyes, the Hart acre or acre in Viccary thereunto adjoining. Also Barragebrarna [Banogetrasna in later transcript], Farrencreddhar [Farrencreehar], Speenke [Speanke], the five acres adjoining to the same called Farrenforfafennell, all in the holding of John Gossidge. Also the meadow behind the above said orchard near the castle of Bray. Also the meadow joining to the said Thady Doyle's garden. Also the acre called Tobberegans Acres. Also Regans' well. Also the acre called Acre Carragh. Also the land called Tarranatra [Fanantra]. Also the four acres called the four acres near Corke and Ardragh in the said town of Little Bray, and also the benefit of commons and commons of pasture and fishing in the said town of Little Bray and River of Bray.'

(Grant to Jeremy Donovan of Little Bray, 1636, in Meath deed 98)

LITTLE BRAY: PROPERTIES GRANTED TO JEREMY DONOVAN, 1636

Another property of the time was the Cherry Garden, one and three quarter acres between Seapoint Road and the Dargle River. The walled outline of the Cherry Garden has been one of the constants in Bray down through the years, surviving into the late twentieth century. In the seventeenth century the Cherry Garden was owned by Robert Sill or Syll, a lime burner, and there were already two lime kilns, convenient for limestone brought in by sea.

One of the key sites in the heart of Bray had a new house, outhouses and stable yards built on it by 1693. This prominent site occupied the corner facing Main Street next to the entrance to Church Terrace and opposite the present Royal Hotel. The new house may already have been an inn, a role it was to fill prominently some decades later.

Little Bray, too, was parcelled out towards the seventeenth century in a flurry of new leases. In 1681 Bartholomew FitzWilliams, who also owned property in Great Bray, leased six acres for thirty-one years. In the same year and for the same term John Robinson acquired the remains of an old house and its garden plot and pledged to build a stone house with a tile roof within two years and to plant hawthorn hedges around the boundaries. The weaver John Ringrose and Widow Margaret Matthews had houses in the vicinity of the present shopping centre; by the 1760s these two houses had passed to Charles Moran, who will be encountered anon.

Equally important as the grants of new long leases to the development of Bray was the first bridge across the Dargle, a four-arch structure built in about 1660. Like subsequent bridges (the present one is the third on the site), it was asymmetrical, sloping down from the cliff in Great Bray towards the low-lying river plain in Little Bray. But at last, nearly five hundred years after the

__3.4.__ Bray barracks, built to protect the town from insurgents in c. 1692, sits above the river between the towers of St Paul's and the Holy Redeemer.

arrival of Walter de Ridelesford's settlers, it was possible to make the journey to Dublin freely without concern about the ford: 'a very large difficult pass over the water after any great rain' as it was described in the Down Survey. The bridge incline was very steep and hard on horses, with an awkward bend on the Little Bray side as the road swung into Back Street — this was to be alleviated much later by the construction of Castle Street — but high tides and river floods were no longer major obstacles. The bridge had some military significance, enabling as it did easy passage into Wicklow. After the battle of the Boyne in 1690 King James is said to have ordered his troops to defend it for long enough to enable him to escape southwards (one tradition has him spending the night in Bray).

Bray acquired another important structure close by with the construction of the infantry barracks in about 1692 — having a regular garrison in the town was both a guarantee of safety and a boost to the local economy. The site chosen was in the old heart of the town, next to the castle and St Paul's Church and with the same dominant position overlooking the Dargle. Built on land acquired by the Crown from the earl of Meath, this rectangular building with a high-walled yard in front was to be in military use for over a century. It survives today, divided into houses, as the oldest relatively unchanged building in Bray.

3.5. *South end of the barracks today. It was divided into three private houses in about 1900.*

3.6. Letitia Bushe's watercolour of Bray in 1736. The bridge is the original one across the Dargle (courtesy National Gallery of Ireland).

If the mists of time hanging over medieval Bray were already clearing in the seventeenth century, as the eighteenth century progresses the picture becomes much more distinct. The first real illumination comes with a watercolour of Bray in 1736 — the first known painting of the town. Letitia Bushe, who would have been in her twenties when she took a position down what is now Seapoint Road, was an accomplished artist and her painting 'View of the village of Bray' is now in the National Gallery of Ireland. She must have been a relation, perhaps a sister, of John Bushe, who was Church of Ireland rector of Bray in the 1730s and who lived at Corke Abbey, the large property just north of Little Bray.

Bushe's charming watercolour has a small figure in a hat, who presumably represents the artist herself, sketching in the left foreground, accompanied by a dog; a carriage is travelling along Seapoint Road. Bray Bridge is in the centre of the view, which was captured five years before this first steep bridge was to collapse in a storm, with a few houses visible on Main Street. St Paul's Church has a large window at the east end and a small bell turret at the west end; presumably this is the church of 1609. The barracks has smoke rising from its chimney and at the bottom of the cliff there is a building at the mill, perhaps the miller's house, with woods behind.

Although there are no houses on Seapoint Road in Bushe's painting, there is a glimpse of the most northerly ones on Main Street. There are also a few houses visible in Little Bray, and an impressive entrance through a high wall that seems to lead to a large house in the vicinity of what is now Ravenswell; which house it might be is unclear. The man with horses close to the river is probably leading his animals from a watering place on the common land at this side of the bridge. The animals and small figures give animation to the scene — the first real glimpse of daily life in Bray.

Chapter 4

'A very small town': Bray in 1760

'Bray is prettily situated on a height over the river [and] is a very small town, with a Barrack in it.'
(*Pococke's tour in Ireland in 1752*, ed. G.T. Stokes, Dublin and London, 1891, p. 163)

If it was possible to get an impression of Bray in the mid-seventeenth century through the partition of 1666 and other documents, then three maps make it possible to paint a detailed portrait a century later. These maps drawn in the early 1760s come at a pivotal moment in the story of Bray. The town was still no more than a small market centre serving the local population, with

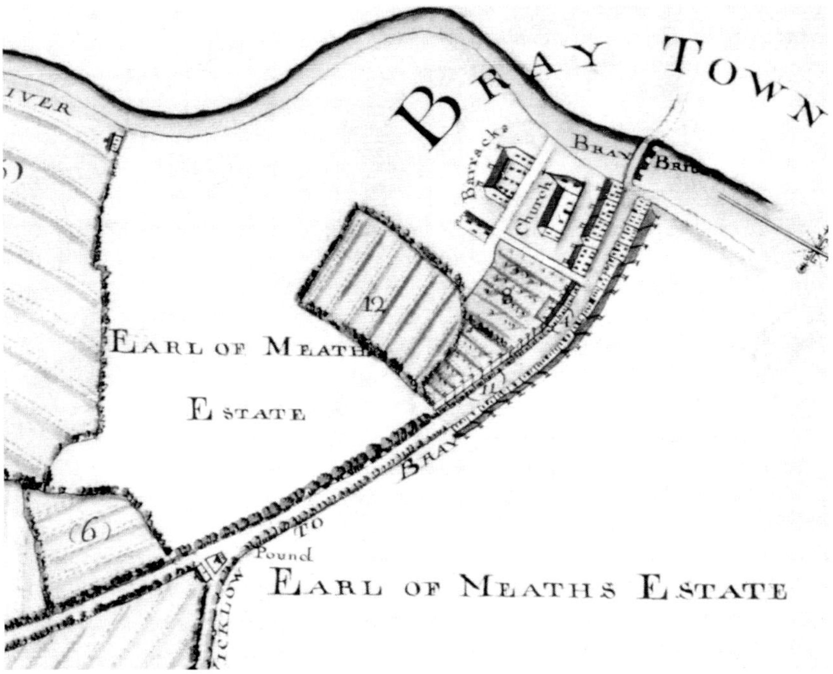

***4.1.** Bray in the 1760s; part of Jonathan Barker's map of 1762 (courtesy National Archives of Ireland).*

its trade boosted by the presence of the infantry companies stationed in the barracks. During the remaining decades of the eighteenth century fresh outside factors were to come into play and lead to great changes and a rapid increase in population. Bray in the year 1760 was poised between the old and the new.

Two of the three maps are detailed estate plans of 1762 and 1764 covering the FitzWilliam and Meath parts of the manor. Both were prepared by competent surveyors of the time. The FitzWilliam map of 1762 was drawn by Jonathan Barker, a Dublin land surveyor. The Meath map was by Jacob Nevill, a surveyor from Kilpoole near Wicklow town, who had prepared a map of the whole of County Wicklow four years earlier and who did other work for the earl of Meath. Both maps naturally concentrate on Great Bray, although the Nevill map shows Meath property north of the Dargle. For a picture of Little Bray, it is necessary to turn to a third map — that of County Dublin in 1760 by John Rocque. This eminent cartographer, of English/French background, spent the years 1754–60 in Ireland, where he prepared a number of town and estate maps, the best-known being his large-scale map of Dublin city.

The two estate maps are on reasonably large scales: Barker's map at twenty Irish perches to an inch, or a little over twelve inches to the mile (about 1:5000) and Nevill's rather larger at twelve Irish perches to an inch, close to twenty-one inches to the mile (about 1:3000). They are very

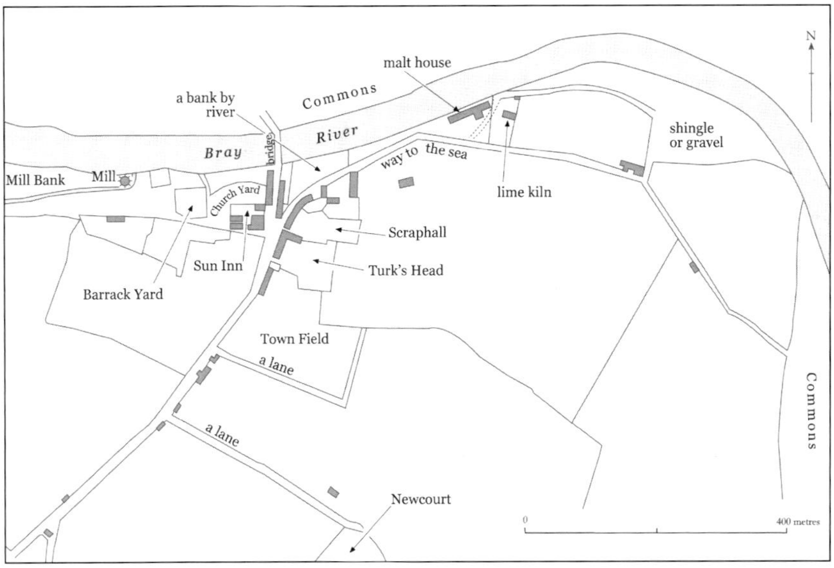

4.2. Meath property from Jacob Nevill's map of 1764, redrawn with names added from the key.

different in style — Barker's map is charmingly pictorial, while Nevill's is entirely utilitarian. Intended to help in the administration of the respective estates, each is accompanied by a reference table that gives the names of the property holders with acreages and brief descriptions. Barker's text records that the Pembroke property was held by five leaseholders and included twenty houses. The third map, Rocque's, covering the whole of County Dublin, is on a much smaller scale at two inches to the mile (1:31,680); although it is less detailed it is valuable as the earliest portrayal we have of Little Bray.

In 1760 the most prominent buildings in Great Bray were still St Paul's Church and the old castle, together with the barracks, all shown as small drawings on Barker's map. The castle was presumably derelict or semi-derelict, any military importance it might conceivably have had by now negated by the building of the barracks. St Paul's had been somewhat modified since Letitia Bushe's time, with the bell turret on the west end replaced by a tower and small spire surmounted by a cross. According to Canon Scott, this spire was 'raised' in 1775, so the elegant one shown in William Cowen's detailed drawing of 1825 (see fig. 5.11) may be higher than the one of the 1760s; it was to remain until about 1840. The barracks is recognisably the same building as today. It held a company of infantry, with seventy-five to a hundred men and three officers. There was a lane leading down to the Dargle between the barracks and the churchyard; later known

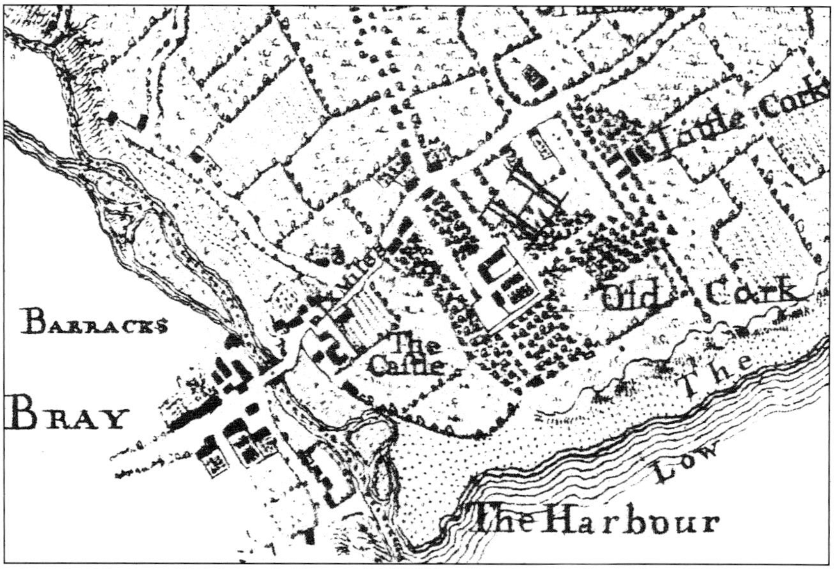

4.3. Little Bray in 1760. Part of John Rocque's survey of County Dublin.

as Jobber's Lane, it was closed off at the end of the nineteenth century although it still exists as a private driveway.

Bray's Main Street had houses and cabins on both sides all the way from the bridge roughly as far as the present Novara Avenue. But the southern part of the street was still surrounded by fields, notably the Mill Park and the Green Park, and bordered with trees and hedges. Close to the bridge on the inland side there was a terrace of three double-fronted, two-storey houses backing onto the churchyard. Next, on the corner of what is now Church Terrace, was a large detached house with two chimney stacks. This large house with its outbuildings stood on a rectangular plot backing onto the churchyard. As we have already seen, it was built by 1693 and by the 1760s it was one of the most important buildings in Bray — the Sun Inn. This corner property must always have been valuable, positioned on the corner of the lane leading to the castle and mill. And it was perhaps more than coincidence that a new building appeared there at the same time that the barracks was opened — every infantryman had to pass by to reach the main street. It is no surprise, then, that it was an inn.

The landlord of the Sun Inn in the 1760s and early 1770s was Charles Moran. He is described in one document as a 'victualler' — perhaps the inn was combined with a shop, or perhaps this was in another of his premises in Bray. In addition to the extensive inn premises, Moran also held a piece of land opposite the barracks, straddling the present Herbert Road and including the area of the present Church Terrace houses. He also held two other major properties in the centre of Bray, the quaintly-named Scraphall plot and the Turk's Head on the seaward side of Main Street, together with a square plot near the mill, and three plots in Little Bray. He must have been one of the most important personages in Bray at the time.

On the opposite side of Main Street there was a house even larger than the Sun Inn, with a central hall door and two windows on either side. This seems to have been Charles Moran's Scraphall, which within a few short years would be opened as Quin's hotel and would replace the Sun Inn as the most important hostelry in Bray. Two more two-storey houses and two or three smaller ones, all part of the same Moran property, took up the frontage as far as the present Quinsborough Road. Here Moran owned another major property, again apparently an inn, the intriguingly named 'Turk's Head'. This building had first appeared in the late seventeenth century as the White Lion — a typical inn name of the time — and later deeds refer to it as the 'White Lion or Turk's Head'. According to Barker's sketch, it was in 1762 a large single-storey building. But it was rebuilt soon after, probably as a much more impressive three-storey structure, one of the main buildings in the town.

Southwards up Main Street these substantial houses gave way to rows of cabins as the town petered out into the fields. The first few cabins were double-fronted, with a central door and a window on either side; the rest were one-roomed cabins. There were gardens behind. There was a forge a little distance out of town on the inland side of the road, busy with the sound of hammering and no doubt exuding a smell of hot coals and singeing hooves. Through the centuries the smith provided an essential service and there was a forge on this side of the street, probably on the same site, as far back as the 1690s. It may be that it stood where no. 89 Main Street is today — Devitt's forge which operated on this site in the nineteenth and early twentieth centuries is said to have carried the date 1725.

TYPICAL CABINS

Cabins *'generally consist of only one room: mud kneaded with straw in the common material of the walls; these are rarely above seven feet high, and not always above five or six; they are about two feet thick, and have only one door, which lets in light instead of a window, and should let the smoke out instead of a chimney … . The roofs of the cabins are rafters, raised from the tops of the mud walls, and the covering varies; some are thatched with straw, potato stalks, or with heath, others only covered with sods of turf cut from a grass field … .'*

(Arthur Young, *A tour in Ireland*, Dublin, 1778, vol. ii, part 2, pp 35–6)

A few more houses or cabins were scattered on the seaward side between two lanes, both dead ends. One of these lanes, a prominent one, already followed the line of the present Novara Avenue; it ended near a large house, perhaps the forerunner of Bay View, today's Novara House, which we shall meet in the next chapter. The second lane, which was L-shaped, also partly survives to the present as the road that leads to Fatima Terrace.

Main Street terminated, as it does now, with a conspicuous structure at the fork between the present Killarney Road and Vevay Road. In 1760, more than a century before the construction of the present Town Hall in the same position, the courthouse and the manor pound stood at this point. Barker shows a building, presumably the courthouse, facing back down towards the town. As was customary, the manor was entitled to a number of minor courts, and the 'petit sessions' were also held in Bray. The pound lay immediately behind, shown by Barker as a wedge-shaped enclosure. A typical pound had a strong surrounding wall — to prevent easy release of the impounded animals — and a shed to store fodder, and this was probably the case in Bray. The pound remained on this site until the 1880s, when the Town Hall was built and it was moved to the rear. It finally disappeared only in the 1980s when the Market Square shops were built.

Another large building faced towards the pound on the south side, and this was probably the Church of Ireland schoolhouse recorded in vestry books as 'adjoining the pound'. There had been a school in the parish from at least as early as 1736 and probably from much earlier and the schoolhouse was to survive until it was replaced by new premises in Little Bray at the beginning of the nineteenth century. Little else is known of education in Bray at this time. There may have been some opportunities for Catholics, perhaps in hedge schools, but the provision of Catholic schools, like the provision of a Catholic church, was some decades into the future.

Most coach travellers passing through Bray would at the pound have taken the mail coach route along the Vevay Road, the way to Wicklow town and Wexford. Going up the hill towards the 'rock of Bray', there was probably already a house on the lands of Newcourt where the Loreto Convent is today, although the property was still a few years away from prominence as the residence of the Putland family. Newcourt House itself was a little further south, on the site of the present Presentation College.

Passing Oldcourt, the home of the Edwards family, on the right, the traveller would soon reach Killruddery House, with the main road at that time passing within view of the house. This was the old 'mansion house' of Killruddery, the plain seventeenth-century house shown in the famous painting of the Killruddery hunt. The passing traveller may have been able to glimpse the gardens, laid out in formal French style in 1682, although such formality was already going out of fashion by the 1760s. Greystones did not exist, and the way south led on through Rathdown and Killincarrig.

The other road at the fork, Killarney Road, continued on towards Kilmacanogue as it does today. With Oldcourt on the left, the farm lands of Killarney and Kilbride lay to the right, part of the FitzWilliam property. There was a field called the College Close, which was glebe land belonging to St Paul's Church. Ballywaltrim and Ballymorris were also separate properties on the west side. The road meandered on past Robert Adair's house, Holybrooke, and Wingfield, home of Colonel Robert Gore.

Back in Bray town, the only other road of any size was the ancestor of the present Seapoint Road. This diverged from Main Street at the market place, curving round in front of the present Royal Hotel. It was then, and for nearly a century to come, the only roadway from Bray down to the shore. On the south side there was a twelve-acre holding that backed onto the gardens on Main Street and extended across the present Quinsborough and Florence Roads. This property, probably already called Fairy Hill, carried a large house, perhaps the same one that became the Quin family's Galtrim House in the nineteenth century.

4.4. *The famous painting of the Killruddery hunt, showing the house and garden as it was in the early 1700s (courtesy Killruddery Estates).*

4.5. *The cliff at the north end of Strand Road — the Dargle once flowed out to sea where the road is today.*

On the north side of Seapoint Road, along the river bank, there was a malt house on the site of the present commercial buildings adjoining Milton Terrace. Next came a narrow rectangular plot with a lime kiln — the ruins of a kiln remain there today. Then came the distinctive Cherry Garden. As far as this Seapoint Road followed its modern line, but at the end of the Cherry Garden it swung sharply to the south-east across what is today the Carlisle Grounds to reach the beach near the present railway station. In 1760 the area around today's Harbour Bar, Martello Terrace and harbour was still either tidal shingle or actually part of the river bed, for the Dargle curved round through ninety degrees and was forced towards Bray Head by a long sand-spit. The river finally met the Irish Sea close to where the road came out to the beach. There was a steep curving sea cliff on the corner, still noticable today below the martello tower. The cliff marked the northern end of the 'two-thirds of Keatley's holding' by this time in the hands of Robert Sharkey.

The view from the top of Sharkey's cliff was vastly different from the view from the martello tower today. Close by at the north side, the river upstream towards the bridge was braided, with large shingle banks in midstream. These banks would have been covered by lapping waters at high tide, and their shapes would have changed from time to time, particularly after major floods. Only the smallest fishing boats could penetrate any distance up river.

The sand and shingle beach that runs along the coast from Killiney ended in the long spit that diverted the mouth of the Dargle. The viewer's eye would travel along the spit and the narrow channel of the river towards the stony storm beach that stretched all the way to Bray Head. The beach had a wide ribbon of short turf on its inland side, forming an open common at least as far south as the Cock Walk, roughly where the Esplanade Hotel is today. This common has a curious distinction — the viewer might have seen the new game of golf in progress, a very early example of this pastime in Ireland. There are mentions of golf in Bray in 1762, when the club members dined at Moran's, most probably at the Sun Inn, and in 1773 when the sea-front commons was described as 'famous for the manly exercise called Goff'. The sport may have been introduced by Scottish army officers based in the barracks and taken up enthusiastically by the local gentry. Elias de Butts, who presided at the golf club's dinner in 1762, lived at Ravenswell, which coincidentally was to be the home of Bray Golf Club a century and half later.

Despite a tradition to the contrary, there were probably already a few small cabins scattered along the edge of the common, the homes of fishermen and others who made a living, legitimate or otherwise, from the sea. The common would have provided grazing for animals. But this sea-front area was not yet part of Bray; separated from the town by green fields, its inhabitants had a lengthy walk via Seapoint Road to reach the main street.

THE GOLF CLUB, 1762

> *'The golf club meet to dine at the house of Mr Charles Moran at Bray on Thursday the 28th of October at half an hour after three o'clock; Elias de Butts Esq. in the chair.'*
> (*Faulkner's Dublin Journal* 23 October 1762)

If the seaside had not yet come to play a part in the story of Bray, there was one important concern that was a continuing focus of life there — the mill. With a pedigree going back to Anglo-Norman times, it was worked in the eighteenth century by a succession of millers including Mathew Casson, Patrick Archbold, Henry Archdall and Thomas Southern. The mill-race, which lay close to the foot of the cliff, is shown clearly on the Meath estate map, and Nevill permits himself a rare pictorial symbol for the mill-wheel. The water was directed into the mill-race by a weir. An adjacent low-lying field called The Island, part of the river flood plain, was also part of the mill property. The mill was still 'the manor mill of Bray'. At some times, at least, it was combined with a tuck mill used for beating coarse woollen cloth into felt.

BRAY MILLS

> *'... the tuck-mill and water-corn mills commonly called Bray mills, with the benefit of the toll, customs of them ... also a small cabin adjoining on the said mills which the said Mathew Casson has built, and also a small parcel of ground adjoining the said mills commonly called the Holmes now and formerly in his possession ...'*
> (Extract from a 21-year lease from 29 September 1691 at £24 p.a. made between the earl of Meath and Mathew Casson of Great Bray, miller)

Leases for properties throughout the Meath estate still stipulated that the lessees should use the Bray mill. The miller in turn agreed to grind in his mill 'all corn, malt and other grist' used at Killruddery House, and there were also stipulations about the miller's use of the Dargle fishery, a concern that was jealously guarded by the earls of Meath. The mill probably served a much wider area than Bray itself. Mrs Frances Jane Seymour in *A hundred years of*

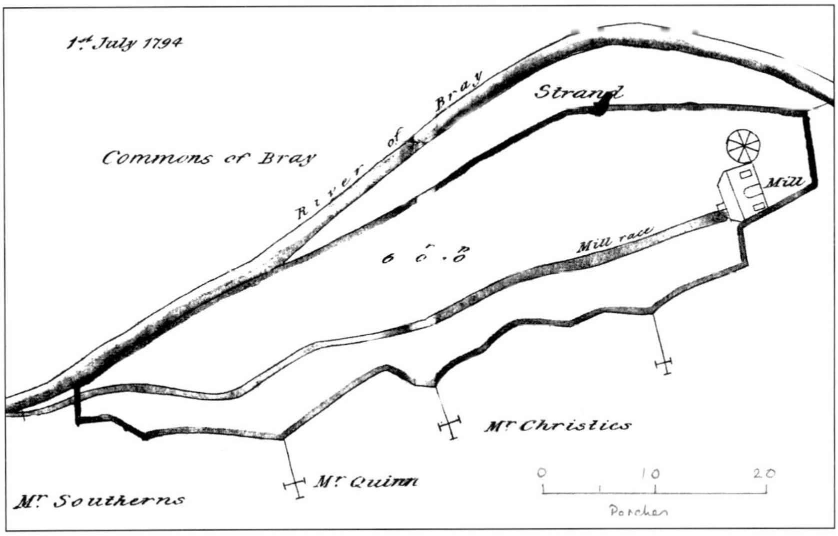

4.6. A lease map shows Bray mill in the late 1700s, still a single building with a wheel fed by the mill race.

Bray and its neighbourhood describes the women from poor farms around Shankill in about 1800 as carrying heavy loads of corn down to Bray and returning with their flour and a few groceries.

To reach the mill the women had, of course, to cross Bray Bridge, which in the century of its existence had helped not only to connect Bray more easily with Dublin city but had improved contact with south County Dublin. Above all it had linked the two parts of Bray, societally if not administratively. Little Bray had been in a different county since 1606, when County Wicklow was created, and it was in a different parish. It had not been included in the 1666 partition and its ownership was fragmented. Little Bray remained a small and relatively impoverished settlement, facing across the Dargle to its larger twin on the other bank.

The actual bridge was by 1760 the second on the site, built after the first one was destroyed by flood waters in 1741. Like its predecessor, it was a four-arch bridge, but with cutwater buttresses on the bases of the piers to protect against the flow of the river. Its appearance is still familiar today since it features prominently in W.H. Bartlett's well-known view of Bray in 1842 (see fig. 6.1). The gradient was still steep and, as before, the road made a sharp turn into Back Street. The view of Bray Bridge by William Cowen in 1825 (see fig. 5.11) shows a small pillar in the centre and this may be the ten-mile (Irish miles) milestone, noted twenty years before as being on the bridge. Rocque's map, however, shows the nine-mile stone on a different site in Back Street and the pillar may instead have marked the county boundary.

Milestones were one of the features that Rocque was anxious to show on his County Dublin map. He claimed beforehand that he intended to include every house, even every cabin, as well as a wide variety of landscape features, including roads, lanes, paths, walls and hedges. This claim was apparently not fulfilled, and his sketch of Little Bray is not to be relied upon. But it does, all the same, give some feel of what the area north of the Dargle looked like in 1760.

One of the most conspicuous features of Little Bray right up until the 1860s was the large area of common land stretching along the river bank on both sides of the main road. The Upper Commons, covering the present People's Park and the area between the Upper and Lower Dargle Roads, was at that time a flat, marshy, flood plain, crossed by a track that meandered from near Bray Bridge towards the present Dargle Tavern. Local landholders had grazing rights, and it is likely that there were already a few poor families living as squatters in tiny cabins around the edge. Upper Dargle Road followed its present route as far as the end of the commons, before turning sharply uphill towards Old Connaught — in 1760 it did not yet continue to Kilmacanogue.

The Lower Commons, on the seaward side of the main Dublin road, was a third of the size of the Upper Commons — 13 acres compared with 37 acres — and until the construction much later of Ravenswell Road its river bank was irregular and indented; Rocque even shows two large islands on this side. While the houses on the west side of Back Street seem to have faced the street, those on the east side, near the castle, were irregularly placed somewhat back from the road. There was a small triangular plot of land at the junction of Upper Dargle Road and the Dublin road, still reflected today in the open space opposite the entrance to Ravenswell House. The avenue leading to Old Connaught was impressive, with a row of trees on either side and a large circular feature in the centre halfway along.

The most prominent house in the vicinity of Little Bray was Corke Abbey, surrounded by trees and named as 'Old Cork' on Rocque's map. The former home of the Revd John Bushe, it was soon to be a base for the lord lieutenant of Ireland and other fashionable visitors to Bray.

Although Little Bray was in most ways poorer than Great Bray it had one advantage: it had an excellent supply of spring water from Broderick's Well. This well, on the north side of Upper Dargle Road some hundred metres beyond the present junction with the Lower Dargle Road, was said to have medicinal qualities, but was most important for providing a reliable supply of fresh water. Otherwise Bray's water supply was drawn from the Dargle, from private wells, or from the minor streams round the town. There was, of course, no public lighting and the darkness at night, penetrated only dimly by flickering candle and lamp light shining from the windows, was still almost as absolute as it had been five hundred years before. There were no proper arrangements for the disposal of waste, human and otherwise. But in 1760 the problems Bray was to face in the provision of clean water, lighting and sewerage facilities for a burgeoning seasonal population were still a century into the future.

Bray from the railway.

PART II

That favourite resort

Chapter 5

'Sea bathing and goat's whey': Bray 1760–1850

'Its vicinity to the sea, the mountains, and to the most agreeable parts of the county of Wicklow, renders it [Bray] a desirable situation during the seasons for goat's-whey and sea-bathing.'
(*The postchaise companion or traveller's directory*, Dublin, 3rd ed. 1805, p. 421)

As the people of Bray went about their daily lives in the 1760s they could not have foreseen the changes that were about to take place in their sleepy little town. For Bray was soon to find itself with natural assets that would transform it into a flourishing tourist resort, well before the nineteenth-century arrival of the railway and the transformation of the town into the place we know today.

Two great movements that were to alter the character of Bray dramatically in the coming decades were already heralded elsewhere. The first of these was the Romantic Movement, which, with its new interest in awe-inspiring scenery, was to make Bray's proximity to the wild Wicklow Mountains a major advantage rather than the disadvantage it had been in the days of raiders and rebels. The second was the new fashion for sea bathing — not bathing as the recreation we enjoy today but for its curative and health-giving powers — which made Bray at last find its sea coast a substantial asset.

From the early eighteenth century onwards, under the influence of the Romantic Movement, the leisured classes in Ireland and Britain began to admire wild scenery: rugged precipices, dramatic waterfalls, steep valleys. Previously such features had been seen as fearsome relics of some dreadful earth-rending catastrophe, most probably the biblical flood; now they represented the 'sublime' in nature, to be looked upon with meditative wonder. Visitors, including many from outside Ireland, began to visit scenic areas among which north-east Wicklow was one of the most popular. The awe-inspiring Powerscourt Waterfall and the rocky wildernesses of the Scalp,

5.1. *Powerscourt waterfall, 1839; Bray was a stopping place on the way to this famous Wicklow beauty spot.*

the Glen of the Downs, the Dargle Glen, and, further south, the Devil's Glen became favourite destinations.

ATTRACTIONS OF NORTH-EAST WICKLOW

> *'The beauties of the county Wicklow, particularly its adjacencies to Dublin, have of late so much attracted the speculations of the wealthy, as very much to enhance the price of lands there. In the charming vicinity of the Dargle, the Glen of the Down, Newtown Mountkennedy, Dunran, The Devil's Glen, etc., lands have almost doubled their rents, and 'tis generally imagined that in less than ten years more, lands there will double even their present price.'* (*Freeman's Journal* 15 June 1791)

Bray became a stopping point for visitors to the mountains, a town where a good meal or overnight accommodation could be obtained. One example of a day's touring involved setting out from Dublin early in the morning and having breakfast in Bray at 9 a.m. before spending the day in the Delgany area. On the return journey another stop was made at an inn in Bray to refresh the horses, and, no doubt, the travellers. Longer visits to Wicklow beauty spots often included one or more nights spent in Bray on the way to and from Dublin. For instance, one three-day excursion in 'an open carriage, called a barouche' with four horses, travelled out via Enniskerry to visit Powerscourt and spent the first night at Newtownmountkennedy; on the second day the party visited Delgany before spending a night in Bray and returning to Dublin through Killiney.

TOURING IN WICKOW: BRAY AS A STOPPING POINT

'This town or village being a great thoroughfare for travellers, and also much frequented by the citizens of Dublin, on account of the extreme beauty of its vicinity, there are no less than twenty-two post chaises kept at this inn.'
([John Gough], *A tour in Ireland, in 1813 and 1814*, Dublin, [n.d.], pp 181–8)

'As a bathing-place, a good Sunday drive from the metropolis, and, above all, as the grand pass from thence to all the principal beauties of Wicklow, it [Bray] maintains an important position on the map of this county.'
(A. Atkinson, *The Irish tourist*, Dublin, 1815, p. 610).

'... we proceeded to the house of Mr. H., in Dame-Street, and shortly after set off from thence in a [jaunting] car, in company with a few friends, to enjoy ourselves during the day in a rural excursion. ... We reached Bray, a small town, ten Irish miles distant from Dublin, at about nine o'clock, where we breakfasted at Mr Quin's well-known hotel. The house is large; the stabling, or livery, as it is termed, attached to it will accommodate 170 horses. Mr Quin is said to be very wealthy, and is said to have mortgages of the estates of the gentry in the neighbourhood. ... After a good breakfast à la fourchette, [with a fork?] for 2s., we proceeded through a delightfully romantic country to Delganny ... . Late in the evening we quitted this interesting neighbourhood and drove to Bray. We stopped at the outskirts of the town, to refresh the horses, and went up stairs in a small public house to wait until they were ready. ... I took a walk through one of the streets, and went into a small china shop, where I conversed a short time with the master of it. ... We reached Dublin at half-past eleven o'clock ... .'
(A.B., *Observations made during a short excursion to Dublin, Delganny, &c. in 1823*, Dublin, [1823], pp 4–5.)

The proximity of this enticing mountain scenery might not in itself have turned Bray into a popular resort — Enniskerry had the same advantages, with the extra benefits of close proximity to both the Dargle Glen and the Powerscourt Waterfall, and with a scenic approach from Dublin through the Scalp. It was the second emerging pastime, the brand-new interest in sea bathing, that was above all to favour Bray.

Just as the mountains had been seen as frightening up to this time, so had the coast. It is difficult at this remove to know how the inhabitants of Bray once thought of the sea. Certainly it was very different to the way we think of it now, sufficiently different to explain why the town had so far turned its back on the shore. The general view at the time was that the sea was unfriendly and dangerous, a place of monsters and unfathomable depths, cruel to seafarers and fishermen. Coastlines were thought to be ugly, with their jagged headlands and islands that seemed to have been torn from the land; some theories maintained that the coast, like the mountain ranges, had been created by the raging waters of Noah's flood. Moreover the seaside was generally held to be unhealthy, with the smell of seaweed and rotting debris on the shore producing air that was bad rather than bracing.

THE PAINS OF SEA TRAVEL

'"The sailing-packet" was a small trader — schooner or sloop; the cabin, of very limited extent, was lined with "berths;" a curtain portioned off those that were appropriated to ladies. In the centre was a table — seldom used, the formality of a dinner being a rare event; each passenger having laid in his own supply of "sea store", to which he resorted when hungered or athirst; finding, however, very often, when his appetite returned, that his basket had been impoverished by the visits of unscrupulous voyagers who were proof against sea-sickness. ... It was not alone the miserable paucity of accommodation and utter indifference to the comfort of the passengers, that made the voyage an intolerable evil. Though it usually occupied but three or four days, frequently as many weeks were expended in making it. It was once our lot to pass a month between the ports of Bristol and Cork; putting back, every now and again, to the wretched village of Pill, and not daring to leave it even for an hour, lest the wind should change and the packet weigh anchor.'

(Mr and Mrs S.C. Hall, *Ireland, its scenery, character, etc.*, vol. i, p. 1)

On a practical level, sea travel was often an unpleasant experience to be undertaken only out of necessity; stormy weather offered the real danger of shipwreck while flat calm meant that sailing ships sometimes could not reach their destinations for long, boring hours or days on end — Arthur Young complained in his *Tour* that his journey from Holyhead to Dún Laoghaire in 1776 was 'a tedious passage of twenty-two hours'. There was another misery, largely forgotten today, in the prevalence of sea sickness, which, combined with squalid conditions, was a terrible trial for passengers. The sea was also a lawless realm, infested with pirates. Before the situation was transformed in the early nineteenth century by the arrival of steamships, it was only the determined traveller who made the journey across the Irish Sea.

But now, too, there was a reappraisal, beginning particularly in England, where the small village of Brighthelmstone — soon to be famous under the name of Brighton — became a fashionable resort from the middle years of the eighteenth century onwards, as did other towns and villages around the coast. The seaside was seen to have health-giving benefits and sea bathing became a fashionable pursuit. Immersion in the sea was thought to renew energies and to strengthen invalids.

For women and girls, bathing involved changing into a woollen bathing dress — later for modesty's sake worn with trousers underneath — inside a cramped bathing hut or bathing machine. A bonnet or cap and, on stony beaches, some sort of footwear, completed the outfit. The bather was then plunged into the cold waves by an attendant, often with the head held underwater to increase the sense of immersion. Once it was soaked through, the heavy bathing dress greatly hampered the movements of its wearer. The time in the water was short, perhaps only five minutes and customarily not more than half an hour, and was followed by a brisk rub down with towels to restore the circulation. Men usually bathed independently and more adventurously, and, both to prevent spying upon the ladies and because male nude bathing was customary, were confined to a different part of the beach. (Women, too, apparently bathed in the nude in eighteenth-century England, the custom in Bray remains obscure.)

Part of this new interest in the seaside arose from the unhealthy conditions prevailing in big cities and the desire by those who could afford it to spend time in more salubrious air. One Dublin writer, John Rutty, complained in the 1770s of: 'the fogginess from the smoke when there is no wind to disperse it, the dirtiness of our streets, which is so great that one is frequently in danger of being up to the knees in crossing them, the putrid animal effluvia exhaling from charnel-houses and dunghills in the middle of the city and in several of the avenues, and dead animals, dogs and cats and the excrements of living ones, butcher's garbage and blood ...'.

Consumption — tuberculosis — was a major problem, and drinking goat's whey was prescribed as a cure. By the 1760s Carrickmines in south County Dublin was one of the localities resorted to by Dubliners looking for fresh air and cures for their 'pulmonary complaints', and a writer in the *Hibernian Magazine* of August 1773 describes how he has taken up residence in a farmhouse on the slopes of the Great Sugar Loaf 'for the convenience of goats whey'. In Ireland, as in Britain and on the continent, there was also some tradition of visiting spas for medicinal purposes. But the emphasis was now switching to the seaside, to Clontarf and Howth north of Dublin city and to Blackrock, Dun Leary (soon to be renamed Kingstown) and, not least, to Bray in the south.

One of the earliest references to sea bathing at Bray dates from 1773, when the property of Seafield, bordering the shore at the southern end of the present Esplanade, was advertised to let in *Saunders's Newsletter*, a newspaper of the time. Among the attractions of this 'genteel country seat' with its bow window in the parlour facing the sea, was the advantage that it was 'well situated for the goat's whey, for bathing, boating and fishing'. The name 'Seafield House' has survived, although the present house of that name is of later date.

LOCAL VILLAS

'Among the numerous villas within the parish are those of Fairy-hill, Bayview, Newcourt, Oldcourt, Killarney, Giltspur, Springfield, Violet-hill, St. Valory, Ballymorris, Herbert, Riversdale, Belleview, Edenview, and Richview.'
(*The parliamentary gazetteer of Ireland*, London, 1846, vol. i, p. 277)

Soon other good houses were available for letting for the summer months, as advertised in the *Freeman's Journal*. Strandville, a 'beautiful bathing lodge' close to Bray was available in July 1809. At the start of the 1819 season Newcourt House, where the Presentation College is today, was convenient for 'marketing, dining, sea bathing and goat's whey'. 'A modern house and garden with stabling for five horses, and five to fifteen acres of ground', name unspecified, was advertised in the *Freeman's Journal* twice in 1821, in May and again, having failed to be let 'for the season', in July.

Violet Hill, described as one and a half miles from Bray, was in the winter of 1834 advertised as a 'select boarding house' for the 'nobility and gentry'. A number of substantial houses let to summer visitors were the property of the same local landowner, the Hon. Sidney Herbert, son of the eleventh earl

5.2. *The bathing lodge Bay View, now Novara House; largely rebuilt a few years ago, the façade is probably original.*

5.3. *Eden View (later Prospect Lodge and later still Carrigbrae), now part of the Marino Centre — a large, elegant bathing lodge of the early 1800s.*

5.4. *This nameplate for Eden View survives over an entrance in Herbert Road.*

of Pembroke and later first Lord Herbert of Lea. Clearly Herbert, who was to have a notable career in British public life, was actively promoting sea bathing in Bray, and in the 1830s he owned four 'bathing lodges' in different parts of the town, evocatively named Bay View, Rich View, Eden View and Bellevue.

Of these Bay View, the nearest to the sea front, has survived on the north side of Novara Avenue; as Novara House, it was largely rebuilt in the 1980s. Eden View, even more substantial and looking down on the town from an elevated site at the corner of the present Church Road, is now part of the Marino Centre. Rich View on Killarney Road was also a substantial house; it was renamed Beechurst in the 1890s and survived until about 1978 when it was demolished and the present Beechurst houses were built on the site. Bellevue was also close to Killarney Road; a square double-fronted house of that name existed until the mid twentieth century. All of these would have been in semi-rural situations at the time.

There was one notable bathing lodge in Little Bray and it, too, has survived. Arbutus Lodge, tucked away behind the Dublin Road and said to have been built in 1802, was described in 1836 by the compilers of the Ordnance Survey name book as being 'generally occupied by persons who come there for the purpose of receiving the salt water'.

VISITORS TO BRAY

'The town has for many years been a favourite summer resort of the wealthier of the Dublin citizens and of the gentry from a large part of Ireland; and it possesses, in a state of high facility and polish, the various appliances required for their accommodation and comfort, whether as lodgers or as tourists. Handsome cottages ornées, boarding houses on different scales of economy, and furnished houses from the small abode to the luxurious mansion, abound both in the town and in its environs, for the special use of visitors.'
(*The parliamentary gazetteer of Ireland*, London, 1846, vol. i, p. 277)

It is much frequented in the bathing season by strangers, who are attracted by the purity of the water which washes its shores, bordering on the Dublin bay, and by the beautiful scenery, with which the neighbourhood abounds. … That stupendous rocky mountain, called Bray-Head, is contiguous to the town, and, although barren, it presents a most majestic appearance.'
(*Pigot's national commercial directory of Ireland*, Dublin, 1824, p. 136)

All these are representative of the best of the houses rented out in Bray, at rents that could be as much as £100 for the season, a considerable sum. A stay in a boarding house or private home, probably for weeks rather than for the whole summer, was another alternative. The proprietor of Woodbine Lodge boarding house, close to Main Street on Seapoint Road, was able to advertise proudly in April 1815 that the premises had been enlarged and were now open for the season 'for the reception of ladies and gentlemen'; convenience for sea bathing and goat's whey was again mentioned. Many other Bray residents already took in summer visitors, just as they were to do for the best part of another two hundred years.

Apart from the places to stay in and around the town, accommodation on a modest scale was available along the sea front. Households catered for visitors by offering rooms or by providing the facilities for simple meals. One tradition has it that in about 1800 there were only two cabins on the shore, one near Bray Head lived in by a beachcomber and pebble seller and her daughters (one version has it that she made a fortune from assisting smugglers), the other a poor fisherman's miserable hovel known as the 'Rat Hole'. Conceivably this had been true earlier, but in the early 1800s there were an increasing number of cottages scattered all along the rough track that ran the length of the bay. John Taylor's map *The environs of Dublin,*

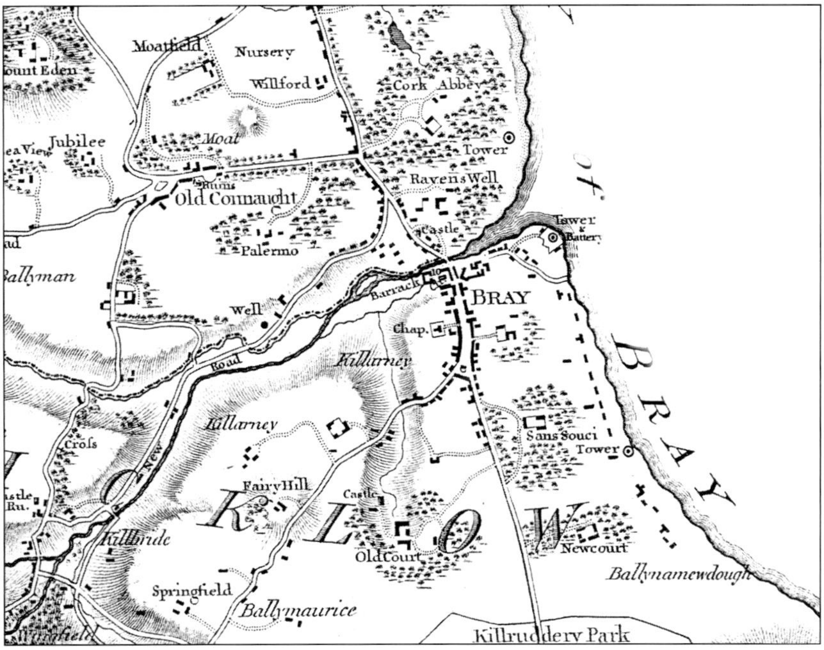

5.5. Bray in 1816 from John Taylor's map of the environs of Dublin. Note the scatter of cottages along the shore and the three martello towers. Only the middle tower, no.2, survives today.

5.6. *Bray Head in the 1770s — the south end of Bray beach has sand dunes and a probable bathing hut (Gabriel Beranger, courtesy Royal Irish Academy).*

published in 1816, shows at least fifteen houses or cabins; the first Ordnance Survey mapped some forty in 1838 and reported that they were 'let to sea bathers in the summer'. Many families probably combined fishing with catering for bathers.

One item from this period that has not survived in any shape or form is that indispensable adjunct to the bathing process, the bathing hut. But we know that they existed — in 1857 Elizabeth Byrne, who lived right on the shore in one of the few cottages that were to remain into the twentieth century, claimed that she had 'for some fifty years erected bathing boxes and used the foreshore by extending planks ... out into deep water for bathing purposes'.

A painting of the 1770s by Gabriel Beranger shows an empty shore in front of Bray Head, but with a small upright structure, perhaps to be explained as the family bathing hut of the landowner, George Putland senior, who had recently acquired San Souci, now the Loreto Convent. If so it is the earliest representation of a bathing feature in Bray. Bathing machines on wheels, often horse-drawn, and offering the extra convenience that they could be trundled a distance down the beach and through shallow water thus preserving modesty, were popular in British resorts right into the twentieth century, but it is not clear whether they were ever used regularly in Bray where water of sufficient depth was easily reachable.

The positive effects of this early tourism — tourism then confined to the

5.7. Early nineteenth-century houses at the south end of Main Street. Still relatively newly-developed in the 1850s and '60s, this end of the street escaped the urban renewal that took place nearer Bray Bridge.

wealthier sections of the community — are clearly to be seen both in the rapid growth of Bray and in the increasing number of shopkeepers and tradesmen. By 1816 the town had doubled in size in fifty years. Houses, some of which still survive, had been built on both sides of Main Street up as far as the pound. The new houses on the west side of Main Street lay mainly on the earl of Meath's Mill Park. The houses on the east side of Main Street were also on Meath land, the Green Park, but were more discontinuous despite the solid row depicted on Taylor's map. There were also small cottages on the northern parts of Killarney Road and Vevay Road.

The population, which was probably some five or six hundred persons in the 1760s, was estimated in 1800 as having risen to nearly two thousand. By the time of the 1841 census, and before the period of stagnation during the years of the Great Famine, it passed the three thousand mark. The ratio of Roman Catholics to Church of Ireland remained much the same over the hundred years to 1850, at about five to one. By 1834 Bray had a modest twenty-three 'dissenters', i.e. Methodists and Presbyterians, a number that was to rise steeply later in the century.

The 1841 census returns also provide an impression of the housing mix of the town. Bray and Bray Commons had just under four hundred dwellings in 1841, twenty-six of which — a very respectable number — were classified as 'first-class', i.e. with more than nine rooms. Of the rest, ninety, or more than a fifth of the total, were one-roomed mud cabins each with a single window. Little Bray had three first-class houses, and its thirty-eight one-roomed cabins represented a near quarter of the total of one hundred and sixty dwellings. But most houses in both Bray and Little Bray fell into the middle two categories 'better' with two to four rooms and 'good' with five to nine rooms, with a modest preponderance of the former.

LUCAS'S DIRECTORY, 1788

'BRAY
COUNTY OF WICKLOW
Brown William, coast surveyor of the Customs.
Brown Robert, soap boiler and chandler.
Byrne Bridget, linen draper.
Connor James, grocer and liquor dealer.
Connoly Bryan, baker and corn dealer.
Cranston Andrew, M.D. and man midwife.
Christie Simon, grocer, wine and spirit merchant.
Delany John, baker and corn dealer.
Doran Bryan, tailor and habit maker.
Edwards John, woollen manufacturer, Old Court.
Hughes Henry, ship owner.
Martin Joseph, brewer.
Mc. Ardle John, slater.
Matthews Constantine, disiller and ship owner.
Moore James, surgeon and apothecary.
Nailer John, corn dealer and miller.
Nailer Daniel, corn dealer and miller, Mullin Ramson.
Pike William, boot and shoe maker.
Quin William, vintner, Meath Arms Inn.
Seymour George, glazier and brewer.
Sharkey Thomas, lime manufacturer.
Southern Thomas, lime manufacturer.
Tobin William, boot and shoe maker.
Toole Tobias, coal, slate, timber merchant, and ship owner.
Warren John, vintner, Mount Cashel Arms Inn.'
(Richard Lucas, *A general directory of the kingdom of Ireland*, 1788.)

Directories of the time help to flesh out this changing picture. In the earliest, Richard Lucas's of 1788, Bray is credited with twenty-five entries, including two corn dealers and millers, two grocers, two bakers, two boot and shoe makers, a linen draper (the only woman in the list) and a tailor. There were also two doctors (one whom was also a 'man midwife'), two brewers, a ship owner and a 'distiller and ship owner'. A third ship owner dealt in coal, slate and timber, and there were two inns.

By Pigot's directory of 1824 the number of shopkeepers had risen to twenty including six grocers and provision dealers, three bakers, two butchers, four linen drapers and a hardware dealer. There were two apothecaries, a haberdasher and — perhaps with a special place in a seaside resort — a straw bonnet maker. There were by now an assortment of craftsmen, including four boot and shoe makers, two tailors, two saddlers and harness makers, a tin-plate worker, a watch and clock maker, and a leather breeches maker. Nine publicans, of whom four were in Little Bray, served the town, as well as the major establishment which by now figured prominently in Bray's story — Quin's Hotel.

The name of William Quin did not feature in the Bray of the 1760s, but he arrived soon afterwards, since Quin's Hotel was opened in 1776. It was apparently at first known as the Meath Arms Inn. The present Royal Hotel is its direct descendant, back now on the original 'Scraphall' site after a lengthy period on an adjoining one. Presumably Charles Moran sold his property to Quin, perhaps at the time that he retired from business himself. Certainly in 1788 the Sun Inn was not listed in Lucas's directory; in addition to William Quin's Meath Arms Inn, John Warren had the Mount Cashel Arms Inn which may have been next door on the south side, perhaps the old White Lion. The Christie family also ran an inn in the latter part of the eighteenth century.

Since William Quin died in about 1811 and had a son born in 1761, he was probably in his late thirties or forties when he arrived in Bray. John Quin senior joined his father by 1800 and his son, also John, came into the

NOBILITY, GENTRY AND CLERGY.

Brady Westby, esq.	*Meath Earl of, Kilruddery*
Grant John, esq.	*Putland Geo. esq.*
Johnstone Mrs.	*Westby Wm. esq.*
Kingsmill Lieut. Parr, H.P.	*Wray Thos. esq. Little Bray*
McMann Mrs.	*Young Rev. Wm.*

BRAY IN 1824: NOBILITY, GENTRY AND CLERGY

BRAY IN 1824: MERCHANTS AND TRADESMEN

MERCHANTS, TRADESMEN, &C.

PROFESSIONAL GENTLEMEN

Heffernan Nesbitt, physician and surgeon, Little Bray

Wray Thos. barrister, Little Bray

SHOPKEEPERS & TRADERS

Anderson John, linen-draper and haberdasher
Belton John, tin-plate-worker and brazier
Brady Ann, linen-draper
Byrne John, tailor
Byrne Michael, grocer
Callagan James, grocer
Carroll James, circulating library
Cassidy J. saddler & harness-maker
Cassidy Robt. apothecary
Charles Richd. Leather seller
Christie Hannah, grocer
Christie H & Son, ale and porter brewers
Coghlan Bryan, butcher
Dunn Thos. victualler
Farrell John, builder
Gilmor Patrick, watch & clock-maker
Healy Patrick, leather breeches-maker and glover
Keane Patrick, baker
Kearney Wm. grocer
McKennew Wm. linen-draper
Miller Charlotte, grocer
Mooney Michl. Saddler and harness-maker
Newcomben Wm. house-painter and glazier
Nolan Dennis, boot & shoemaker
Nowlan Eliz. boot & shoemaker
Pike Patrick, boot & shoemaker
Reilly Michael, baker
Reilly Stephen, carpenter & builder
Roche Mary, provision dealer
Rolan Thos. tailor
Ryon [sic] *Thos. boot & shoemaker*
Schooles Alex. apothecary
Seymour Geo. coal and slate merchant
Shepard Henrietta, haberdasher
Wallace Jane, straw bonnet-maker
Waller Robt. hardware dealer
Wilson Wm. linen-draper
Winders Jeremiah, baker

TAVERNS AND PUBLIC HOUSES

Quin John, (hotel)
Byrne John
Collins John, Little Bray
Fennell Wm.
Jenkins Henry, Little Bray
Jordan Ralph
McCabe Michl. Little Bray
McGorrin James
Rooney John
Synnott James, Little Bray

(*Pigot's national commercial directory of Ireland*, 1824.)

5.8. *Royal Hotel,* c. *1950. The central and left-hand portions were Quin's Hotel in the early nineteenth century; the right-hand block is the post-1854 addition.*

business to add a third generation of entrepreneurs. The name Quin's Hotel dates from the early years of the nineteenth century — the French 'hotel' only replaced 'inn' for the better kind of establishment towards the end of the 1700s. (The term 'tourist', too, apparently dates from about 1800.) Quin's was soon mentioned very frequently in newspaper reports and in visitors' eulogies of the time, for the Quin family rapidly made a reputation for their hotel as one of the best in Ireland.

Its site was a good one. The inn was immediately visible, as is the Royal Hotel today, to travellers arriving over the bridge from Dublin; it faced across to St Paul's Church, and Bray's markets and fairs took place outside its windows. When the courthouse was built in 1841, the legal profession had to take only a few steps to reach the hotel's door. The site had another advantage, quickly exploited by the Quins, in that it lay on the coastal side of the main street. Before long the Quin family owned all the fields behind the hotel, including from 1810 onwards the northern part of the coastal 'two-thirds Keatley's holding', and were able to lay out a 'broad gravel walk' from their premises to reach the shore in the vicinity of the present railway station. Passersby who today stroll along the inner road in front of Duncairn Terrace are following in the footsteps of the fashionable throng that sauntered down 'Quin's Walk' to take the sea air two hundred years ago. The Quins also provided hot and cold baths, which were by now regarded as a necessary adjunct to bathing in the sea itself. They provided bathing huts on the sea front. They expanded into transport, and were said to have twenty-two post chaises available for travellers and stabling for 170 horses. John Quin ran a coaching service between Bray and Dublin — 'Quinsbray' — and kept stables in Dublin's Pembroke Street. He was also listed as a 'coach and car builder' in the 1840s, perhaps using premises behind the hotel. Apart from his commercial enterprises, John Quin senior was a shrewd investor, and documents have survived showing that he was in a position to lend substantial sums of money at highly profitable rates.

With some sixty bedrooms in 1835, Quin's Hotel was by far the largest hotel in east Wicklow. In 1852, just before the great upheavals that were to follow the arrival of the railway, it charged 2s 6d a night — more than any other hotel in Ireland with the exception of a few in Dublin and one other Wicklow hotel, Hunter's, further south at Rathnew. The fashionable crowd who flocked to Bray included a lord lieutenant of Ireland, Earl de Grey, who stayed at Quin's Hotel several times, including a visit prescribed by doctors for his 'flying gout' in March 1842 when 'many distinguished people called on him'.

In the 1840s an 'omnibus' ran three times a day from Quin's Hotel to the Dublin and Kingstown Railway terminus at Kingstown. There was also a direct omnibus from Quin's Hotel to Dublin every morning at half-past eight; according to Mrs Seymour in *A hundred years of Bray and its neighbourhood*, this was 'much patronised by ladies who wanted to do a day's shopping in Dublin, and who did not find it convenient to bring their own horse and man so far'. Other services to Dublin also left Bray twice a day

5.9. *Andrew Nicholl's view of Main Street from the east in about 1840; Quin's Walk leads down to the sea where Quinsborough Road is today, cows graze on the site of Florence Road.*

from close to the hotel, one from outside Isaac Mason's public house, later called the Anchor Tavern — the building closest to Bray Bridge on the west side of Main Street, today's no. 116.

QUIN'S HOTEL AND COACHING SERVICE

> *'TO FAMILIES GOING TO THE COUNTRY. THE proprietor of the BRAY HOTEL, takes leave to inform his Friends and the Public, that since last Season he has made such additions and improvements, as he trusts will be found to obviate every objection that may have hitherto been made to his House. Families taken to Board in their Private apartments as usual. Baths, Fresh and Salt, Hot and Cold, with Shower ditto, always ready, for the accommodation of Families in the Hotel and those residing in the neighbourhood. An elegant appointed Coach with Four Horses, leaves the above Hotel every Morning at Half-past Eight o'Clock and arrives in Town at Ten. Returns every Afternoon, leaving No. 2, LOWER PEMBROKE-STREET at Half-past Four o'Clock, and arrives in Bray precisely at Six.'*
> (*Freeman's Journal* 30 April 1832)
>
> *'Bray, which we have selected as the first station for those desirous of seeing the beauties of Wicklow, has long been a favourite resort; and the excellent hotel and posting establishment of Quin have greatly conduced to the increase of visitors. Connected with the hotel are cold and tepid baths; and for those who prefer the sea, bathing-boxes, with a private walk through pleasure grounds to the beach. From the lower end of this walk a fine view is obtained of Bray Head, the coast, town, and suburbs of Bray, and of the beautiful circular outline formed by the surrounding mountains. Pews are reserved in the different places of worship for the frequenters of this hotel; and, in short, every accommodation is afforded, as well to travellers as to sojourners. In summer, Bray is considerably frequented as a watering-place, the air being found highly salubrious; and, in addition to the hotel, there are inns and numerous lodging-houses in and around the town, suited to the various ranks and conditions of visitors.'*
> James Fraser, *Guide to the county of Wicklow* (Dublin 1842), pp 6–7.

The Dublin, Wicklow and Wexford coaches passed through Bray's Main Street until the early 1800s, when a new mail coach route was built via the Glen of the Downs. The new Wexford road bypassed the centre of Bray, following the present Upper Dargle Road and extending it south-westwards along the Dargle before swinging southwards towards Kilmacanogue. The Upper Dargle Road was to form part of the principal route to the south-east until the M 11 by-pass was built in the late twentieth century.

Apart from Quin's hotel and the other attractions of Bray itself, the town was encircled by large country houses belonging to wealthy gentry and professional families, many with town houses in Dublin but anxious to spend part of the year enjoying the south Dublin and Wicklow scenery. Many of these large houses were built or rebuilt during the late eighteenth and early nineteenth centuries; some were available for letting and most had residents who contributed to the social life of the neighbourhood. Corke Abbey, just north of Little Bray, was a favourite with successive lord lieutenants and their visits involved some pomp and ceremony. Thus when Lord Camden paid a visit, not his first, in 1796, he arrived by sea in the 'Dunleary barge' and was 'saluted by frigates off the coast as he passed along'. In 1814 Viscount Whitworth had a bodyguard of grenadiers from the Royal Cheshire Militia, and all visits must have involved a considerable retinue.

In the late eighteenth century Corke Abbey was home to a member of the lord lieutenant's privy council, Theopolis Jones, which may account for some of the lord lieutenant's visits; in the early nineteenth century it was the property of Colonel Edward Wingfield, son of Lord Powerscourt. It was let to the lord lieutenant for the whole summer of 1814; it was also let to other

__5.10.__ View looking downstream, c. *1800. St Paul's Church and the barracks are at the right; the ford in the foreground may be the one by the mill weir.*

members of the aristocracy, for instance to Lord Lismore for the season in 1811. The *Freeman's Journal* also found it worthy of note that various personalities from across the Irish Sea visited major houses in the neighbourhood. For example, in 1824 the British foreign secretary George Canning was at Old Connaught House, home of the barrister and politician Lord Plunkett, as well as at Killruddery, while the agriculturist and writer William Cobbett stayed with General Sir George Cockburn at Shanganagh Castle, north of Little Bray, in 1834.

FASHIONABLE VISITORS

> *'The Lord Lieutenant and the Duchess of Dorset have been for a few days past on a visit to Lord Powerscourt, at his beautiful residence near Enniskerry. His Excellency and her Grace were at Powerscourt Church on Sunday last. The Lord Lieutenant and suite are expected to move to Cork Abbey about the 15th instant, having taken it for four months from the Hon. Colonel Wingfield. A number of fashionables are, in consequence, collecting in Bray.'* (*Freeman's Journal* 6 July 1814)

On the other side of Bray the earl of Meath's Killruddery House was, of course, predominant and the Meath/Brabazon family, together with the Wingfields of Powerscourt and the Moncks of Charleville, represented the pinnacle of the local social scene. The family was not always in residence, however, and Killruddery, too, was let periodically; in 1826 the lord lieutenant, Marquis Wellesley, eldest brother of the duke of Wellington, took it for the summer.

The story of Bray's growth in the late eighteenth and early nineteenth centuries was not, however, entirely one of uninterrupted and happy progress. Just as external factors were responsible for that growth, so the great national cataclysms of the time impinged on the life of the town. The first of these was the 1798 rebellion, in which County Wicklow was much involved, with the number of subsequent claims for compensation second only to those of County Wexford. The rebellion broke out on the night of 23–4 May, and had largely collapsed by late July, though the aftershocks

5.11. View looking upstream, 1825, part of a pen and ink drawing by William Cowen.

reverberated on into 1799 and well beyond. The United Irishmen had already spread rapidly in Wicklow in 1797, with a well-organised group in the Powerscourt area as early as 1796.

Bray was soon affected by the government response, the quartering of the military, both in Bray barracks itself — strategically important as one of only two in County Wicklow — and in the large camp at Lehaunstown (Loughlinstown). The presence of troops was viewed, of course, with contrasting feelings, very welcome as a promise of security to those loyal to the Crown and equally repugnant to those planning the uprising. The soldiers must have brought extra business to Bray, but at a high cost, for their methods of keeping order were often harsh.

As the unrest deepened, Bray barracks was crammed with prisoners not yet brought to trial. There were a number of executions. Two prominent Bray republicans, Richard Kennedy and Thomas Ledwich, were hanged in Little Bray. Two others, Patrick Burke and Tom White, were shot on the sea-front commons for administering the United Irishmen oath. By late May 1798 the loyal inhabitants of Bray were once again as in medieval times gazing apprehensively over their shoulders towards the mountains, where fires from the rebel camps were visible from a great distance. At the same time republicans were looking towards the sea; munitions were being secretly shipped into County Wicklow, and it may be that Bray beach and Bray Head were among the convenient landing places.

With the outbreak of the rebellion, Bray became an important stopping point for government forces moving southwards; the town must have been filled to bursting point, both with infantry and with cavalry, with all the need for provisions and accommodation such crowding entailed. Of the two locally recruited units, Bray town was guarded by the Bray yeoman infantry, under the liberal Captain John Edwards of Oldcourt House, while the Bray cavalry, based at Killruddery under the tenth earl of Meath, patrolled the wider neighbourhood.

The key engagement in north Wicklow was that at Newtownmountkennedy on 30 May and the defeat of the rebel forces there reduced the threat to Bray. It also incidentally reduced the pressure on the town, as troops moved away to pursue the rebels into the mountains. Bray remained in a state of high alert, however; the *Freeman's Journal* reported that on 7 June 1798 they 'were under arms all the night' after reports, that proved to be false, of rebels assembling near Killruddery.

The town was, ostensibly at least, on the government side; the inhabitants carried arms and the poor showed their loyalty by wearing blue or red rags as badges on their hats. Nonetheless among the followers of the United Irishmen were, apparently, seventeen men employed by a Bray brewer, who left to join the rebels. Although not named in the newspaper report, the brewery was probably the new Bray Brewery next to the mill, and the number of men involved suggests that this brewery was already a major employer in the town.

Bray felt some of the after-effects of the engagements at Arklow and Vinegar Hill in June 1798, when wounded troops were brought to a temporary infirmary in the town. It seems appropriate to imagine, although

5.12. *Bray mill, 1807, by Jean Claude Nattes. The corn mill has by now been joined by a brewery and malthouse, shown clearly in Cowen's view (opposite). Seventeen employees may have joined the United Irishmen.*

there is no evidence, that injured soldiers were housed in Quin's Hotel in a situation analogous to the quartering of convalescents in the International Hotel during the first world war. From July onwards the Wicklow rebels were mainly confined to the mountains, and the north-east of the county gradually quietened. The army camp at Lehaunstown was phased out; most of the soldiers had left by April 1799 and the land was sold in 1812, a reflection of government confidence echoed in the closing of Bray barracks in 1818.

UNITED IRISHMEN

'From Bray, a similar account was heard yesterday of servants in that quarter — Seventeen men employed by a brewer, it was said were of the number who eloped from thence, one of whom left behind him, a written note to his employer, stating his reason for going away, which he said was in consequence of a notice from his officer, (a Rebel) ordering him to join his ranks directly.'
(*Freeman's Journal* 12 July 1798)

AFTER-EFFECTS OF THE REBELLION

'Disturbances and nocturnal robberies still continue to annoy the peaceable inhabitants of Co. Wicklow. Scarcely a night passes in the vicinity of Bray, Newtown Mount Kennedy, and Delgany without some outrages of this sort being committed by detachments of rebel bandits.'
(*Freeman's Journal* 13 December 1798)

Less than half a century later, within a lifetime, Bray was to share in the sufferings of the Great Famine of 1845–8, even though to some extent as a spectator given that the worst privations were in western counties and rural areas. There were also mitigating factors. As we shall see in a later chapter, preliminary work on the coastal railway line provided labouring employment in 1847–8, in addition to the usual public works such as road building. Proximity to the coast meant that herring and other fish were available, while nearness to Dublin offered an easy opportunity to migrate to the city. Major local landlords — Lord Meath, Charles Putland of Sans Souci, Sir George Hodson of Holybrooke — took an active part in relief measures.

The potato blight was reported in Wicklow in October and November 1845, a month or so after its first appearance in Ireland. Reports show that many Bray labourers were soon in difficulties. In April 1846 forty Bray men went to the nearest workhouse, that at Loughlinstown in south County Dublin, looking for work or outdoor relief, neither of which was available, only admission for those destitute; when refused they 'went quietly away'. The Rathdown Union Workhouse at Loughlinstown had been opened in 1841 to serve three north Wicklow electoral divisions, Bray, Delgany and Powerscourt, as well as a large area of south county Dublin. Its board of guardians included Bray residents John Quin, George Seymour of Seapoint House and Isaac Weld of Ravenswell, under the chairmanship of Sir George Hodson. More than half of the paupers had come from Bray even before the famine.

THE FAMINE: RELIEF EFFORTS

> *'TO THE EDITOR OF THE FREEMAN. Bray, February 12th, 1847. Sir — I wish to avail myself of this opportunity to inform you that destitution to an alarming extent is on the advance amongst the poor of this neighbourhood, although great exertions have been made, and are making, by Lord Meath and the resident gentry to raise subscriptions in aid of the funds of the relief committee established here to check its progress. Lady Meath is also most bountiful in administering coals, blankets, and warm dresses to the poor located in her own immediate vicinity, and has contributed largely towards the erection of a soup kitchen in Bray. The zealous co-operation of the shopkeepers and other respectable inhabitants of Bray in this work of mercy is beyond all praise; but from the inclemency of the weather at present, and so many broken days hitherto, and the government wages being so parsimoniously dealt out, the labouring class now engaged on the public works is almost reduced to the verge of death. Their spirits are depressed, their marrow is wasted — they are not able to work.'*
> (*Freeman's Journal* 13 February 1847)

Bray Relief Committee was formed in May 1846 and free food tickets were issued in June and July; one of the distribution points was martello tower no. 1 on the beach where food, mainly 'indian meal' (maize) and oatmeal, was given out twice a week under the supervision of the coastguards. After the crop was totally destroyed in 1846 the destitution in the winter of 1846–7 was far greater than a year before and frequent reports must have come into Bray of areas further south running out of food supplies. A meeting was held in Bray courthouse in November at which proposals for relief works were discussed, given that about 270 heads of families and about 400 able-bodied people in the barony of Rathdown needed work. Among the proposals passed, though perhaps never fully implemented, were two for Bray, one to build a road across Mr Putland's estate from Bog Hall to Bray Head, the other to 'make 65 perches of road' from the coast guard station to the shore.

Severe snowstorms in February 1847 added to the hardships. A letter to the *Freeman's Journal* reported that the effects of bad weather and the low wages paid on the public works meant that many of the Bray poor were starving despite the efforts of the local relief committee. Some170 local men were employed on public works that winter. There was a temporary improvement in the summer of 1847, but this was followed by the general failure of the potato crop in 1848. The famine was now at its worst, and Bray traders must have shared in the deep economic recession that spread throughout Ireland. The Loughlinstown workhouse was grossly overcrowded. Bray fever hospital in the old barracks had already been under great pressure as 'famine fever', including typhus and dysentery, spread, and in early 1849 an outbreak of cholera added to the problems. Sixty-eight persons died of the disease in Bray that year.

The population of both Bray and Little Bray did not increase in the decade 1841 to 1851, although it did not decline in the same dramatic fashion as happened in some parts of County Wicklow. Taken together Bray and Little Bray were virtually stable, with 3178 persons recorded in the 1851 census compared with 3209 in 1841; Little Bray, in fact, showed a minute increase, offset by a small fall in Bray and Bray Commons. Some of these may have been people moving in from the countryside, replacing others who, following the common pattern, left permanently for Dublin and further afield. County Wicklow as a whole experienced a high rate of emigration, which must have had some effect, however small, on the prosperity of Bray.

One very different, though frequent, source of alarm — and excitement — for the people of Bray arose from the town's proximity to the coast. Having fishing as a resource was of benefit to the neighbourhood, and must have been of particular value during the famine years, but the Irish Sea was also the scourge of shipping during the era of sailing ships and before the provision of proper lighthouses and rescue services. The coast could be treacherous, given the twenty-five kilometre long Arklow bank and the rocky headlands of Bray Head and Wicklow Head. Wrecks, some of them involving tragic loss of life, were regularly reported in the newspapers. Two coasters were sunk off Bray Head in a violent storm in January 1781, and another two in December 1784. A Liverpool ship with wool, hardware and other goods was 'driven on shore at Bray and dashed to pieces' in February 1799, the 'Eliza', carrying copper ore from Wicklow to Neath in South Wales sank at Bray in December 1803, and the sloop 'Invincible' was lost on Bray beach in a gale in April 1810. Bray's own shipowners were not immune; Robert Seymour of Seapoint lost a coal sloop in a great March gale of 1844, when the crew all perished.

SHIPWRECKS OFF BRAY'S COAST

'Last Friday evening a merchantman bound from Cadiz to this port [Dublin], laden with wines, was wrecked in a tempestuous sea off Bray-head. She had struggled a long time against the impetuosity of the tide and storm, and finding herself beyond a possibility of making land, being almost full of water, she fired several signals of distress, whereupon the inhabitants of Bray humanely inclined to run every danger for her relief, and having for that purpose provided a boat, one brave adventurer committed himself singly to the mercy of the waves, without sail or rudder, and providentially reached the crew, just as the ship was split asunder, and went to the bottom, whereby every soul on board (consisting of the Captain and twelve men) was saved; and on Saturday morning they came into town in a most pitiable condition. Her cargo is said to have been worth £80,000 [sic]*.'*
(*Freeman's Journal* 11 September 1786)

'MELANCHOLY SHIPWRECK. The Friends, *of, and from Liverpool to Dublin, was unfortunately lost within sight of Bray on Sunday last, at three o'clock. The Captain, Thomas Kirkham, his son, John Kirkham, aged two years and a half, and William Sto[r]t, seaman, perished. The Captain's wife, Mrs. Kirkham, and William Robinson, the mate, were, with much difficulty, saved.'*
(*Freeman's Journal* 30 April 1819)

Shipping safety improved in the first decades of the nineteenth century, with lightships on the Kish and Arklow banks and a new lighthouse, less obscured by mists than the old one, erected on Wicklow Head in 1818. Bray's first coast guard station was built on the sea front by 1832, providing a formal rescue service.

Fishermen, of course, also suffered in severe gales. Five Bray fishermen died, apparently of exposure, after their boat was caught in a storm in March 1811, and in December 1843 four were drowned when their boat, which belonged to the coal merchant Mr Cuthbert, capsized opposite martello tower no. 2. On a lighter note, there must have been much excitement on the sea front when great shoals of fish appeared. In September 1786 a shoal of herrings was 'a column upwards of a league broad' and the boats were filled in a very short time; unfortunately the wind was blowing the wrong way, and the fish could not be shipped to Dublin 'so the fishermen had no other market than the villages of County Wicklow and what could be sent in kishes to Bray.'

A more agreeable source of excitement was provided by the annual boat races held each July in the early nineteenth century and organised by a 'committee of gentlemen' in aid of the poor fishermen and providing a 'good deal of amusement and a crowded and fashionable company'. In June 1843 the fishermen and locals had a unique diversion when a balloonist from Dublin passed over Bray and landed in the sea near Bray Head. It fell to the fishermen to rescue both balloonist and balloon and, apparently, to make 'exorbitant demands' for the balloon's return.

The view out to sea, too, must occasionally have been spectacular. In windless spells ships were often becalmed on their way into Dublin Bay and in early August 1788, according to the *Freeman's Journal*, the onlooker on the sea front could have gazed at no less than thirty square-rigged ships all becalmed off Bray Head.

SMUGGLING

'A revenue cutter pursued and captured a smuggling wherry on Saturday morning off Bray Head. The wherry was laden with geneva [a spirit rather like gin, distilled from grain & flavoured with juniper berries, made in the Netherlands, also called hollands,], tobacco & raw silks. Some boats from the shore seeing the situation of the wherry, put to sea and received all the silk, which they landed before the cutter could come up.'
(*Freeman's Journal* 22 June 1789)

'It was yesterday reported that, about two or three o'clock, an engagement took place, off Bray between a smuggling cutter and one of his Majesty's cruisers, supposed to be the Mary, [commanded by] Captain Griffith. The action continued brisk for near an hour, but it was said the King's boat was necessitated to give up a contest rendered very unequal by the superior number of the crew and weight of metal of the smuggler.'
(*Freeman's Journal* 14 November 1791)

Proximity to the coast provided more than access to sea fisheries. Smuggling was rife in the eighteenth century and during Napoleonic times; gin from the Netherlands and brandy from France were favourite commodities, together with tobacco and tea. Just as smugglers' routes in England led to London, so Dublin with its well-heeled citizens was the main Irish destination, and the Wicklow coast was a convenient landing place. Bray Head's involvement is still commemorated in the name of Brandy Hole cove, set in the cliffs half a mile from the south end of the beach. Apparently a concealed shaft led from a cave up to a point on the Head, up which contraband was hauled — a feature which, passing through solid rock, would have required considerable initial planning. Organised gangs would have had the assistance of local people, some of it pre-arranged, some of it, like the 'rescue' off Bray of silk from a smuggler's boat about to be seized by customs officers, opportunistic. The customs boat house built near the Dargle mouth in the 1820s was probably regarded with less than enthusiasm by many of its neighbours.

'PLUNDERING THE CARGOES' OF WRECKED SHIPS

'The barbarous custom which prevails on the sea coasts of these kingdoms, of plundering the cargoes of ships driven ashore by stress of weather, is degrading to humanity. The shipwreck which lately happened at Bray is a recent proof of the existence of this horrid practice; the particulars whereof are known to almost every gentleman in that neighbourhood. On Christmas Day last, the ship Friendship, of Bristol, last from Oporto, laden with port, oil, fruit, etc. of the value of £400 and upwards, was driven ashore opposite to Bray, and within half a mile of that town; the captain and crew were providentially saved, having got out of the vessel before the night came on, but the ship and cargo were entirely carried away before six o'clock the next morning; the town and country people carried off not only the whole cargo but every plank in the ship.'
(*Freeman's Journal* 3 February 1784)

Wrecks, too, did not represent tragedy for everyone. While flotsam and jetsam would have yielded serviceable items, both for immediate use and for sale, a wreck close to shore would have been much more valuable. Whether or not actual 'wreckers' — men who put out false lights to mislead passing ships — operated on Bray Head, certainly the locals were not slow to profit from natural disasters.

The events of Christmas night 1783, when an entire ship, the 'Friendship', driven ashore on Bray beach, and its cargo apparently vanished by morning, may represent an extreme — and perhaps exaggerated — example, but it was by no means the only such happening. Public-spirited locals and, later, customs officers, often had to protect stranded vessels until they could be floated off or until their cargoes at least were salvaged.

Bray town had its own 'happenings', albeit of a more law-abiding kind. There were various celebrations, whether national or local, for which the town was decorated with arches and greenery. According to the *Freeman's Journal*, there were 'rejoicings' with illuminations at the barracks and at Quin's Hotel for the jubilee celebrations of October 1809, Bray was 'splendidly illuminated' in April 1814 to celebrate the abdication of Napoleon, and 'green branches, flags and handkerchiefs, streamed in the air' on the occasion of King George IV's visit to County Wicklow in 1821.

Daniel O'Connell was twice greeted in the town; there was a Repeal of the Union meeting in December 1840 followed by dinner at Quin's Hotel, and he breakfasted at the hotel again in May 1845 on his way to Wexford. On the latter occasion great crowds gathered, the band played patriotic airs and the town was decorated with greenery cut from Sans Souci's shrubberies. Shortly beforehand, in March 1845, a number of bands from surrounding areas had also enlivened a visit to Little Bray by the founder of the total abstinence movement, Father Theobald Mathew, when he delivered a sermon in St Peter's Church in aid of the newly-opened national schools and also administered the pledge to 'several thousand' persons.

DANIEL O'CONNELL IN BRAY

'the Liberator, Daniel O'Connell left Dublin for Wexford on the 22nd, On arrival at Bray he alighted at Quin's Hotel and was received by the parish priest and clergy. He then joined them in a public breakfast. During his stay the street was crowded to excess, and the area in front of the hotel was almost impassible. Mr Putland intended joining the party but was prevented by illness. However he gave his men the day off and carte blanche *to use his shrubberies to decorate the town with green boughs. During the breakfast a band played patriotic airs outside the hotel. When Daniel O'Connell left at 9.45 am. amid the enthusiastic acclamation of thousands the members of the band tastefully attired in crimson and blue were drawn in cars in front of his carriage.'*

(*Freeman's Journal* 24 May 1845)

The local gentry had their moments too. The Putland family of San Souci gave an annual harvest-home dinner, with 'primest joints of beef, mutton and veal, with strong ale and porter' served to a hundred and fifty or so of their tenants and labourers. When they held a 'fête champetre' in June 1835 for five hundred guests the town was decorated in style; when they returned from a stay abroad two years later there were illuminations, bonfires, dancing and free refreshments. Similar festivities — perhaps even grander as befitted their higher social standing — took place when the Meath family returned to Killruddery after an absence.

FÊTE CHAMPETRE AT SANS SOUCI

'Fête champetre (from Morning Register*).*
One of the most splendid fêtes ever witnessed in this country was given on Monday last at San Souci, the residence of Geo. Putland, Esq., near Bray. At an early hour the town presented a most animated and picturesque appearance, a number of triumphal arches having been thrown across the principal street, tastefully decorated with green boughs, flowers and banners of different coloured silks. From the centre arch was suspended a large banner bearing the name of his excellency splendidly emblazoned, and underneath the hospitable Irish inscription, "céad míle fáilte". ... From three to half-past five the company, consisting of upwards of 500 of the principal nobility and gentry of the metropolis and its environs, continued to arrive. ... the dejeune was served up in splendid style, and consisted of every rarity and delicacy which the season admitted of, and which the most profuse expenditure could supply. The ices, confectionery, etc, were served in marquees erected upon the lawn, and covered with fine grey cloth and linen. The band of the 15th Hussars played some beautiful airs during the evening ... an excellent quadrille band was also in attendance. ...'
(*Freeman's Journal* 8 June 1835)

The most prophetic celebration, however, was that which took place on 25 August 1847, when a ceremony took place at Bray Head to mark the commencement of work on the proposed railway line. The guests assembled at Quin's Hotel, proceeded along a new road made by Lord Meath for the occasion and then scrambled down to a 'small piece of table-land about seventy feet above the level of the sea' with a flagstaff, near the Brandy Hole. Stakes already marked out the line of the track. A sod was turned by the chairman of the railway company, the work was formally signalled by setting

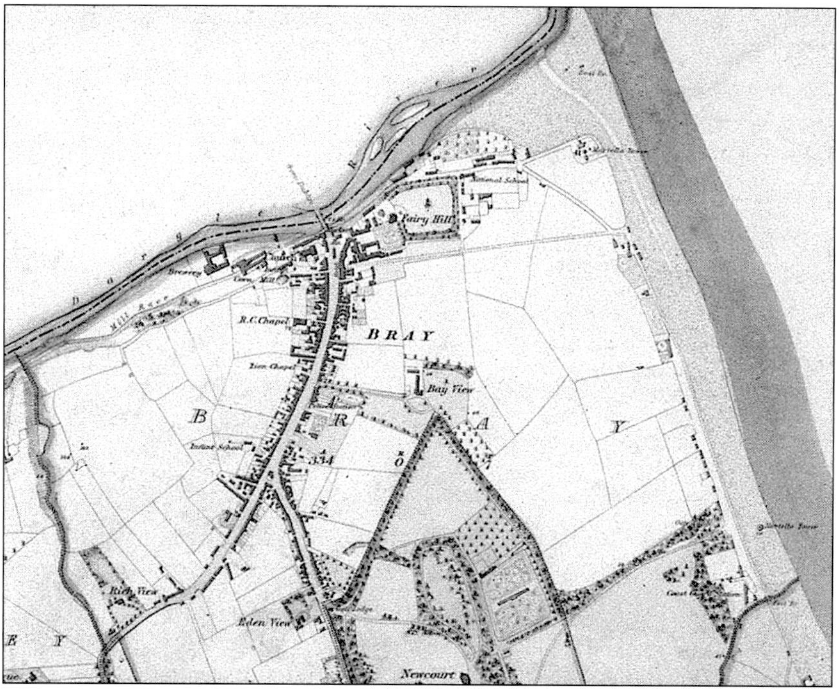

5.13. *Bray in 1838 from the six-inch Ordnance Survey map.*

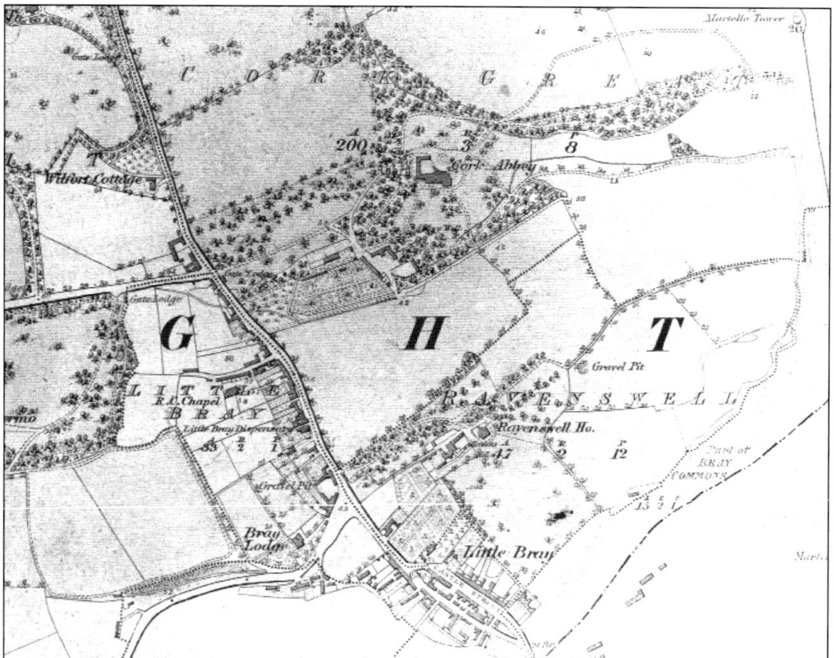

5.14. *Little Bray in 1837 from the six-inch Ordnance Survey map.*

off the first blasts, and the guests headed back up the hillside as best they could.

> *'The vehicles passed round the hill along the new road made by the Earl of Meath, and the descent to and ascent from the flagstaff, where the cortège halted, tried the energies and agility of all whom curiosity and love of the picturesque attracted to the scene.*
>
> *We saw some elegant equipages on the ground, and in every respect the scene was one of the most gratifying and exhilarating character. ... The heath and fern-clad hillside was literally thronged with gentle and simple folk clambering down to the chosen site, and their progress was cheered by the gay sounds of the Bray Temperance Band, which led the way.'*
>
> (*Irish Railway Gazette* 26 August 1847)

WORK BEGINS ON RAILWAY LINE

> *'From its situation on the coast, and in the vicinity of several admired parts of the county of Wicklow, this place is rendered busy and cheerful in the summer months by numerous visitors, having health and pleasure for the objects of their travels. An excellent hotel, and several convenient lodgings, must be noticed amongst the solid attractions of this gay town.'*
>
> (J.N. Brewer, *The beauties of Ireland*, London, 1825, p. 283.)

BRAY'S 'SOLID ATTRACTIONS'

The daily lives of the people of Bray were thus enlivened, for good or ill, over the years in which Bray first evolved as a resort town. But Bray in the first half of the nineteenth century was usually still a sleepy place out of season; in the summer months it was awake and lively, the main street bustling with visitors and loud with the sound of horses' hooves from passing chaises and jaunting cars. There was already by 1850 no other town like it in County Wicklow, and the mountain scenery behind gave it an ambience noticeably different from that of other bathing resorts around Dublin. As one traveller wrote, Bray was already a place with 'solid attractions'.

Chapter 6

A 'favourable bathing place': Bray in 1850

'Bray, the property of the earl of Meath, is a more favourable bathing place than either Wicklow or Arklow, a preference to which it is justly entitled. It has an excellent hotel, every facility for hot and cold baths, a pleasant promenade to the sea beech [sic], *and a series of thatched cottages, kept with great neatness, which furnish accommodation to summer visitors, at a rent of £40 and upwards for the season.'*
(Alexander Knox, The Irish watering places, *Dublin, 1845, p. 150)*

By 1850 Bray had undoubtedly grown into a resort of some consequence. Besides the steadily increasing number of houses and shops along the main street and in adjacent areas, it had churches and schools, the sea front had undergone a degree of transformation, and there was an abundance of large houses, the homes of professional families and gentry, in the neighbourhood. In some respects it had already become recognisable as the present town; some of the actual buildings have survived and many property boundaries and most of the laneways off Main Street are the same. In other ways it was totally different; all the land between Main Street and the shore remained in fields and the area where Strand Road and the Esplanade are today was still no more than a shingle storm beach with a scatter of thatched cottages.

The traveller from Dublin crossing Bray Bridge in 1850, the same bridge shown in Bartlett's drawing of 1842 and by this time a hundred years old and quite dilapidated, would have seen St Paul's Church rising on the right above the row of old houses that fronted the road. St Paul's had undergone some improvements as the congregation had increased and therefore the need for accommodation had increased with it — the congregation more than doubled with visitors in the summer months. New pews, which were paid for by individual parish families who, as was customary, then had exclusive rights to their use, were added in about 1770; a gallery was added in 1779, and in 1816–18 the church was enlarged at the east end to give it a roughly T-shaped plan.

6.1. Bray Bridge (rebuilt in 1741) and neighbouring parts of Bray and Little Bray, the well-known view by W.H. Bartlett, 1842.

ST PAUL'S CHURCH

'The church is a neat but plain structure, rebuilt in 1609. A considerable augmentation has been recently made to the eastern part, but without the least attention to architectural beauty. The interior is destitute of sepulchral monuments, and has no embellishment, unless such a term may be applied to the arms of the Earl of Meath, which, in large proportions, are worked in stucco on the northern wall.'
(J.N. Brewer, *The beauties of Ireland*, London, 1825, vol i, p. 283).

'The church [St Paul's], *situated in the town, is an old building, and was repaired in 1818, by means of a loan of £941 10s 9 1/4d, from the late Board of First Fruits. Sittings 450; attendance 500 in summer, and about 200 in winter.*
(*The parliamentary gazetteer of Ireland*, London 1846, vol. i, p. 277)

One feature of the time, much commented upon, was the pair of fireplaces that heated the interior — these were positioned high up on the east wall and must have been a serious trial to the sexton, whose job it was to attend to the fires. The short spire that had been notable in the eighteenth century was removed in about 1840; instead there was the familiar battlemented, pinnacled tower, also shown in Bartlett's view. The graveyard,

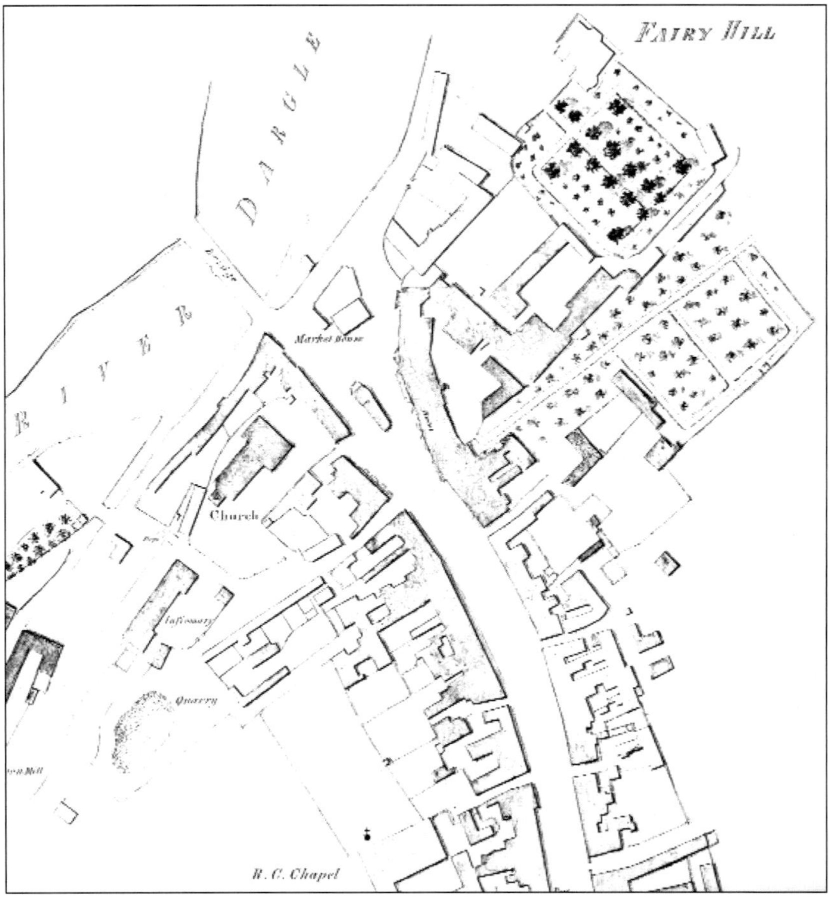

6.2. The core of Bray before the arrival of the railway from the Ordnance Survey, 1838 (original scale 1:1056).

where the oldest surviving stone was a broken one of 1697, still served the whole town, as it would for another forty years.

The area behind St Paul's had lost some of its importance. The barracks had been closed in 1818. The tenth earl of Meath purchased it for £100 and donated it to the dispensary district as a fever hospital at a time, during the typhus epidemic of 1817–19, when funding was made available for such hospitals. It provided a valuable service, too, during the cholera epidemics that hit Bray in 1832 and 1833. By 1850, after the pressures of the Great Famine abated, it was either already closed or due to close, leaving a considerable lacuna in the life of the town.

Another significant loss was the destruction of Great Bray Castle, ending an important link with Bray's Anglo-Norman past. The fate of the castle after the 1760s is unknown — presumably it was seen as a good source of dressed

***6.3.** The last unmodernised cottage in Church Terrace photographed in about 1980; this one, too, has since been altered* (Bray architectural heritage).

stone and demolished for use in a building project, probably the enlargement of the mill buildings nearby. No one seems to have mourned its passing.

Despite its closure in 1850, the outward appearance of the barracks remained unaltered. And by this time Bray's most charming row of cottages, Church Terrace, faced onto it and St Paul's churchyard. These six quaint single-storey houses, with their round-headed window frames and decorative chimney stacks, were presumably built at some date near to 1800. The terrace survives today, although all the exteriors have been radically 'modernised' to varying degrees. The end cottage does, however, retain its unusual curved granite coigns (projecting corners) at the east side.

South of Church Terrace, the shopper on Main Street had the choice of a row of substantial shops, interrupted by the railings and gates of the Catholic chapel, forerunner of the present Holy Redeemer Church. The chapel's history was a chequered one. The first Catholic church in Bray was built on the site in about 1784, so that the local Catholic population no longer had to go as far as Old Connaught or Kilmacanogue to attend Mass. (The old chapel at Raheenacluig may also have been used in penal times.) John Quin, senior, was one of the trustees who leased the site. But despite such well-to-do patrons the parish was so impoverished that in about 1800 the parish priest and congregation were evicted for non-payment of rent, services were discontinued and the chapel roof was removed. Local builder John

Donnellan, who owned the site, then filled the chapel yard with new buildings — two houses facing onto the road and a range of cabins behind — leaving only an eight-foot-wide passage as access to the ruined chapel. The sight must have been a sad one.

REPAIRS TO THE CHAPEL

'We find that the inhabitants of Bray, taking into consideration the ruinous and even dangerous state of their church, have come to a resolution to use their utmost efforts towards securing and repairing it. The rising population of the neighbourhood, and unusual concourse of people on Sundays, whom business or pleasure may lead to this charming outlet to the city, and to whom the inhabitants would wish to offer every accommodation in their power, render moreover the enlargement of their chapel absolutely necessary. From the small number enjoying any degree of affluence among them, (their congregation chiefly composed of labouring poor) and the enormous price of building materials, finding their best efforts unequal to the task, they are forced to appeal to the well-known liberality of the citizens of Dublin on such occasions, for their assistance.'
(*Freeman's Journal* 25 September 1809)

The chapel did not remain roofless for long. In 1809 a wide appeal was made for funds to repair and enlarge the building, given that the local congregation was too poor to bear the full cost itself and that many who attended mass were visitors who came out from Dublin on Sundays. The funds were forthcoming; with 'liberal donations' from 'the earl of Meath, Colonel Keating, and other respectable Protestant families', the chapel was restored and services resumed.

This chapel was T-shaped, and stood on a rectangular plot back from the road with a central pathway to Main Street. It was soon replaced by a new church, built largely in 1824 and ambitious in scale, which, again presumably because the parish was not a rich one, took at least five years to complete. A 'gothic altar screen' was due to be installed as late as 1832. A plain oblong building, the church's side walls were over thirty feet high; at the front there were three entrance doors with windows above. A pencil drawing by Andrew Nicholl (fig. 5.9) shows this building, rising high above the surrounding houses with three arched windows and with the east end surmounted by a cross. It stands out in the sketch as one of the largest buildings in Bray.

While the buildings along the northern half of Main Street mainly had shops on the ground floor, from about midway these gave way to small blocks of houses, some with cabins behind, facing directly onto the street. Most of these modest houses would by 1850 have been fifty or sixty years old, the first houses built at this upper end of the town. Some of the present two-storey buildings on both sides of Main Street are survivors of this time, and the back garden walls still mark the old line that divided the town from the fields. Hall's Court, part way along, was a cluster of five cottages belonging in 1852 to Daniel Hall, of which two survive today.

Other houses have not survived, including a row of picturesque thatched cottages not far from the present Town Hall; these particular cottages, of which a painting hangs in Bray Library, were demolished only in the mid twentieth century. Among the houses stood Devitt's forge, as it may have done since the early 1800s. Next door there was a 'plain but neat' Presbyterian chapel, of almost square plan, built in 1817. It was set back from the street, with a gate and short path. Bray's Presbyterians, at this time a very small group of fifteen to twenty, had previously held their services in the old courthouse and in a private house in Little Bray. As their numbers increased the plain chapel was soon to be superseded by a far grander edifice on a new site.

The first Methodist chapel in Bray, built between 1838 and 1846, still stands on Brighton Terrace with an almost unchanged exterior. A steep-roofed, granite building, with three windows on the west wall and one on the south, it belonged to the Primitive Wesleyan Methodists, and was closed when this splinter group was reunited with the Wesleyan Methodists in the 1870s.

Nearby a Church of Ireland infant school was set in the fields, although today the building adjoins the south side of the Brighton Terrace road. The wall plaque which records that this school was built by Lord Powerscourt in 1829 is still visible, somewhat worn, high on the east wall of the building, above where the entrance door once stood. The school was in its early days funded by Lady Powerscourt; as it was for infants only the numbers were not very large, with 58 pupils in 1835. It was in use until the end of the nineteenth century. The 1870 Ordnance Survey map shows that the building consisted of a large open room, with three windows on the north and two on the south. The wide space in front was part of School Lane, which provided access to Main Street and which still partly exists as a short laneway between nos 59 and 60.

From the school it was possible to look across a field towards the low, windowless backs of some of the poorest cabins in Bray. These were clustered in Critchley's Lane, otherwise Pound Lane, a triangular piece of ground

6.3. *The short-lived Methodist chapel in Brighton Terrace; dating from the early 1840s, it was closed by 1880.*

roughly on the site of the present Kilmantain Place, and some were the property of William Critchley himself. The forty or so mud cabins, thatched and one-roomed, were ranged in two rows facing onto a central open area. They probably accounted for nearly half of the one-roomed mud cabins listed for the town in the 1841 and 1851 census returns. The cabins had no yards, and the open area would have been busy with people and animals. Patrick Ledwich or Ledwidge's forge was also at this top end of Main Street in a yard just north of the cabins; it was soon to close and was in ruins by 1857.

Apart from Bray Cottage, a late eighteenth- or early nineteenth-century house set in a good-sized garden which during the late twentieth century was part of the Bray Health Centre, the buildings at the north end of the

Killarney and Vevay Roads were all small cottages. The poorest were those immediately behind the pound, which were more tiny cabins of irregular shape and size.

> *'The mansion is a chaste and elegant structure of the Tuscan order, with an embattled roof, from which are obtained extensive views of mountain scenery and of the sea;* [leading] *from the drawing-room antechamber is a noble conservatory of polygonal form, erected at an expense of £5000, and containing a fine collection of the most choice and rare exotics; the pleasure grounds and gardens are laid out with the greatest taste and kept in the finest order, presenting one of the principal attractions in this truly picturesque and much frequented part of the country.'*
> (Samuel Lewis, *A topographical dictionary of Ireland*, London, 1837, vol. i, p. 222)

THE PUTLANDS' HOUSE

Further along Vevay Road, opposite to Eden View (Marino Centre), by now renamed Prospect Cottage, lay the entrance to the Putland family's house. This imposing property was standing empty and neglected in 1850,

6.4. The former Sans Souci, embellished by George Putland in the 1830s, and in 1850 soon to become the Loreto Convent.

but it was poised to undergo a major transformation. Variously known as Sans Souci, Bray Head and, confusingly, Newcourt (as distinct from the 'real' Newcourt further south, now the Presentation College), it had been the home of the Putlands since soon after 1771 when an original sixteen acres, quickly extended, were bought by George Putland, senior, from the Edwards family of Oldcourt. His son George Putland, junior, added the adjoining Newcourt to his estates, and he lived at Sans Souci for thirty years. After his death it was sold by auction in July 1850 to the Loreto Order by his brother and heir, Charles Putland, senior. As the Loreto Convent it has played a major part in the life of Bray to this day.

The Putlands were prominent in Bray. Their late-eighteenth-century house was transformed by George Putland, junior, and his wife Anna (Nancy) in the 1830s, when it had thrown over it, in the words of a modern writer, 'an elaborate sugar-icing of gothick frivolousness'. Cast-iron crenellations were added to the parapets and chimney stacks, together with a square porch also largely of cast iron. An ornate, twenty-one-sided conservatory of timber and cast iron embellished with elephants' heads was the final touch. The house stood just below the summit of the hill on spacious grounds extending from Vevay Road to the sea shore; a large walled garden had a central range of glasshouses with a vinery and there was a wilderness area on high rocky ground and an orchard. The front grounds

6.5. *Killruddery as rebuilt in the 1820s (J.P. Neale, London, 1821).*

commanded views through more than 180 degrees from the Dublin mountains and Carrickgolligan, Dalkey and Howth in the north to Bray Head and the Little Sugar Loaf in the south. It was and still remains — an impressive property in an impressive situation.

Beyond Sans Souci, Newtown Vevay was still a distinct village of some fifty houses and a little under two hundred inhabitants. Oldcourt House, adjacent to Oldcourt Castle, and its one hundred and forty acres of land remained the home of the Edwards family. Newcourt House, after a period of doubtful fortune — it is not shown at all on the 1838 Ordnance Survey map — was just gaining a new lease of life. Charles Putland, senior, obviously preferred not to live in his brother's house and he chose instead this adjoining property as home to his large family; renovated, or perhaps largely rebuilt, in about 1848, it was renamed Bray Head House. Charles Putland owned virtually all of the townland of Newcourt, extending the length of the present Putland Road and southwards and eastwards to encompass the northern portion of Bray Head and the coast. The Putlands were to live in Bray Head House for two more generations, but after the death of Charles junior's unmarried son, another George, in 1876, the property was divided by remaining family members. The Bray connection of the Putlands ended when Bray Head House was finally sold in 1917; it became the nucleus of today's Presentation College.

Together with Oldcourt, the Putland estate served to divide the earl of Meath's portion of Bray from his extensive Killruddery lands further south. The Putland lands gave way to those of the earl at the then junction of the Boghall Road and the present Newcourt Road. Killruddery House had been rebuilt in 1820–22 by the tenth earl as a massive Elizabethan-revival mansion, designed by the foremost architect Sir Richard Morrison. It has been praised as the most successful example of this style of architecture in Ireland. The formal seventeenth-century gardens at last had a house of grandeur to match. There were impressive entrance gates to the demesne on the main Greystones road, dating, probably, from about 1820. At that time, after it ceased to be the main route to Wexford, the road had been moved eastwards to a new line further away from the house.

One more property at this side of Bray deserves a mention. Holybrooke House, to the south-west, was in 1850 the home of Sir George Hodson or Hudson, who has a place in the later story of Bray's development. Holybrooke House was built in Elizabethan-revival style in 1835 with Sir Richard Morrison's son, William Morrison, as architect. Unlike Killruddery which, probably because it was often rented out, did not join in the Wicklow

6.6. *St Cronan's, built in about 1826 as Bray's presbytery.*

6.7. *Bray Courthouse, now the Heritage Centre.*

landlords' general practice of admitting the public to their scenic demesnes, the grounds of Holybrooke were open to the public every day except Sundays.

Back at the south end of Main Street, the pound was still a prominent feature, with its gates and entrance pillars on the south side. Two substantial houses abutted onto it facing back down Main Street; these may have been the old courthouse building divided. The upper part of east Main Street had fewer houses than the west side; those opposite the pound were quite large, with the same wide street frontages as today. St Cronan's, built as a commodious presbytery in about 1826 and sited well back from the road, also had the same wide street frontage as today and a large garden. The present Novara Avenue was still the private road leading to the bathing lodge of Bay View. The property on which it stood was variously spelled 'Navarra', 'Navara' and 'Navare' before the present spelling became current in the late 1860s. One small laneway off the street that had already existed a hundred years earlier now had nine cottages; this lane was to become the entrance to Hudson's Terrace, a notoriously insanitary row of mid-nineteenth-century cabins; today it leads to Fatima Terrace.

The most northerly properties on the east side, like those across the street, were substantial, with the three properties closest to the bridge in the hands of John Quin. The central one, with an extensive frontage, was his hotel, which had a valuation almost twice that of any other property on Main Street.

Until 1841 the market house, a two-storey, three-bay building erected by the ninth earl of Meath in 1790, stood close to Quin's Hotel, together with a

***6.8.** Galtrim House before 1914 (Joe Loughman collection).*

narrow, coffin-shaped building that probably sheltered market stall-holders. The area in front of the market house, spilling over onto the bridge, was one of the places where Bray's fairs were still held, by 1850 with six cattle fairs a year and four for frieze, a coarse woollen cloth. Although the market house was only fifty years old, it was replaced in 1841 by a fine new courthouse or 'Petit Sessions House', today's Heritage Centre. The handsome new building must surely have pleased the Quin family as they stepped out of their front door. It was used for twice-yearly quarter sessions and fortnightly petty sessions. Behind the hotel, Quin's extensive livery stables occupied a considerable area, with the start of Quin's Walk passing through gardens alongside them. Woodbine Lodge boarding house was just north-east of the hotel and behind was one of the most notable houses in Bray. In 1850 this house was still called Fairy Hill (not to be confused with the house of the same name on Killarney Road), although it is better remembered by its later name of Galtrim House. It seems to have dated back to the middle, at least, of the eighteenth century, and certainly the interior, as seen in the 1980s, appeared to have mid eighteenth-century features. The house and lands belonged to Thomas Tisdall in 1789 and were sold to John Donnellan in 1793, but Donnellan overstretched himself and was forced by his debts to sell Fairy Hill, which John Quin senior agreed to take over in 1807.

6.9. *Martello tower no. 2, seen from across the Dargle, 1836, by Capt. Edward Jones; the cliffs and the mud banks in the estuary are well shown (Society of Antiquaries of London Library).*

Fairy Hill was a valuable adjunct to Quin's Hotel, and the tradition is that it was the Quins who renamed it Galtrim House, after the family's home village in County Meath — by the time of the valuation records of the 1850s it was being referred to as 'Galtrim or Fairy Hill'. It may have been the Quins who remodelled the house to give it a more fashionable appearance or the renovations may have been the work of Donnellan; there were also formal gardens to the south and a large garden surrounded by trees and a perimeter walk, with a massive tree at the centre, to the east. Galtrim House was almost as impressive as the Putlands' Sans Souci, although, of course, the Quins were 'in trade' and so further down the social scale, however much they benefited the town.

The Quin family probably continued to live in the hotel, rather than in the house, for it was described by the Ordnance Survey as a bathing lodge. John Quin did, however, make good use of the wider grounds for it was here that Quin's Walk was laid out across the fields. Although the walk was a fashionable route to the sea front, Nicholl's sketch (fig. 5.9) shows it as no more than a long straight path edged on either side with posts and chains and flanked by what looks more like rough grass or rushes rather than by any kind of ornamental planting. There are cattle grazing in the adjacent field, but safely at a distance from any strolling ladies of a nervous disposition.

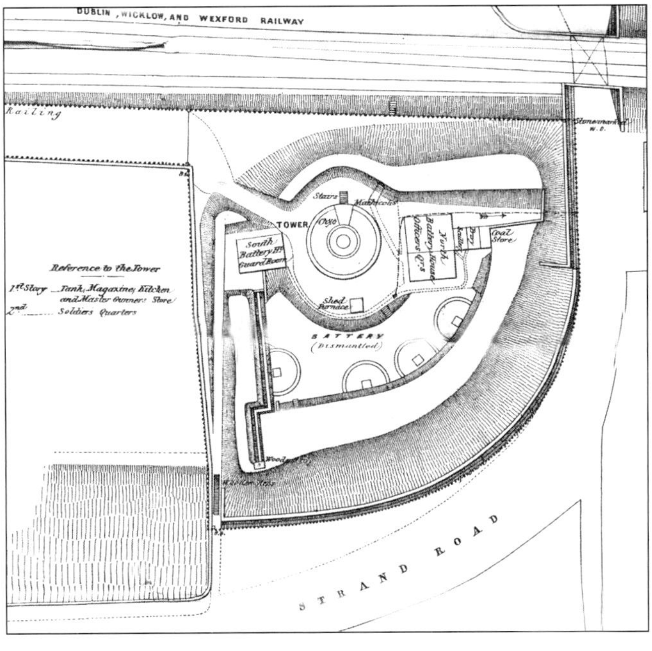

6.10. Martello tower no. 2, Mount Park, from a survey of 1859.

6.11. Martello tower no. 2 survives, well-hidden, as a private residence.

Hotel guests as they crossed the fields would have found themselves heading towards a cluster of thatched cottages on the sea front occupying the site of today's railway station. The most noticeable structure visible across the fields must, however, have been the martello tower at the mouth of the Dargle. This tower, which still survives although not nearly so prominently, was no. 2 of a series of fourteen extending northwards from Bray to Sandymount in south Dublin, with yet more north of the city. Taking their name and design from a tower at Cap Mortella in Corsica, they were intended as protection against invasion during the tense Napoleonic times. The cliff-top site of tower no. 2 lay on the lands of Mount Park and had been acquired from the earl of Meath. Like the others from Bray to Dalkey, this tower was begun and largely completed during the summer of 1804; it was ready for occupation by September 1805.

The tower, strongly built of granite at a cost of some £1,800, contained as was usual a tank, magazine, kitchen and master gunner's store on the ground floor and soldiers' quarters in the large circular, stone-roofed room above. In addition to an eighteen-pounder gun on the roof, there were four gun emplacements for twenty-four pounders on the seaward side, three facing out to sea with the fourth facing southwards towards the strand. There were also two substantial outbuildings: the South Battery House guard room and the North Battery House officers' quarters with scullery, 'privy' and coal store. One officer and twelve artillery men were stationed there.

'Bray is a neat little town, most charmingly situated near the coast, about half a mile distant from the sea, into which the Powerscourt river falls here. On each side are Martello towers; that on the right, as you front the sea, mounts one long eighteen pounder, moving on a pivot, on the summit of the tower; and five twenty-four pounders on the rampart of turf, below. It is built most substantially, with hard granite brought from the sea side; its walls are seven feet thick, and twenty-one feet high; are circular, having the top bevelled so that balls striking it may glance off. It contains only one chamber, to which you ascend by means of a ladder, through a door about twelve feet from the ground, above which is a place similar to those in ancient gateways, for the purpose of showering down stones, &c. on assailants.'
(Anon, *Journal of a tour through several of the southern counties of Ireland during the autumn of 1809*, London, 1810, pp 12–14.)

MARTELLO TOWERS

'The trade, exclusively of what is requisite for the supply of the town, consists principally in the importation of coal, timber, slates, and limestone, in which two vessels of 70 tons each, one of 50 tons, and one of 25 tons, belonging to the place are regularly employed. … The small haven is very incommodious, having a bar at the entrance, and only eight feet of water at spring and five feet at neap tides: from a change in the channel of the river, an outer beach has been formed, which breaks in some degree the violence of the sea.'
(Samuel Lewis, *A topographical dictionary of Ireland*, London, 1837, vol. i, p. 222)

LACK OF A GOOD HARBOUR

Bray *'is much frequented in the bathing season from its local attractions and its contiguity to the enchanting rural scenery with which this vicinage abounds, but as long as its harbour is suffered to remain destitute of either quay or pier for the accommodation of shipping, it must continue a summer lodging and bathing station, for which purpose it is extremely well adapted, but can never enjoy the benefit derivable from the establishment of a main factory, requiring plenty of fuel cheaply conveyed by water.'*
(Anon, *The traveller's new guide through Ireland*, Dublin, 1815, pp 58–9.)

The observant visitor strolling eastwards along Quin's Walk would also have had a distant view of at least one other martello tower. Tower no. 1, the most southerly of all, was built on a far less commanding site than was tower no. 2. It lay on the storm beach not far above high-water mark opposite the present Esplanade Terrace. The inside accommodation was the same as that of no. 2, but this tower was a simpler affair in that it lacked a gun battery and the only structures outside, catering for twelve men but no officer, were a privy, a poultry house and an ash pit. Its lifetime was to be comparatively short, ending in the 1880s. Tower no. 3, similar to no. 1 and which may also have been visible from Quin's Walk, was to have an even shorter lifespan. It lay north of the Dargle mouth on a headland in the crumbling cliffs just north of the Woodbrook stream and fell victim to coastal erosion as early as 1865.

The sea front had undergone some degree of transformation by 1850. The most noticeable change was the diversion of the Dargle, which instead of turning to the south now flowed out directly into the Irish Sea. This 'navigable cut' had been made in 1787, at the expense of local inhabitants.

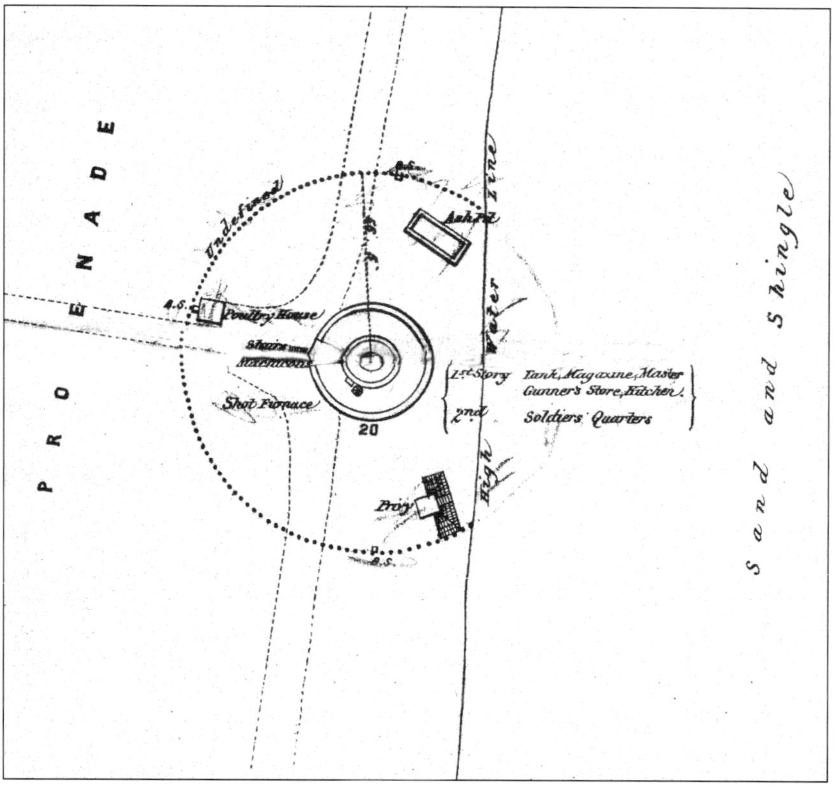

6.12. Martello tower no. 1, Bray Head, from the survey of 1859. Note that the tower was then above the high water mark as were the ash pit and privy.

The prime movers in this must have been the local ship owners, listed in Lucas's directory of 1788 as Matthews Constantine, Tobias Toole and Henry Hughes. By the early part of the nineteenth century the principal ship owner was Robert Seymour of Seapoint House and a small quay, known as Seymour's Dock, was cut into the bank just below Seapoint House. The visitor would have seen his boats unloading in the dock, many of them carrying coal from Britain. Coal merchant Mr Cuthbert's 'William and Margaret' of 60 tons, newly built in 1846, might also have been seen unloading at the river bank. But despite the improvement to the course of the river, it was still only possible for small vessels to get into the estuary, and then only at high tide. The larger vessels, such as the 'Robert Seymour' of 89 tons which carried coals from Whitehaven to Kingstown and Bray, could barely manage to dock. The idea of building a harbour pier was mooted, but came to nothing at this time.

The previous course of the river was still marked by a long narrow gully along the sea front, filled by the tide twice daily. The area below Seapoint House, where the Seapoint Court houses are now, was an extensive shingle bank, in the process of silting up but still below high-water mark. The boat house belonging to the Customs Service, built in 1822, was positioned on the part of the bank that lay out of reach of normal tides, although it can hardly have been a comfortable place in an easterly storm.

STORMS

'The fishermen's cottages at Bray Head are in a deplorable condition; the poor inmates had to rush out to save their lives in the middle of the night and their houses were soon after all but under water. There are two large vessels stranded at the mouth of Bray river, both coal laden; one the William and Margaret, newly built, belonging to Mr. Cuthbert, of Bray, coal merchant — the other the Robert Seymour, the property of Mr. Seymour, also of Bray. ... Both vessels dragged their anchors during the gale, and came into collision before going on shore. They are both blown high and dry up the beach, and it is supposed that considerable difficulty will be had in getting them afloat.'
(*Freeman's Journal* 21 November 1846)

The cluster of cottages at the end of Quin's Walk lay on either side of the sea-front track that led from this point towards Bray Head. Of the ten or so cottages that visitors would have seen in 1850, four of the outer ones were to survive until the 1960s as an 'island' on the later promenade near to the present level crossing. The tenants in 1841 included the Byrne family, with Elizabeth Byrne's bathing boxes on the foreshore nearby. Once past these cottages, if the stroller turned southwards on the track towards Bray Head, the next house was a rather larger one facing the sea and standing on an extensive yard. This was probably the one remembered many years later as the only slated house on the sea front at this time; certainly it was sufficiently substantial to survive the drastic changes to come. The building survived until the late twentieth century, and its successor on the same site still abuts somewhat uncomfortably onto the most northerly house in Fitzwilliam Terrace.

The bathing huts belonging to Quin's Hotel must have been close to high-water mark somewhere in this area. The stroller would then have passed a number of thatched cottages facing seawards along the edge of the cultivated fields and separated from the track by a strip of grass. After the first row of eight, crowded together where Claddagh Terrace is today, some stood alone, others were paired; a few, at least, were no more than tiny cabins. In 1838 there were some forty cottages in all, including a few in ruins, and there may have been more by 1850. The cottages faced across the track to the shingle beach, some three hundred feet (eighty metres) wide at high tide. Like later sea-front residents, their inhabitants had much to fear from easterly gales, when breaking waves swept across the shingle piling pebbles and seaweed against their front walls and scorching the grass with salt spray.

The scene, with Bray Head as a backdrop, must have been a picturesque one for the visitor, further enhanced by the fishing boats drawn up on the beach with their nets stretched out to dry. Towards the southern end of the shore, opposite martello tower no. 1, there was also the impressive curved entrance and gate lodge, surrounded by trees and shrubs, leading to the grounds of Sans Souci. The visitor, pausing at the entrance, could look up the long sweeping drive to glimpse the Putlands' house in its commanding position on the hill. Perhaps a few visitors would gaze with particular interest, knowing that the gateway was the spot where Roman-style graves were said to have been unearthed a few years earlier.

A little further south, where the Esplanade Hotel is today, there was the first coast guard station, built on the lands of the Cock Walk by 1832. Two buildings joined, one square, one rectangular, it faced the sea backed by a plantation of trees on Mr Putland's land and with a small watch tower in front. Houses for four boatmen and their families were included, as well as that of the commanding officer. Since it was whitewashed, the structure must have been a very conspicuous feature on the sea front.

The visitor then had a footbridge to cross over the Cockbrook, before reaching the next row of small cottages and, most importantly, Mrs George Putland's school. This private school, which cost Mrs Putland £100 to build and which was run at her expense, was much praised. It catered for about a hundred poor children, mainly girls, and flourished from the 1820s until about 1850. Mr and Mrs Putland also supported a linen and woollen factory that employed some forty local women; this may also have been on the strand although its location is unknown. Mrs Putland's support of the local poor was highly praised although, writing anonymously at a much later date, in *A hundred years of Bray and its neighbourhood*, Frances Seymour was more critical: 'Mrs Putland was kind to the poor, but not very judicious in her charities. Crowds of beggars waylaid her at the gate when her carriage-and-four passed in or out'.

The school with its small scholars must have made a lively focal point at the southern end of the strand. Beyond it the beach tapered out at the rocky declivities of Bray Head, with a last few cottages and their gardens on the site of the present Fontenoy Terrace.

'CHRISTIAN BENEVOLENCE. (FROM A CORRESPONDENT.) — On Wednesday the 14th inst., an annual festival was given by Mrs. Putland, at San Souci House, Bray, to upwards of one hundred poor female children, all of whom are clothed and educated without religious distinction, and at the sole expense of this truly amiable and philanthropic lady. It was most delightful to behold this patroness of everything that can cast a lustre round the female character, exerting herself to make her young guests happy. On grace being given by the Rev. Mr. Roche, P.P., an elegant band struck up "God save the King", "Patrick's Day", with many other cheering and appropriate airs, which were encored during the entertainment. The order, cleanliness, and decorum of the children on this interesting occasion gave infinite satisfaction to a vast crowd of spectators, who were attracted to witness this feast of mercy ... .'
(*Freeman's Journal* 24 September 1831)

'... a manufactory of flax and wool is supported entirely by Mr. and Mrs. Putland, in which more than 40 poor women are employed; the materials, when woven into linens and linseys, are distributed gratuitously among the poor of the neighbourhood.'
(Samuel Lewis, *A topographical dictionary of Ireland*, London, 1837, vol. i, p. 223)

MRS GEORGE PUTLAND: 'PATRONESS'

Although it entailed taking a less scenic route than the one along the sea front, the visitor who strolled down Quin's Walk could also return to the town by turning northwards and following Seapoint Road. In 1850 this was still the only public way to the sea front from Main Street, cutting across the present Carlisle Grounds. Seapoint House stood, as it does today, on a corner site, looking down over the Dargle mouth. The ship owner Robert Seymour owned a property complex including this house, with the large D-shaped Cherry Garden, the dock, coal yards and three slated houses facing the road. In 1850 these houses still had a clear uninterrupted view across the fields all the way to Bray Head.

6.13. *Bray seen across the Dargle from James Fraser's* Guide to the county of Wicklow, *1842.*

6.14. *Bray Bridge and the cottages in Mill Lane from Fraser's guide.*

At the town end, the girls' national school was on Seymour's land. The boys' national school, a more substantial building, was across the road on John Quin's land. Schools for male and female pupils had been opened for its parishioners by the Catholic parish in 1820, both apparently accommodated originally in what was later the girls' school. Before their incorporation into the national schools system in 1833, they were largely supported by means of annual 'charity sermons' in the chapel and subscriptions from the parish. There were close to a hundred male pupils and a similar number of females, although newspaper reports of the time give an inflated picture.

CHARITY SERMONS

> *'BRAY SCHOOLS. On SUNDAY next, 29th JULY, 1821. At Two O'Clock. A CHARITY SERMON will be Preached in BRAY CHAPEL by the Rev. C.V. DOWLING, O.S.D. in aid of the extensive Male and Female Schools of that town, in which nearly 400 children receive the benefits of a Literary and Moral Education, are trained up to habits of industry and virtue, and qualified to fill their humble spheres in life with propriety and decorum. "Blessed is he that considereth the Poor, the Lord will deliver him in the time of trouble." — Ps. xl. v. 1.'*
> (*Freeman's Journal* 26 July 1821)

Seapoint Road led back to Main Street, and reaching Bray Bridge, Bray's mill and brewery would have come into sight where The Maltings are today. By 1850 this was a considerable commercial complex. The mill had been repaired and enlarged after it was leased from the ninth earl of Meath by Thomas Southern in 1794 and, with its malt-houses, consisted of two long, tall buildings with the mill-race and wheel between them. The adjacent brewery buildings formed two sides of a rectangle with a yard at its centre, and extended right to the river's edge. The brewer's house stood facing the mill-race with an ornamental flower garden in front and a formal walled garden at the side; it was demolished in the 1990s.

An engraving from James Fraser's guidebook of 1842 shows the mill and brewery complex, with the tall chimney belching smoke. A second engraving with Bray Bridge in the foreground shows the approach to the mill, with the row of cottages in Mill Lane that were finally removed in about 1900. In 1850 the mill was still in the hands of the Southern family, who also held the fishing rights in the Dargle. The salmon and sea trout fishery, with its venerable history, was soon to undergo close scrutiny; in 1853 the Commissioners of Public Works and Fisheries in Ireland would formally decree that drift nets could not be used in the river, or within a half-mile radius of its mouth, nor 'stake, bag or fixed nets' within a mile radius. This was to be one of the reasons, if not the main one, why local fishermen were soon concentrated at the southern end of the strand close to Bray Head. And after a bitter dispute with the miller, Alfred Southern, the earl of Meath as lord of the manor was able to reassert his ownership of the fishery in 1855.

BRAY BREWERY

'TO BE SOLD BY AUCTION. On THURSDAY, the 1st of November, 1810. THE extensive BREWERY at BRAY, Co. Wicklow, with every Utensil fit for immediate Work, equal to the manufacture of 100 Barrels of Malt per week, comprising extensive Stores, Vattage, Casks, Drays, Horses, etc., all in complete order, with Malt House capable of making 3000 Barrels of Malt per year and stores for 5000 Barrels of Grain. It is at present adapted for 2000 Barrels per year, in all respecting accords to the Revenue Laws. There is a neat Dwelling-House and Garden, etc, etc. the Lease is for ever, and an abundant supply of water. The Proprietor paid a Fine, and has since expended £1000 on the Concerns. — The advantages of this Situation are too obvious to need comment.'
(*Freeman's Journal* 27 October 1810)

'Bray Brewery. R. & J. Watkins beg leave to acquaint the nobility, gentry and public that they have purchased Mr Darley's Brewery at Bray, where they have commenced brewing ale and table beer, which they beg leave to recommend to their notice. They will have a constant supply of their West Indian XX and XXX stout in casks, to suit private families. Orders, per post or otherwise, addressed to Bray Brewery, or to R. & J. Watkins Brewery, Ardee Street, Dublin, will be respectfully attended to.'
(*Saunder's Newsletter* 1 January 1839)

Across the river in Little Bray, Upper Bray Commons still formed an unbroken green space grazed by roaming animals. Some forty cottages were scattered around the margins, of which a considerable number belonged to squatters who paid no rent. The commons had a few years of glory in the 1830s, when a racecourse was laid out complete with a stand at the winning post and a wall alongside the river. Improvements apparently involved the removal of some gardens, presumably those of squatters, and it would seem that the work was done with the complicity of those, such as Lord Meath, who held grazing rights. The flat flood plain, edged by the higher ground of the Upper Dargle Road, must have made an admirable, if somewhat boggy, venue.

Race meetings were held annually in the seven years 1832–8 as two- or three-day events. They were supported by the local gentry, some of whom served as stewards, and the crowd was estimated as eight to ten thousand on well-attended days. The annual races must have brought great excitement and trade to Little Bray; Quins' Hotel benefited too, for the *Freeman's Journal* recorded that after the 1832 race a hundred 'gentlemen' sat down to dine.

6.15. Little Bray, showing Castle Street (right) and Back Street (left) leading away from Bray Bridge; a postcard of the early 1900s.

6.16. One of the surviving buildings on the east side of Castle Street and its original street nameplate.

BRAY RACES, 1833

'BRAY RACES. Yesterday these races (in professional parlance) "came off" on the Bray course. The morning was very unfavourable, being incessantly wet up to 12 o'clock. In consequence the concourse of spectators was not so numerous as it otherwise would have been; but the sports were, however, far from being badly attended. Crowds of citizens poured out from Dublin, and the gentry and peasantry of the surrounding country thronged the course in great numbers. The coup d'oeuil *from the course was most picturesque. The racing ground is formed from the strand of the river and the common, on the Dargle side of the bridge, and is completely encompassed with hills. These were thronged to their summits by the peasantry, while the arena in the centre was crowded with carriages, cars, etc. We heard it remarked that none of those who constitute the aristocracy of the Dublin side of the county Wicklow attended the races. The Powerscourts, Meaths, Rathdownes, etc. were all absent. The people, however, contrived to do without them, and even to be happy notwithstanding their absence ... . The sports of the day concluded by an admirable hack race, which afforded a great deal of amusement. The only accidents we heard of were caused by a large quagmire in the middle of the course, into which many a gallant Nimrod was precipitated. Only one gentleman, however, was hurt severely. He, we understand, had his collarbone broken. Excellent sport is expected today. In consequence of the late rain the road is most agreeably free from dust.'*

(*Freeman's Journal* 5 June 1833)

BRAY RACES, 1834

'THE TURF — BRAY RACES. THE Nobility, Gentry, and the Public, are most respectfully informed that the Stand-house of Bray is now fitted up for their reception, under the immediate inspection of the Committee, for the sale of every description of Refreshments, of the primest quality — Dinners, Lunches, Snacks, etc. Parties may, therefore, rely on the very best attention and accommodation being afforded them, every arrangement being made on the best possible scale. Three hours sufficient notice for the supplying of hot Dinners, etc, First-class Wines, Bottled Ales, Porter, Soda Water, Ginger Beer, etc.'

(*Freeman's Journal* 17 June 1834)

BRAY RACES, 1834

'BRAY RACES. These races commenced on yesterday, and were very numerously and fashionably attended. The afternoon continued fine throughout, although, during the morning, the variable winds, some few showers and the continuance of what sailors call a "dirty sky", betokened a far different result. The course was in excellent order ... The public is indebited for much of its enjoyment to the excellent arrangements completed by the Bray committee of management. A commodious stand-house, capable of accommodating several hundred persons, has been erected contiguous to the winning-post, from which a splendid view of the surrounding, and of every part of the course, is obtained. The course was kept clear by several men furnished with stout staves; and those accidents whose occurrence so frequently throws a gloom over meetings of a similar character, were thus altogether avoided.'
(*Freeman's Journal* 18 June 1834)

Bray Commons was inundated, however, when the Dargle flooded after heavy rain in late July 1839 and the racecourse was destroyed. In the summer of 1844 an attempt was made with the aid of local subscriptions to rebuild the course and resume racing, but this was thwarted when opponents of racing intervened, led by the Revd Sir Samuel Synge Hutchinson of Palermo in Little Bray and presumably connected with the Bray Temperance Society. Hutchinson and his supporters issued summonses claiming that the levelling work was 'skinning and destroying the surface of the commons'. Although the case did not succeed, momentum seems to have been lost and Bray forfeited its racecourse for good — within a few years the Upper Commons was destined, as we shall see, to become building land.

The part of Little Bray near the Dargle had undergone a major change by 1850, with the construction of Castle Street, laid out in about 1808 as a wide new road to make access to Bray Bridge easier — the sharp turn at the bottom of the bridge into what became Back Street was apparently responsible for many accidents. At its north end Castle Street skirted Little Bray Castle, which now came to face directly onto the street; in the 1830s the castle had been used for a few years as a police station, but it was vacant by 1850. John Donnellan, the local builder, was responsible for Castle Street, having donated the land, and he may also have built the new houses that lined both sides — some of those on the east side survive today.

Castle Street was busy, with four public houses and two forges in the area.

Like the north end of Main Street, it was a venue for Bray's fairs; as was customary the cattle would have been herded on the street, with booths set up on either side to sell 'fairings' to the farmers. Fair days were lively and profitable occasions, but the amount of cleaning up afterwards was considerable.

The Church of Ireland national schools for girls, boys and infants, occupied a row of three buildings built in 1819 on a site on the Lower Commons acquired from the tenth earl of Meath. The row still exists as the present Belton Terrace. Like their corresponding Catholic national schools in Seapoint Road, there were close to a hundred each of boy and girl pupils. Although all three buildings seem originally to have been school premises, by 1850 the most northerly of the three was in use as Bray Savings Bank, which dated back to 1831. The premises had also had another function before 1841, the monthly manor court and weekly petty sessions were held there, presumably at a time when the old courthouse by the pound was no longer fit for use.

LITTLE BRAY HOUSING

Little Bray *'is let in tenements from £7 to £18 per annum viz one room a kitchen and a small patch of garden generally let at £7 per annum and so upwards in proportion to the quality and size of the tenement ...'* (OS field name book, Old Connaught parish, 1836).

Both sides of what had formerly been the main road but was now aptly rechristened Back Street were lined with small cottages — most of the one-roomed mud cabins in Little Bray probably stood here. Across the present Upper Dargle Road, by now the mail coach route to Wicklow, there was one good-sized house standing on its own grounds with a gate lodge at its entrance. This was Bray Lodge, built before 1829, which under its later name of Ardilaun House survived until the mid twentieth century. One of the three properties on the corner may already have been the Wicklow and Wexford Hotel, which continued into the 1960s as the precursor of the Sunnybank Inn. (Under its most recent name of The Pickled Pig the building was destroyed by fire in 2001.) The houses and gardens along the Dublin Road included Arbutus Lodge, hidden away, as it is today, behind a pair of substantial houses that also still exist. Little Bray dispensary had formerly been adjacent to Arbutus Lodge, but by 1850 was in a smaller house further towards Dublin. It was opened to serve the parishes of Old Connaught and Rathmichael in 1836.

Chapel Lane already led to St Peter's Church, built in 1837 and dedicated on 11 September 1838 to replace the older Catholic church further north at Crinken. The church is little changed today. The adjoining graveyard was consecrated soon after, on 8 May 1842; originally quite limited in extent, it has been extended twice in the twentieth century. Next to it St Peter's National Schools had been opened for the children of the parish in 1844, with girls upstairs and boys downstairs, and together they formed a new vibrant focus for life in Little Bray. Unlike St Peter's Church, the school has not survived in its original form; it was rebuilt in 1874 and is today St Peter's Parish Hall (with the date 1864).

'DEDICATION OF THE NEW CHURCH OF ST. PETER THE APOSTLE, AT LITTLE BRAY. This interesting ceremony took place on Tuesday last. — In the absence of His Grace Dr. Murray, the ceremony was performed by the Rev. Mr. Woods, assisted by the clergy of this rural deanery, and a number of gentlemen from Dublin and various parts of the country. The Litanies and Psalms were intoned by the Rev. Mr. Laphen, in his usual effective style. The High Mass was celebrated by the Rev. Walsh, assisted by Rev. Messrs. Murphy and Sohan. After the High Mass most appropriate and eloquent sermon was delivered by the Rev. Thaddeus O'Malley. — The reverend gentleman's observations in general, but particularly in reprobating persecution, and inculcating universal benevolence, left a deep impression upon his numerous and diversified auditory. His compliment to the estimable pastors of the parish was delicate and just. In the evening the numerous clergy were hospitably entertained by Mrs. Segrave, at Jubilee Hall, and the musical department met an equally hospitable reception from the kind-hearted and urbane Rev. Mr. Fagan.'
(*Freeman's Journal* 13 September 1838)

ST PETER'S CHURCH, LITTLE BRAY

Sherman's public house, on the corner of Chapel Lane was a stopping point for the mail coaches to Wexford — called 'The Coach and Horses' until comparatively recently, its past is still commemorated in its present name 'The Coach Inn'. It was distinguished by a painted board showing a coach-and-four. Cottages and small houses extended all the way up the west side of the Dublin road as far as, and slightly beyond, the junction with Old Connaught Avenue.

On the seaward side of the Dublin Road there were no houses, only demesne lands, gardens and fields. Cork Lodge, built in 1840, was a major

6.17. St Peter's Church, Little Bray, built in 1837.

6.18. Little Bray in the early 1900s from a postcard; Bray Bridge was a hiring place and the men may have been hoping for work.

property in 1850; it survives today. The gate lodge and driveway of Corke Abbey lay opposite Old Connaught Avenue. The house itself stood in the middle of large ornamental grounds with a winding pathway down to the beach near to martello tower no. 3; it was demolished in the mid-twentieth century. One large field, where the industrial estate is now, separated its walled garden from the entrance drive to Ravenswell House. Ravenswell, with gardens stretching back down to the Dargle, was by far and away the largest property actually in Little Bray. Dating back to at least the 1770s, its name had been changed from the earlier one of Bolton Hill at the turn of the century to mark the well, Ravens or Regan's well, close to the house. Isaac Weld, the traveller and writer, had bought the house in 1814, and lived there until his death in 1855. Facing down towards the Dargle, the rectangular house still forms the core of the present Ravenswell convent.

BRAY IN 1837

'The surrounding scenery is exceedingly romantic, and combines with its short distance from Dublin to render this place a favourite resort during the summer season for bathing. A number of thatched cottages of great neatness, and containing, exclusively of offices, from three to eight rooms each, have been appropriated to the accommodation of visitors, to whom they are let furnished at rents varying from £40 to £50 and more for the season. The hotel and posting-house, conducted by Mr. John Quin, jun., is fitted up with every regard to the superior accommodation of families and visitors of the highest respectability; hot and cold sea water baths may be had at all hours without delay, and the house has long been a favourite resort of parties on excursions of pleasure, and of wedding parties to spend the day in festivity and in the enjoyment of the beauties of the surrounding scenery. A spacious gravel walk, half a mile in length and perfectly straight, has been made from the rear of the hotel through the private grounds to the sea, forming a beautiful promenade, and commanding fine views. On the Dublin side of the river a race-course has been formed and races are held annually.'
(Samuel Lewis, *A topographical dictionary of Ireland*, 1837, vol. i, p. 222)

Ravenswell House commanded, as it still does, wide views across the Dargle estuary and Bray town towards Bray Head, views just as extensive as those of Sans Souci further south. As the nineteenth century passed the halfway mark, the residents of Ravenswell, like the Loreto nuns newly installed in Sans Souci, were to have a bird's-eye view of startling changes. The Dublin & Wicklow Railway was already under construction and with the opening of the line from Dublin in 1854 Bray was soon to be transformed into a new kind of seaside town.

Chapter 7

'The Brighton of Ireland': Bray 1850–70

'The aristocracy and the wealthy merchants of London go down to Brighton and give — not uncommonly — a hundred a-month for houses facing the sea. They travel fifty miles of railway to reach it, and when they get there what is it? An arid, glaring chalky place, with a fine open sea-side certainly, but without a background of mountain scenery. ... We cannot conceive any more delightful day than a fine one spent quietly at Bray. To stroll on the Esplanade, to lie on the beach, to linger over the panoramic grandeur presented around the face of the Head, indeed merely to breathe the life and health-giving air of the mountain, and the sea, is happiness of a high degree in itself.'

(G.R. Powell, *The official railway handbook to Bray*, Dublin, 1860, p. 22)

The construction of railways began the transformation of some English and Welsh coastal towns into a new kind of seaside resort, accessible to a wider cross-section of the public than ever before, and in Ireland this was mirrored in the transformation that took place in Bray after the Dublin & Wicklow Railway was opened in July 1854. As a holiday resort, Bray nearly doubled its population in the twenty years from 1850 to 1870, at a time when much of the country was stagnating after the Great Famine. The twin advantages of seaside location and striking mountain scenery that had already made the town far more than a local market centre were turned to good use by a small group of entrepreneurs, including some from outside, and by the local landlords. Their enterprise and foresight were responsible for the birth of a new resort modelled on the English pattern. The model was specifically Britain's most fashionable seaside town, Brighton.

The railway had been heralded even before the Dublin to Kingstown (Dún Laoghaire) line, the first in Ireland, was opened in 1834. A line to Bray had been suggested as early as 1832, although it was the mid 1840s, after the extension of the Kingstown line to Dalkey by the short-lived atmospheric railway, before serious plans were made. The advantages for Bray seemed

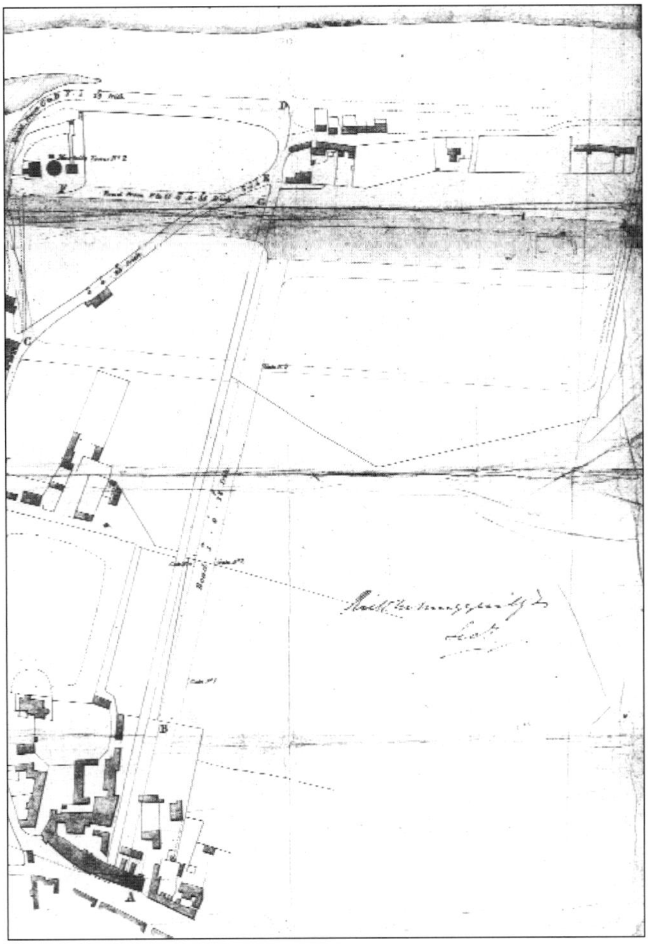

***7.1.** Lease map showing part of the route of the railway, as agreed between John Quin junior and the Dublin & Wicklow Railway Co. Quinsborough Road is marked alongside Quin's Walk. Note the sea inlet still close under martello tower no. 2 (top left) and the old route of Seapoint Road diagonally across what is now the Carlisle Grounds.*

obvious. Improved access to Dublin was causing a building boom in villages such as Blackrock and Dalkey, and around Kingstown, and extension of the line would surely do the same for Bray. The atmospheric railway was attracting Sunday excursionists as far as Dalkey and Killiney. The sight of seaside towns mushrooming up in North Wales after the London–Holyhead line was opened in 1848 was soon to encourage further the idea that Bray, with its existing reputation as a healthful resort, was ideal for similar development.

There was also pressure from a different direction, with the proposal by the Great Western Railway company in England, whose engineer was the eminent Isambard Kingdom Brunel, to establish a route via Fishguard and Rosslare with a rail link to Dublin. After protracted negotiations between the

Dublin & Kingstown Railway company and the G.W.R.'s Irish company, the Waterford, Wexford, Wicklow & Dublin Railway, agreement was reached, and a year's work began on the Bray Head section of the line in August 1847.

In 1848 there was a pause during the economic depression caused by the Great Famine, and it was the summer of 1851 before the project was resumed. By now the main party involved was the Dublin & Wicklow Railway, a less ambitious version of the W.W.W. & D. Railway. The two routes agreed upon were those that were to become familiar to generations of travellers: the coastal line via Dalkey and the Harcourt Street line via Dundrum, the lines merging just south of Shankill. But in determining the future shape of Bray, the main consideration lay in the choice of route through or past the town.

The route selected, very close to Bray sea front and with a spectacular but difficult section around Bray Head, was not the only possible one. The line might, for instance, have been sited further inland, nearer to the Dublin road and Bray's Main Street. But this would have meant crossing the grounds of a number of estates — Corke Abbey, Ravenswell, the newly-established Loreto Convent, Charles Putland's Bray Head House — which might well have entailed paying large sums to the owners. Bypassing Bray Head would have meant running the line through the Killruddery demesne and there is a tradition, undocumented, that the tenth earl of Meath provided the eastern route around the Head free of charge in order to avoid this. In any event, the

7.2. The railway embankment and low bridges limit access to the sea front.

selected route was a logical continuation of the line that already hugged the southern shore of Dublin Bay, and it was the one that involved the minimum number of changes of gradient.

North of the Dargle the new railway skirted the grounds of Corke Abbey and Ravenswell, traversing the flat boulder clay deposits rather too closely, as it proved, to the cliff edge — the track had later to be moved further inland. Spanning the mouth of the Dargle involved, as well as building the railway bridge, throwing up a 130-metre-long embankment across the shingle at Seapoint, greatly changing the appearance of the river estuary. The rail-track then ran southwards just inland of the beach, cutting off the two martello towers, the coastguard station, and the straggle of sea-front cottages and their gardens from the fields behind. The section around Bray Head required all Brunel's engineering skills, with an embankment, wooden trestle viaducts, and three tunnels: the Brabazon, the Brandy Hole and the Cable Rock.

The choice of route profoundly affected the appearance of Bray, as it has to this day. It created the problem of how best to reconcile the railway's needs with those of the projected resort, where a neat grid of new roads was planned for the coastal fields. Generous access to the sea front was essential, and the solution adopted was to provide one major level crossing and to elevate the rest of the line onto an embankment, its gradient steepening upwards towards Bray Head, so that the track passed over the new west–east roads by means of a series of low, narrow bridges.

SEEING THE SEA

'The house that the Fitzpatricks had taken in Bray for the winter was not situated in what is known as the fashionable part of the town. It commanded no view either of the Esplanade or of Bray Head; it had, in fact, little view of any kind except the backs of other people's houses, and an oblique glimpse of a railway bridge at the end of the road. … its crowning claim to distinction was the fact that by standing just outside the gate it was possible to descry, under the railway bridge, a small square of esplanade and sea that was Mrs. Fitzpatrick's justification when she said gallantly to her Dublin friends that she'd never have come to Bray for the winter only for being able to look out at the waves all day long.'

(E. Œ. Somerville and Martin Ross, *The real Charlotte*. London, 1894, p. 356)

This had inevitable consequences, perhaps regrettable ones. The constricted strip of land between the railway and the beach offered only

7.3. The railway and above it the cliff walk skirting Bray Head, from a postcard of the early 1900s.

limited sites on which to build private homes, hotels and boarding houses with that most desirable of resort amenities, a view of the sea. Most of the new part of Bray was cut off from the beach by the railway station buildings and the embankment, with enticing glimpses of water only from the upstairs windows of tall buildings and through the arches of the bridges. (One might, of course, argue that the latter provided visitors with a truly theatrical experience — a sudden emergence from the damp shade of the underpass into the sunshine of the Esplanade.)

If the positioning of the track was important, so too was the siting of the railway station, destined to be the focal point of the new resort. There was also the need for an impressive link road between it and Main Street. And here the Quin family had a most important role. John Quin senior died in 1852, having already transferred part of his property to his son, and in 1854 it was John Quin junior who was firmly in control of much of the land between Main Street and the northern part of the seafront. Quin sold the necessary land to the Dublin & Wicklow Railway, and the agreement as finalised between the parties was responsible for the positioning of the railway station on its present site. It also stipulated that the railway company would build a new road, parallel to Quin's Walk, from the station to Main Street. This road was given the dignified name of Quinsborough Road, although in practice it has always been popularly known as the Quinsboro' or 'Forty Foot'. It is still today the second most important road in Bray.

Quinsborough Road was to be forty feet wide where it replaced the existing houses, back gardens and fields close to Main Street, as far as the present Eglinton Road, and fifty feet wide as it was carved across the fields for the remaining distance. It reached the sea front at the point where Quin's Walk already merged with the then end of Seapoint Road, just by the cluster of cottages. The original agreement was for a railway bridge at this point, but instead the railway company agreed to build the level crossing, thus providing one wide, inviting connection between town and sea front. Quin had displayed to the public a bird's-eye view of his development plans for Quinsborough Road, including terraces, villas and ornamental lawns, as early as November 1852, only days before his father's death at the age of ninety-one. John Quin senior must have looked back with pride on his own lengthy involvement in Bray's growth; he lived to see imaginative plans for the future, if not their implementation.

IMAGINATIVE PLANS FOR THE FUTURE

> *'PROJECTED IMPROVEMENTS AT BRAY.*
> *From the terminus to the hotel, the railway company will construct a spacious avenue through Mr. Quin's grounds; and on either side of this avenue the spirited proprietor has planned a variety of delightful terraces, detached villas, and ornamental lawns, forming altogether the beau-ideal of a suburban paradise. Judging from the view, it would appear that such improvements are designed in the appearance of the hotel that it cannot be recognized as the same on the outside. The interior arrangements, we believe, cannot be much improved.'*
> (*Freeman's Journal* 25 November 1852)

The agreement with John Quin also determined a major road realignment that was part of the change from the old Bray to the new. The diagonal portion of Seapoint Road across the present Carlisle Grounds was closed off and the railway company continued Seapoint Road down to the sea along its present course under the most northerly of the railway bridges. At the seaward end Seapoint Road was curved round into a new section of road extending from the present Martello Terrace to the end of Quinsborough Road — creating the earliest part of a new sea-front roadway, Strand Road, which was soon to extend all the way to Bray Head.

In addition to John Quin, there were also important new players on the scene. One of them, the railway engineer and entrepreneur William Dargan, has received full credit over the years for the considerable part he played in moulding the new resort, although in monetary terms it was to cost him far more than he benefited. Dargan's associate, Edward Breslin, a leading businessman in Bray for over forty years, and the builder John Brennan are less well remembered, although the latter's name is still evoked in Brennan's Parade and Brennan's Terrace, both of which he built, and indirectly in Adelaide Road which was named after his daughter.

William Dargan was in his fifties and at the height of his fame when he purchased shares in the Dublin & Wicklow Railway and as director and later as chairman galvanised work on the completion of the line. His success in organising and financing the 1853 Great Industrial Exhibition in Dublin, coming on top of his many railway ventures, made him one of the best-known figures in Ireland. Perhaps his early experience of working on the London–Holyhead line had provided the germ of his vision for the development of Bray, at any rate it was he who financed — and in some cases donated to the town — many of the necessary resort amenities.

Edward Breslin, a small farmer's son from Baltinglass in west Wicklow, had served with Dargan as caterer to the Exhibition and his primary role in Bray was to lie in developing the hotel and catering business — he was soon to replace John Quin as the premier hotelier in the town, although as an incomer he complained of having met some initial jealousy. But, unlike Dargan, Breslin was to live in Bray, first at his hotel and later at 4 Fitzwilliam Terrace nearby, and make it the centre of his life from his mid thirties onwards. By the time of his death in June 1897 he had served as a town commissioner for most of the full forty years of the Township's existence, including fifteen years as chairman, and his obituary in the *Freeman's Journal* could report that he had risen 'from an extremely humble position to be the chosen associate of the gentry of his native county'. At his death he was apparently worth some £40,000, a considerable fortune at the time. Edward Breslin was a formidable force in Bray. His hotels have not survived, however, and he has no memorial in today's Bray. John Brennan, who according to his newspaper obituary had made his fortune in 'distant lands' and returned to invest it in Bray, died in 1866, so his period of involvement, though intense, was comparatively short.

Bray Station was almost finished by January 1854 and the line around Bray Head and on to Wicklow was proceeding with 'amazing rapidity' thanks to Dargan — two years earlier five hundred men had been reported as being employed on the Bray Head part of the line alone, which gives some indication of the work involved. It was in fact to be almost another two years,

October 1855, before the Bray–Wicklow line opened for traffic. In May 1854 tenders were sought for the building of a hotel, the first of the new hotels and boarding houses that were to spring up along the sea front. This was Breslin's hotel, soon to acquire the proud title of Royal Marine Hotel, which was built

7.4. *William Dargan (1799–1867).*

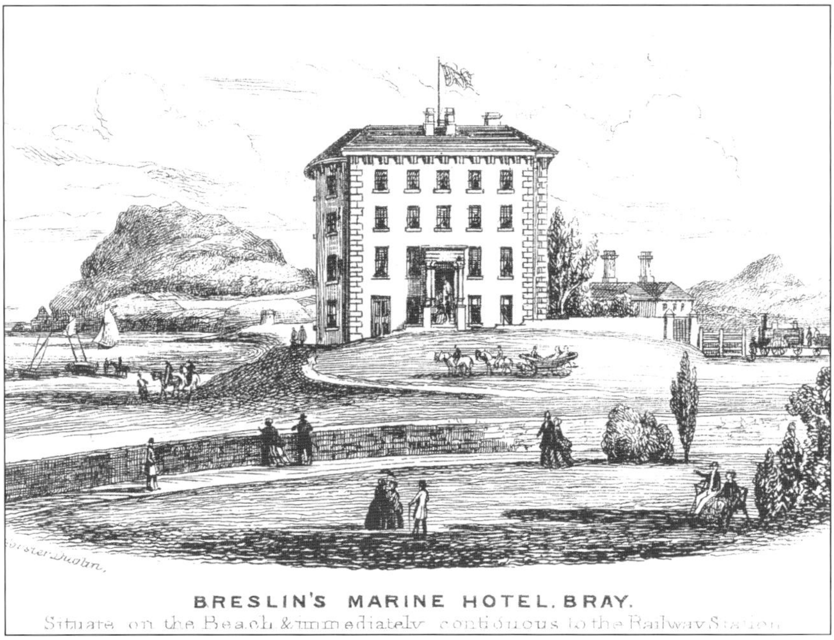

7.5. *Edward Breslin's hotel, the first on the sea front, as opened on 29 May 1855. The first Esplanade has not yet replaced the storm beach, martello tower no. 1 is visible in the distance and the railway station and level crossing are at the right, although the train is approaching from an unlikely angle. (Courtesy National Library of Ireland)*

on the commanding but constricted corner site next to the level crossing where Katie Gallagher's public house is today. After a year's building work its doors opened to the public with a celebratory dinner on 29 May 1855.

DUBLIN AND WICKLOW RAILWAY

'DUBLIN AND WICKLOW RAILWAY.
Those portions of this line between Dublin and Bray, and between Bray and Dalkey, having been inspected and approved of by Captain Wynne, the government inspector, on Tuesday last, and it being intended to open the line for public traffic on this day, the directors determined to give the shareholders an opportunity of viewing the line and works previous to the final opening. According on Saturday three trains, each consisting of twelve or fourteen very handsome and comfortable carriages, were started from the Harcourt-road Terminus at twelve, two, and four o'clock, and conveyed a large number of shareholders and their friends to Bray. The trip — twelve English miles — was accomplished in each instance in about twenty-eight minutes, and the motion of the carriages was extremely smooth and regular. On the arrival of the trains at the terminus in Bray, the visitors having examined and admired the very handsome station-house there, refreshed themselves with the good things provided by Mr. Breslin, whom many of them recollected as having catering to their wants in the Exhibition, broke off into little parties, and dispersed themselves, some to enjoy the cool sea breezes on the strand, others more adventurous to climb the hill and luxuriate in the magnificent views to be had while reclining on the soft and verdant turf of Bray Head. Others, again, and not a few, took advantage of the opportunity thus afforded them of seeing some of the far-famed beauties of the county Wicklow, and drove off to the Dargle, the Glen of the Downs, Bellevue, and other places of interest. The day was beautifully fine — it was, in fact, quite a "pet" day, and the sun shone out, for the first time during the week, *gloriously and brilliantly. The splendid band of the 1st Dragoons went down by the four o'clock train, and contributed greatly to the pleasure and enjoyment of the visitors, by playing several very admirable selections of music during the evening. The whole of the works have been executed under the immediate supervision of Mr. Dargan himself, who undertook the construction of the line ; and it is sufficient to say that they have been executed in the same excellent and substantial manner which characterises all the undertakings of that gentleman.'*
(*Freeman's Journal* 10 July 1854)

When the directors of the Dublin & Wicklow Railway and their friends were ferried down to Bray in three special trains on 8 July 1854, the area around the station must have been little more than a building site. This does not seem to have detracted from the festivities, which included a dance on the single platform then in commission, with a military band in attendance. The only new facility in place when the railway was officially opened to the public on 10 July was the station refreshment rooms, divided into first and second class, and run by Edward Breslin. The refreshment rooms quickly became a popular part of a rail trip to Bray. Ten days after the opening, for instance, the Dublin Natural History Society held their annual dinner there from six to ten p.m., having travelled down by a special evening train.

The railway caused a spurt of commercial activity. Quin's Hotel quickly advertised its table d'hôte dinners, served at five o'clock on Sundays with 'soup, fish, meats and pastry' at three shillings a head. Enniskerry innkeeper James Shirley, presumably fearing a decline in his business, immediately started a service from Bray Station to the Powerscourt Arms at a fare of 3d. In Delgany Fitzsimons Hotel, today the Delgany Inn, mentioned the railway in advertising that dinners and luncheons were available at 'shortest' notice; it served table d'hôte dinners on Sundays at two shillings. This suggests that jarveys with their jaunting cars — a peculiarly Irish form of two-wheeled

7.6. Breslin's hotel in 1865. It had been extended by 1859 to provide 90 bedrooms and 12 sitting rooms.

7.7. The surviving 'footprint' of Breslin's hotel.

horse-drawn vehicle — were already plying for hire at Bray station within weeks of the railway opening, an activity that was to be a major business well into the twentieth century. (The more commodious four-wheeled vis-à-vis, in which passengers travelled face-to-face in an open carriage, was also to become popular with visitors.)

When Breslin opened his new hotel at the start of the 1855 season he provided Bray sea front with a major new amenity, and one that was on a pivotal site. At last visitors spilling out from the trains had a fine establishment nearby to patronise, or at least to admire, as the hotel enhanced the as yet largely undeveloped sea front. So successful — and optimistic — was Breslin that he almost immediately extended his hotel on the landward side, so that by 1859 it offered a total of ninety bedrooms and twelve sitting rooms.

Meanwhile the network of new roads was taking shape. Quinsborough Road was, of course, the most important. Although the corner carries the date 1854, it is not clear exactly when the old White Lion properties at the Main Street end belonging to John Quin were demolished and Quinsborough Road itself was not transferred to the control of the township until the late 1860s. A second new road leading from Main Street on the seaward side was Novara Avenue, following the pre-existing avenue to Novara House and curving round southwards into Sidmonton Road. The completion of Florence Road, the third main road planned for this side of

Main Street, was still fifty years into the future. Parallel to the railway and the sea front, Meath Road provided a very long straight vista all the way to the lower slopes of Bray Head. It was crossed at right angles by the short roadways of Quin's Passage, Kingsmills Avenue, Novarra Avenue and Nunnery Avenue (the present Albert, Sidmonton, Victoria and Convent Avenues), which passed under the railway to the sea front.

Logically, there would have been space for another road leading from Main Street to the sea, starting close to the present Town Hall, and one might have been built had the Putland family still lived in their old home. But Sans Souci was now the preserve of the Loreto nuns, and the grounds were to remain largely unaltered until the late twentieth century. It remains necessary, even today, to travel a kilometre along the Vevay Road to reach the next seaward road, Putland Road. Although he did not act until the early 1860s, Charles Putland had no qualms about completing the road, the seaward part of which had been built as famine relief, through the lands of Bray Head House and quite close to the house itself. Putland Road is, in fact, one of the most attractive roads in Bray, starting at a height and offering an inviting view of the distant sea.

The construction of Quinsborough Road turned Seapoint Road into something of a backwater, while on the other side of Main Street the minor road past the barracks via Church Terrace was to become even more redundant. Like Charles Putland, another landlord, the Hon. Sidney Herbert,

***7.8.** Meath Road provides a long straight vista all the way to the lower slopes of Bray Head.*

7.9. Church Road, laid out on Pembroke estate land in c. 1859, and the massive spire of Christ Church, visible for miles.

7.10. Herbert Road, laid out in 1858–9; the truncated yards of the Church Terrace houses are at the right.

already encountered here, second son of the eleventh earl of Pembroke, decided to construct a new road across the Pembroke lands and open up the area west of the town. Herbert Road was laid out in 1858–9 at a cost of £2,000; aligning it with Quinsborough Road meant a delicate operation, slicing diagonally across the backyards of the Church Terrace cottages to leave the end cottages with their back windows only a foot or two from the new pavement — and with no sanitary provision whatsoever. The west end of what had been Barrack Lane became no more than an alley and today has mostly disappeared. Instead Herbert Road formed a fine new roadway, although it was to be the twentieth century before much housing was attracted to this side of Bray.

The Pembroke estate was also responsible for a new road in a quite different part of Bray. It provided Church Road as a curving link between Killarney Road and Vevay Road, a few hundred metres south of their junction and just beyond Prospect Cottage. Church Road was laid out in about 1859, at the time of the construction of the Church of Ireland's prominent new Christ Church.

'BRAY, COUNTY WICKLOW — BUILDING GROUND.
TO BE LET, a few Lots of Ground laid out for BUILDING, admirably circumstanced for the erection of detached or semi-detached Houses, within a few minutes walk of the Bray Railway Station, and convenient to the sea shore.
Also, several Lots of Ground varying in size from One Acre to Twenty, situate on the slopes of Bray Head, commanding unrivalled mountain and marine scenery, and peculiarly adapted for the erection of Villa residences or Terraces.'
(*Freeman's Journal* 4 May 1855)

NEW BUILDING PLOTS

The development of the sea front was, of course, crucial to the new Bray. For the first three or four years rail visitors must have found the area not greatly changed. Although building lots were advertised almost immediately after the railway was opened, it was the late 1850s before much development other than Breslin's Hotel was actually completed. A 'Plan shewing the disposition of the roads and intended improvements of Bray Strand', surveyed for Lord Meath and dated 1859, marks Strand Road 'to be widened and improved' and shows more than a dozen of the old cottages still intact.

But the rough track was soon replaced by an impressive new road, while a flurry of building transformed the landward side. The building was mostly on plots wide enough for several houses and with 61-year ground leases either from 1860 or, further south, from 1867.

Within a few years there were many glowing newspaper reports describing new properties in Bray. Already in October 1859 the *Freeman's Journal* was able to boast that fifty new houses had been built along the sea front, and that although a few cottages remained, they were 'likely to be gone by next summer'. Many terraced and individual houses were occupied by 1862, the first year in which *Thom's Directory* considered Bray to be of sufficient importance to be covered street by street. The *Dublin Builder* noted that 'houses of every imaginable class, shape and capacity are springing up', and the inland side of Strand Road had by then acquired some of the appearance it has retained to this day.

THE ESPLANADE UNDER THE 'UNSPARING HAND OF THE IMPROVER'

'It [the Esplanade] *has been reclaimed from the wild shingly shore at the sole cost of Mr. Dargan, and is open to everyone who chooses to enjoy its delightful expanse. It was originally dotted here and there with the unsightly huts of fishermen and bathing-women; these were swept away by the unsparing hand of the improver, but not without ample compensation to the owners, for whom neat cottages were provided in other parts of Bray. Over the arid sand of the shore tons of maiden soil were laid, and a quantity of grass-seed carefully sown. Along its whole enamelled surface nothing now interposes between the beholder and the Head; the Railway Baths on the sea edge, and the Martello Tower about mid-way — once like a lonely pioneer of civilisation — are the only erections on the enclosure. At an additional expense of three hundred pounds, Mr. Dargan caused a vulcanized wire fence to be run along the road edge of the esplanade, thus preserving the evenness and beauty of its surface.'*

(G.R. Powell, *The official railway handbook to Bray*, Dublin, 1860, pp 27–8)

The seaward side was also transformed, thanks to the involvement of William Dargan. In 1859 he took a 99-year lease at the peppercorn rent of a shilling a year on Lord Meath's portion of the old storm beach, and had it levelled as a lengthy esplanade, an essential sea-front amenity. Previously visitors 'taking the air' had had to content themselves with a stroll along the storm beach, now they had a strip of flat grass; paths were subsequently

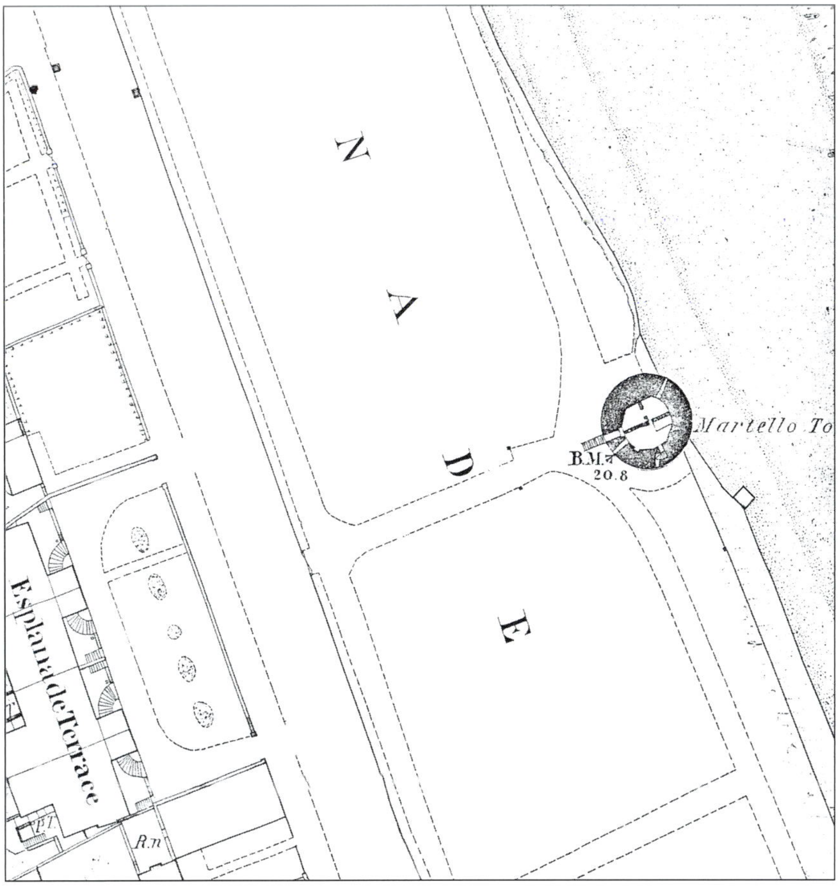

7.11. *Martello tower no. 1 in 1870 — the seaward side is unprotected from the waves and part of the new path on the edge of Dargan's Esplanade has already disappeared (see chapter 8).*

7.12. Esplanade and Strand Road from Gaskin's Irish varieties, *published in 1869. The path laid out on the seaward side of the Esplanade before 1870 is not shown. Fitzwilliam, Claddagh and Brennan's Terraces are at the right — with little protection from the sea.*

added on either side. Dargan fenced the Strand Road side with granite posts and chains, spending his own money and refusing contributions. Apart from improving the look of the Esplanade, this served, in theory at least, to keep wandering animals off the grass. And in 1861 he made a present of the Esplanade to the town.

Bray had Dargan to thank, too, for other amenities provided for the nascent resort. John Quin had assigned thirteen acres adjacent to Quinsborough Road to Dargan in 1858 and this gave Dargan the opportunity to develop the area. The most unusual of his new amenities was the Turkish Baths, opened a year later in an astonishing edifice on Quinsborough Road which unfortunately has not survived the commercial imperatives of the late twentieth century. Dr Richard Barter was a pioneer in this area who had opened the first modern Turkish baths in Ireland and Britain at St Anne's, near Blarney, County Cork, in 1856; by 1860 in addition to the Bray baths he had eight establishments around Ireland, including ones in Belfast, Dublin, Killarney and Limerick.

The baths took about a year to build at a cost of £10,000. According to the *Freeman's Journal*, Sir John Benson was the architect, although Dr Barter's architect nephew, also named Richard Barter, seems to have been involved with the interior. They were elaborately built of red and white brick on a base of cut granite from the quarries at Dalkey, embellished with tall minarets at the corners and with a seventy-foot high ornamental chimney. Photographs and drawings of the exterior survive and although the building was in poor condition when it was demolished in 1980, many people still remember it with affection. The interior was as novel as the exterior. According to a detailed description of the Bray baths in a lecture given in England just after the opening, the decoration was sumptuous (or aspired to be): the windows were of coloured glass, the interior floor was of Staffordshire tiles in imitation of Roman pavements and a marble fountain surrounded with plants stood in the centre of the grand entrance hall. As a final touch, the attendants were to wear Turkish costume.

The Turkish Baths were opened on 2 November 1859 — not the most auspicious time of year since the winter clientele would have been mainly confined to local residents. Nonetheless they opened on an optimistic note. The hours were from 6 a.m. to 11 p.m., except for Sundays, when they closed for five hours in the middle of the day. There was a choice of public or private bathing, and bathing dresses, sheets and towels were included in the charge. Shampooing — which was not allowed on Sundays — cost extra.

The baths received publicity, both harmful and beneficial, from a major attack aired in the medical press in 1860, contrasting genuine Middle-Eastern Turkish baths that used hot, humid air to create a vapour bath with new ones, like Bray, that used hot dry air conducted through underfloor piping; it was claimed that the latter worsened symptoms instead of relieving them. The charges were vigorously contested by Dr Barter. But Bray's Turkish Baths were not to be a success. Perhaps the season was too short, or perhaps they were too great an innovation for Bray and the criticisms produced an element of doubt in the minds of potential users. Unlike Dr Barter's similar establishment in Lincoln Place, Dublin, which operated until 1900, Bray Turkish Baths were, as we shall see, to have only five years of somewhat dubious glory. In the winter of 1862 visitors were being enticed by the offer of free entry, while as early as 1864 Dargan was trying to sell the baths for £4000 — a massive loss.

Dargan was also responsible for another short-lived therapeutic concern nearby. He bought Galtrim House from John Quin in 1858 and by 1860 set up 'Bray Hydropathic Establishment' in conjunction with the Turkish Baths. Hydros, where the treatment was based on the action of water to cleanse the system and included swathing patients in cold, wet wraps for lengthy periods, were also being pioneered in Ireland at the time — St Anne's at Blarney included one as well as its Turkish baths — and Dr Edward

7.13. *Quinsborough Road looking eastwards, 1865; Quin had displayed his plans for terraces and villas to the public as early as 1852.*

Haughton, who became physician and manager of Bray's hydropathic establishment, was a former patient of Dr Barter at St Anne's. 'Conducted on Eclectic Principles', a stay cost £2 to £3 a week, similar to a good hotel. But the Galtrim House hydro was to be no more successful than many others in Ireland, including a second Wicklow hydro set up by an English practitioner in nearby Delgany. There was a swift change of emphasis to general medicinal care and it vanished from the scene within a year or so. (Haughton moved to England in 1861 as physician to the new Oriental Baths in Liverpool.)

TURKISH BATHS

'The building cost £10,000; it is extremely handsome, of an Oriental style of architecture — of red and white bricks alternately placed, and faced with stone. The interior is very appropriately decorated, and composed of several apartments admirably adapted to their respective uses. There is a grand entrance hall, or reception room, divided into a dozen small apartments on each side of the hall, each fitted as a dressing room, with a couch, &c, to lie down upon after the use of the Bath; divans or couches placed around the room for the purposes of reposing, smoking, and conversation. The ceiling is painted in arabesque, and richly coloured with the favourite Turkish colours — green, red, and blue. The windows are all of coloured glass, and the light of the apartment is most agreeably diffused by the hues of the glass. The centre is ornamented with a handsome marble fountain; flowers and aquatic plants, and ferns, interspersed amongst shells and rock-work, adorn the fountain. The flooring is richly inlaid with tessellated pavement — made for the purpose at Minton's Porcelain Works, in Staffordshire in imitation of the pavement of ancient Baths. The warm and hot air rooms are also beautifully constructed, with marble seats and tessellated pavement; the domes are enriched with stars of variegated glass, which give a brilliant appearance. There are, in recesses connected with the hot rooms, chambers for ablution, where tepid and cold water are plentifully supplied as Shower and Dash [i.e. douche] Baths; and there are to be attendants in Turkish costume to shampoo the bathers; coffee and sherbet, cigars and pipes, will be added, to complete the whole ceremony of the Turkish mode of bathing.'
(Description of Bray Turkish Baths from Robert Wollaston, *The sanitary advantages of baths, especially the Turkish or Roman bath: a lecture* [at the] *Literary and Philosophical Institution, Cheltenham, 15 November 1859,* Cheltenham, 1860)

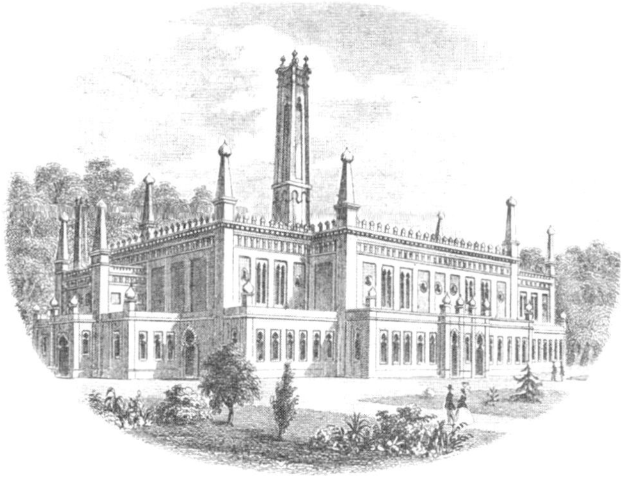

***7.14.** The Turkish Baths took a year to build at a cost of £10,000 and opened in optimistic mood on 2 November 1859.*

***7.15.** Dr Richard Barter, the pioneer of modern Turkish baths.*

There was, however, another truly major project underway, the most ambitious by far. Edward Breslin's Royal Marine Hotel had by 1862 enjoyed seven years as the premier hotel of the new resort, but now it was to be more than matched in size by the monumental International Hotel, built by John Brennan on William Dargan's site at a cost of £30,000. John Quin had leased the site to Dargan in October 1860, with the stipulation that a hotel and/or houses were to be built fronting onto Quinsborough Road within two years. The hotel was completed eighteen months later with the assistance of a labour force of some hundred artisans and labourers. The position chosen for this, the largest hotel in Ireland of the time, was an interesting one. Placed

THE INTERNATIONAL HOTEL

'IMPROVEMENTS AT BRAY.
Those who have visited Bray of late must have noticed within a stone's throw of the railway station an extensive building, occupying a wide area of ground, fronting the Quinsborough-road and with more plate glass windows in all its sides than one would care to have to count. This is the great International Hotel, which has been built by Brennan, and which when in full working order, will be a remarkable feature in connection with this beautiful locality. After one has travelled through the entire building, which, by the way, is no small journey — involving as it does, the ascent and descent of numberless staircases, and the traversing of long corridors and apartments of all dimensions, the great difficulty is attempting to describe, even in a general way, what has been seen is to know where to begin. The most intelligible and natural mode, probably, is to commence at the bottom, and accordingly, going doing to the basement floor, we go through a range of servant's apartments — knife room, boot room, glass room, servants' hall, and under-servants' dormitories. On this floor we find the kitchen, where steaming and hot water apparatus are being fitted up, after the most approved system, by Messrs, Turner and Hodges. After looking into the larder and other necessary and important apartments of a similar character, we find our way into the wine cellars — cold and dark — which are built on a very extensive scale, capable of storing 15,000l. worth of wine. We now ascend to the ground floor, where we find a large, cheerful, well-lighted room, where it is intended the table d'hôte shall be established. This room is 90 feet by 30. On this floor there are a splendid coffee room, a very fine billiard room, and a public restaurant. Going up to the first or principal storey, we see pleasant sitting-rooms and airy bed-rooms in large numbers; then up another staircase to the next floor, the principal feature of which is a fine apartment, which will be used as a ladies' sitting-room, and which will be provided with pianofortes and chess tables, and furnished in the richest style. On this floor there are more bedrooms and sittingrooms looking out on the beautiful scenery. Now we go up a grand staircase, most elaborately finished, lightened by a handsome stained-glass window, by Sillery, Dublin, and here we find more bedrooms and fine sittingrooms, commanding still finer prospects, both by land and sea. Higher up still we go until we come on the roof, from which,

as may easily be imagined, from such an elevation and in such as district, a magnificent prospect is enjoyed. Commencing with old Bray Head, we have before us a beautiful panorama of mountains, terminating in Killiney Hill. Then we have "Sweet Dublin Bay", and a view away out to sea as far as we please. The intention is to furnish the roof, on which a delightful promenade can be enjoyed with seats, and to have a communication established between it and the regions below, where the servants are to be found, so that all who have a mind may enjoy the air and the prospect, weather permitting, and summon the waiter to attend to their wants, just as they would in their sittingrooms. There are altogether about 250 apartments, 212 of which are bedrooms, in the house, which it is estimated can accommodate between 300 and 400 people. Every storey is furnished with bath rooms and water-closets, and so well has the vast building been erected, that even the smallest apartments are well lighted and ventilated. It has an elevation of 70 feet, each storey being from twelve to 20 feet; it has 200 feet of main frontage, and 200 feet each wing, and the main corridors are 430 feet from end to end. As to the principle on which the hotel will be conducted, an erroneous impression prevails that it is to be what has been called "a first, second, and third class hotel". The intention is to make it in every respect a first class establishment, to be conducted somewhat after the Continental system, the chief feature of which, as is known, is the table d'hôte. The bill of fare will be marked, as in clubs. So that visitors can have dinner for two shillings or ten shillings, or higher, just as may suit their purses, or inclinations, and wines will be supplied on the same principle. By this system people of moderate means will not have the enjoyment of their meals marred by thoughts about what's to pay when the dinner is over. … The servants will all be paid by the house, and there will be no charge for lights in any of the apartments. Private apartments can, of course, be had by those who may not wish to dine at the table d'hôte. … Bray owes much of its rapid progress to the admirable hotel accommodation provided by Mr. Breslin, which is equal to that of any hotel in the United Kingdom. The extension of such accommodation will not fail to add further to the development of that beautiful locality, destined before long to become the Brighton of Ireland.'
(*Freeman's Journal* 25 April 1862)

on Quinsborough Road, rather than on one of the more constricted sites on the sea front, it formed a majestic conclusion to the impressive terraces newly erected on each side of the road. John Brennan and Edward Breslin were in turn to be involved in the early years of its management; later in the century it passed into the hands of John Brennan's son-in-law Charles Dufresne.

Although the International Hotel had glimpses of the water only from some of the upper windows, it had the convenience of the railway station just across from its side entrance. (The accompanying inconvenience for guests at both the International Hotel and the Royal Marine Hotel was the noise of the steam trains, particularly at night in the nearby shunting yards.) Designed by Edmund O'Kelly, a local builder involved in various Bray projects of the 1850s and 1860s, the frontage onto Quinsborough Road had a grand portico in the centre with bay windows at each end; three-storey over basement, there were a further seven windows at the front on each floor. There were 212 bedrooms, more than twice as many as in Breslin's hotel. Despite the absence of public mains, there were bathrooms and water closets. The gardens behind, laid out in lawn, extended to the end of the present Florence Road. The first stone had been laid on 18 February 1861 and the hotel opened on 31 May 1862 to coincide with the opening of the International Exhibition in London, after which it was named. (The inaugural dinner was presided over by Sir George Hodson of Holybrooke,

7.16. *The monumental International Hotel, seen here in a view of 1865 (see fig. 7.21), was built by John Brennan on William Dargan's site; it had 212 bedrooms at the time of its opening in 1862.*

who, although only marginally involved in the development of Bray, was a powerful figure in the neighbourhood; Dargan was vice-chair.) But despite its auspicious beginning there were not sufficient numbers of wealthy visitors to Bray to make such a large hotel profitable, and its existence over the coming years was to be precarious.

> *'BRAY ATHLETIC GAMES.*
> *The ground is already marked out by directions of Mr. Dargan, and will be finished in a first rate manner and for a permanency. It will be of vast extent, and inclosed on all sides. A handsome entrance will face the road leading to the reserved seats. On the left, where you enter, there will be a ladies' refreshment saloon; on the right a saloon for the sterner sex. There will be also second and third-class places outside the ropes, so that all can have an opportunity of viewing the sports carried on therein. The interior, or arena, round which prizes for walking matches, running matches and hurdle races will be competed for, will be reserved for cricket, croquet and archery.'*
> (*Freeman's Journal* 2 July 1862)

CARLISLE GROUNDS

The front windows of the International Hotel, although they may not have had a good view of the sea, did look out onto another of William Dargan's provisions for the resort, also later the property of Edward Breslin. In the summer of 1862 residents would have seen the laying out of his 'Bray Athletic Ground' or 'racing ground', opened with a fireworks display on 29 September 1862 for 'cricket, croquet and archery'. The opening ceremony was performed by the lord lieutenant, Lord Carlisle, hence the title of Carlisle Grounds still in use today. The Carlisle Grounds were intended as a centre for genteel entertainment in the resort, and there was an entrance charge. At first, at least, there were refreshment rooms and other facilities. The entertainments, which included band performances and firework displays, may not have suited the convenience of some of the new neighbours, however, and apparently there were soon complaints. The Grounds were nonetheless to play a significant role in providing amusements for visitors, particularly in the last quarter of the nineteenth century, a role that continues today, though differently, in their use by Bray Wanderers Football Club.

The hotel windows also had views across Quinsborough Road onto Dargan Terrace (the present Duncairn Terrace), which William Dargan built in 1859 and which until 1870 carried his name. By this time Quinsborough Road was taking on much of its present form, and Main Street was being revitalised by the demolition of some of the old premises, particularly at the northern end, and their replacement by new commercial buildings. At the junction of the two, John Quin moved his hotel to fine new premises that curved around the corner site, although it was to be a few years later before his hotel acquired the stately title of Royal Hotel.

BUILDING OPERATIONS AT BRAY

'LATEST INTELLIGENCE. (BY MAGNETIC TELEGRAPH.)
Building operations at Bray are likely to be more extensive next year than they have been hitherto. Mr. Dargan is about erecting two pair of semi-detached villas and terraces of commodious dwelling-houses, also Turkish baths on a large scale, of which we understand Mr. Cunningham is the contractor. For the former Mr. Wilkinson is the architect, and the latter Sir John Benson. A new church is in progress from designs by Mr. Barre, architect of Newry; as also are some works of a domestic class from the designs of Messrs. E. Carson, Burne, and J.J. Lyons, architects respectively.– The Irish Builder.'
(*Freeman's Journal* 31 December 1858)

Across the bridge there were also changes afoot, ones that were to give Little Bray, too, the beginnings of its present-day appearance. The untidy open space of Bray Commons, a 'resort of loiterers' with roaming animals and squatters' cabins, fell under the critical gaze of the promoters of the new resort, and in 1858 proposals were put forward for its enclosure. After some brief opposition, these proposals resulted in the passage of the Bray Commons Inclosure Act of 1859. The enclosure of common land was no new thing, and although ancient rights were extinguished, there were in this case many benefits: former squatters acquired security of tenure; housing was provided for working-class families (although it has been suggested that this was to corral them away from the more up-market parts of Bray); the fairs that had sprawled messily along the main streets were contained on a new fair green.

The Upper Commons was largely partitioned between various claimants, including Lord Meath as lord of the manor, some thirty-five long-time squatters, and a few others proving grazing rights. Ten acres along the river bank were fenced in for public use — the People's Park — as compensation

7.17. Heffernan's view of Breslin's Hotel, as first opened in 1855 with gardens on the west side.

7.18. Heffernan's view of Quin's Hotel in the 1860s, with new premises on the corner of Quinsborough Road. Unable to compete with the brand-new hotels nearer the sea, however, it became for a few years no more than a boarding house.

for the loss of recreational rights on the commons, a two-acre fair green was provided for and a regular pattern of streets was laid out. Of these, the longest was the straight expanse of Lower Dargle Road, thirty feet wide, dividing the People's Park from the short streets on the inner side. At first access from Castle Street to this new road was via Sheridan's Lane, a short laneway that had formerly petered out into the Commons. A second, narrower road, Green Park Road, was curved around below the existing Upper Dargle Road, with very small lots facing the road on the uphill side. There were 124 lots altogether, including four large ones on the northern side of Upper Dargle Road which were also part of the commons.

7.19. The construction of Ravenswell Road caused the Dargle to take a straight course to the sea.

7.20. Erskine Nichol's view of the sea front in 1862. (Courtesy National Gallery of Ireland)

The river side of the Lower Commons was also tidied up with the construction of a lengthy riverside wall and Ravenswell Road in 1861; the Dargle estuary lost its irregular, sloping banks and the river was forced to take a straight course to the sea. Later in the 1860s the new street pattern of Little Bray was completed when access to the Lower Dargle Road from Castle Street was improved by extending the former all the way to the bridge, forming the present stretch of road that divides Little Bray Shopping Centre from the river.

Unlike the new roads in 'Great' Bray, those of Little Bray were to be lined with small houses and cottages for the working class, rather than with substantial houses for the wealthy. And siting houses on the Dargle flood plain was to create periodic problems for the residents. Despite the fact that the 1835 flood that destroyed the racecourse was well within living memory, it was perhaps optimistically hoped that the Dargle would not burst its banks again, or perhaps it was hoped that any future flood waters would be confined to the new park. But these hopes were to be in vain.

A day excursion to Bray by train from Dublin must have been a wonderfully novel entertainment in the late 1850s and 1860s, available not just to the wealthy but to anyone who could pay the fare. The opening of the Harcourt Street line and the Bray–Dalkey line was followed by that of the Kingstown–Dalkey line, replacing the atmospheric railway, so that from the season of 1856 onwards excursionists could enjoy the full pleasure of the journey along the coast with its wide views of Dublin Bay and Killiney Bay. Special fares were offered. In the summer of 1855, for instance, there was an excursion train from Harcourt Street at 11 a.m. daily, returning at 8 p.m., for the price of a single fare. The same rate operated on two trains that August, when the lord mayor of Dublin asked railway companies to provide cheap trips on the 29th to replace Donnybrook fair, which had been suppressed because of its rowdiness. (Whether this was the kind of visitor that the new Bray was trying to attract is another matter.) There were regular Sunday excursion rates at 1s. 2d return.

On public holidays great crowds poured out from the steam trains, presumably to spend most of the day on and around the sea front. There are occasional glimpses of the numbers involved. Four thousand visitors — equivalent to the whole resident population — arrived by train at Easter 1861, and at Whitsun that year one packed train alone from Dublin is said to have carried 930 day trippers.

This was in addition to those who chose to stay in the fine hotels, the boarding houses and the many other new houses of all sizes offering accommodation. Bray was aiming to attract an up-market clientele and hotel titles such as 'Royal Marine Hotel' and 'International Hotel' were intended to provide impressive addresses to their residents, to be flaunted on headed hotel notepaper when they wrote their letters home. It was a general practice for holiday resorts to acquire a slogan for promotional purposes, often dreamed up by the railway companies and used on their posters; 'Sunny Rhyl' and 'Skegness is so bracing' are typical British examples. Kingstown called itself 'The gate of Ireland' in railway handbooks. Bray quickly adopted the imposing title 'The Brighton of Ireland', which was probably already current when it appeared in the *Dublin Builder* in 1860. Bray also later used 'The gateway to the garden of Ireland' and 'The Irish Riviera'.

The railway company, renamed the Dublin, Wicklow & Wexford Railway Company in 1860, was instrumental in enticing visitors to Bray by advertising the resort's attractions in Britain. It promoted Bray still further with G.R. Powell's *The official railway handbook to Bray*, published in Dublin in 1860. Powell's role, of course, was to paint a glowing picture of Bray, and he tried to set the tone, claiming that Breslin's and Quin's hotels were crowded in summer with 'aristocratic visitors'. In 1869 J.J. Gaskin went even further in *Irish varieties*, claiming that Breslin's Royal Marine Hotel was patronised by 'the nobility of Great Britain and Ireland, as well as of France, Italy, and Germany'. The visitor books would make interesting reading.

Improvements in sea travel with the coming of steam ships had, of course, played a part in encouraging visitors from Britain to holiday in Ireland. The route from Holyhead to Kingstown, favoured as the shortest at four to five hours at sea, involved a lengthy rail journey on the Welsh side

7.21. *A passenger train leaving Bray Station in 1865; the International Hotel and Prince of Wales Terrace rise dramatically in the background.*

from main centres of population in England. Visitors from Lancashire could avail of the ten-hour sea journey from Liverpool to Dublin, while those from Scotland could travel from Glasgow or Greenock and disembark at Dublin eighteen hours later. There were twice daily services on most of these routes during the summer months. A sea voyage on a fast, reliable ship was seen as part of the holiday, although the ordeal of sea sickness remained a likely accompaniment to journeys across the choppy Irish Sea.

> *'The voyage across the Irish Channel from either of the ports above mentioned* [Holyhead, Liverpool, Glasgow] *is generally attended with much of the disagreeable, as the turbulence of the sea there is not surpassed even by the dreaded straits of Dover. The shortest route, therefore,* via *Holyhead, should always be adopted if possible.'*
> (*Black's guide books for tourists: Dublin and the Wicklow Mountains*, Edinburgh, c. 1875, p. 9)
>
> *'The hotels — Breslin's and Quin's — especially the former, are usually crowded in summer with aristocratic visitors. The modern part of Bray — Dargan Terrace, about the station, Breslin's Hotel, the residences on the esplanade — affords ample and suitable accommodation for wealthy families. Indeed this portion of the locality has risen as a first-class and select sea-side resort of wealth and fashion — but of wealth and fashion without ostentation. The spirit of the place is essentially quiet; there is nothing flashy, or noisy or obtrusively convivial met with; but a sense of natural and thorough enjoyment is apparent in every face one meets.'*
> (G.R. Powell, *The official railway handbook to Bray*, pp 22–3)

SUMMER VISITORS

Once in Bray, visitors, whether there for a day or a month, needed facilities on the sea front to keep them amused. Provision for sea bathing was, of course, fundamental. As we have seen, there were already bathing boxes, and the railway company tendered for a range of twelve of its own in May 1857. The short-lived Railway Baths were built on the seaward edge of the Esplanade by 1859; this was a rectangular building, with two rows of bathing boxes on the beach, opposite the north end of Fitzwilliam Terrace. In the summer of 1861 local entrepreneur Joseph Kelly built 'extensive hot, cold and sea-water baths' also right at the water's edge at the north end of the Esplanade adjoining Martello Terrace; as Kelly's Baths and later as the property of the town they were to feature among the seaside attractions of Bray for almost a hundred years.

KELLY'S BATHS

'The sea walls of some extensive, hot, cold and open sea baths were commenced on Saturday at the northern end of the Esplanade. These will present an Italian façade to the Esplanade of about 40 feet, the sea front being 72 feet. A large enclosed basin will be prepared for ladies, and every convenience provided for bathers of both sexes. The baths will be the property of Mr. J. Kelly and are from the designs of Mr. Edward Kelly under whose eye the Bray Turkish Baths were erected.'
(*Freeman's Journal* 8 April 1861)

BATHING REGULATIONS

'1 that from and after the second day of May 1870 in lieu of the byelaws for the above mentioned purposes … the following byelaws shall be substituted:
2 That the female bathing place shall extend … from Quinsboro Road south to the Martello Tower … "No 1" and that bathing machines shall be fixed at such places within that distance as the Commissioners may from time to time direct, but not elsewhere … .
3 That all bathing machines shall be open to the public at all reasonable times, and that at such times attendance shall be given.
4 That all machines shall be kept in a proper state of repair and be cleansed at least once a week and kept properly painted … .
5 That the name of the owner or conductor as the case may be of each bathing machine be neatly or legibly painted or otherwise inscribed on … the machine … .
6 That all requisites and proper conveniences for Bathers shall be kept at each machine … .
7 That boys over 10 years of age shall not be permitted to bathe at the female bathing places.
8 That the male bathing places shall extend from the estuary of the Bray River to the south corner of Mr Joseph Kelly's Baths and no further and that every male bathing within the boundary of the Township shall wear drawers.'
(Bray Township bye-laws of 2 May 1870)

Given the strict code of behaviour of the time, the sexes were still carefully segregated when bathing in the sea in a way that would seem ridiculous today. Following a code that was usual in Irish and British resorts, women, girls and boys under the age of ten had the greater share of the beach, from the bottom of Quinsborough Road to martello tower no. 1, with bathing machines for their sole use. Men had to bathe in the area north of Kelly's Baths, where the harbour is now, 'wearing drawers', or near Bray Head, and to keep their distance from the women's areas. No doubt this was both limiting and titillating, although to what extent the regulations were strictly obeyed is hard to tell — the town commissioners, recipients of all the town's complaints, seem not to have received a large number on this score.

END OF THE SEASON, 1865

'[7 October] *There is a walk immediately facing the sea, and behind a very broad esplanade, intended to be covered with turf but become very dry. Here there are seats. Altogether Bray possesses a good situation and fine sea, but the shore is pebbly and bad for bathing. There are ladies' machines or boxes in front of the esplanade. There was only one lady bathing this morning. She walked into the sea along a plank, and kept up by a rope held by an old woman. ... The season here is evidently now quite over. Few people are walking about. A solitary carman is driving up and down, and offers for a moderate sum, which he would probably have scorned a month ago, to take me to Powerscourt, and the Waterfall, and the Devil's Glen ... .*'
([W.W. Barry], *A walking tour round Ireland in 1865,* London, 1867, p. 352)

Boating was another popular pastime — one that augmented the 'uncertain livelihood' of the local fishermen — although again the boatmen were required to keep their distance from the women's bathing areas 'during the time of bathing'. This must have meant that they were largely confined to the southern end of the beach, where in any case most fishing boats were based. Besides bathing, boating and enjoying fresh air while strolling along the Esplanade, a certain amount of organised gaiety gave life to the sea front. Visitors could enjoy the regular performances of military bands; in August 1857, for instance, on the 3rd they could have spent the afternoon at the bandstand listening to the band of the 16th Regiment, while on the 31st it was the turn of the 94th Regiment.

The earlier annual boat races, held to benefit the fishermen, were recast as regattas from August 1860, and were accompanied by fireworks on Bray

Head. The railway company helped to revive Bray races, with a two-day steeple chase meeting on Lord Meath's Boghall land in August 1855. The following July excursions were run by rail from Bray to Wicklow races, enticing visitors to enjoy the pleasurable frisson of rounding Bray Head over trestle bridges and through tunnels. In May 1856 there were special rail fares from Bray to Dublin when a firework display was put on in the Phoenix Park to celebrate the ending of the Crimean war earlier that year; the same applied in March 1863 for the Prince of Wales's wedding celebrations.

47TH REGIMENT BAND

'THE BAND AT BRAY. — A more brilliant day than yesterday, as far as the weather was concerned, could not be conceived for the inauguration of the military band performance on the Dargan Esplanade at Bray. The Monday excursion train — the ten a.m., from Harcourt street — was crowded to excess. The twelve and two trains, if they conveyed a more aristocratic class of travellers, certainly did not bring down any persons more keenly alive to the beauty of the day and of the scene. The trains of the Kingstown branch also added a goodly number to the fashionable crowd of promenaders. The admirable band of the 47th Regiment arrived punctually to its advertised time. The music performed consisted of the splendid overture from Guilleume Tell, *Farmer's insinuating walse, "First Love". It is needless to say that poor M. Jullien's* "Hibernian Quadrilles" *were the most acceptable. The climax of the day's performance, however, was found in the grand selection from Donizetti's* Pasquele. *Amongst the distinguished attendants were the Countess of Clonmel, Lady Lurgan and her youthful and interesting family, Lord Downs, Lord Mahon, of the 1st Fusilier Guards; Captain Packenham, of the Guards, &c; the Ladies Scott and Boyne. Several fine yachts stood in from the bay, lying to during the performance, and adding greatly to the gaiety of the scene, amongst others the schooner yacht Rosalind, J.B. Vernon, Esq., owner. Taken as an opening performance, at an early part of the season — which promises to be a long and settled one — today's may be accepted as a decidedly successful one. —* From Our Correspondent.'
(*Freeman's Journal* 28 May 1861)

Edward Breslin, shrewd businessman as he was, continued to exploit his link with the railway company. When, for instance, a bazaar to raise funds for the new church at Enniskerry was held in the gardens of his hotel at Whitsun 1859, the admission fee was combined with a special rail excursion rate from Harcourt Street. Those who could afford the entrance charge could also enjoy the various entertainments put on in the Carlisle Grounds, such as the 'Grand Musical and Fashionable Promenade' held there every Tuesday in the summer of 1863, and there were concerts and other entertainments in the International Hotel. After 1867 when, as we shall see, Assembly Rooms were opened in the previous Turkish Baths, this too became a concert venue.

Driving out to the local beauty spots was, of course, also part of the holiday for the more well-to-do visitors. Powerscourt and the Dargle remained favourite destinations and cards for admission could be obtained at Breslin's and the International Hotels.

The jaunting-car fare from the railway station or Bray post office to the waterfall was three shilllings for two, or four shillings for three or more. A full-day excursion, for which the fare was ten shillings, might take in all the main northern beauty spots circling from the Dargle, Enniskerry, Powerscourt, Glencree, the Sally Gap, Luggala and Lough Tay to the Glen of the Downs, thirty miles or so in all. One guide book noted optimistically: 'No gratuities to be demanded by drivers'.

THE IRISH JAUNTING CAR

'Our note of the town would also be incomplete should we forget "the Irish jaunting car". This vehicle is peculiar to the Emerald Isle, and its advantages and glories have been sung by poets at various times, but nowhere in the country has the "outside car" attained such a point of excellence, and nowhere is it horsed in such perfect form and taste as in the town of Bray. The Bray cars will bear comparison with any outside cars in Ireland, and the horses which work them are not excelled, and scarcely equalled, by any post-horses in the world; and the natural courtesy and wit of the "jarvies" who drive them, are amongst some of the most pleasing recollections of this place.'

([Craig], *A guide to Bray and the picturesque scenery in its vicinity, Co. Wicklow: published by authority of the township commissioners*, Dublin, 1884, p. 12)

Catering for this summer population of visitors, now arriving on a vastly increased scale compared with the pre-railway numbers, involved setting up a whole new infrastructure. On the one hand, the visitors needed appropriate resort entertainment, largely the concern of private entrepreneurs and the railway company. On the other hand, and more

THE BRAY REGATTA

'SPORTING INTELLIGENCE: THE BRAY REGATTA.
It is no wonder that the weather should at all times be the topic of general conversation, as a good deal of social happiness and enjoyment are entirely dependant on it. The summer now just closed furnished a strong contrast to several that preceeded it, as during its continuance we have had a long succession of glorious days of brilliant sunshine. Yesterday, fixed for the aquatic sports at Bray, furnished one of the exceptions to the rule, and was as unfavourable a day for a regatta as could be well imagined — a day on which torrents of rain fell at frequent intervals, with little or no wind. The projectors of the regatta made every preparation, and the railway company was not behind hand in making the necessary arrangements for the accommodation of the public, who were expected to be present in large numbers to witness the sports; but the weather spoiled all, and hundreds who had intended to spend the day at the sea-side had to remain in town. The morning was dull and hazy, and many banks of clouds hanging to windward showed that we were in for a genuine wet day. A stiff breeze was blowing from S.S.E. as the several vessels entered for the different races beat down from Kingstown to take up the positions assigned to them; and, notwithstanding the unpromising appearance of the day, the scene was charming. ... About a quarter of a mile from the shore, in front of the esplanade, the fine schooner yacht Bella, C. Putland, Esq., R St.G.Y.C., lay moored as a flagship, gaily decorated with many-coloured bunting. On

fundamentally, the fine new hotels, boarding houses and eating places that served the visitors needed reliable lighting, water supply and sewerage facilities, the streets needed lighting and cleaning, and the town needed bye-laws to regulate everything from sea bathing to street vending and proselytising on the Esplanade. Responsibility for all these matters fell on the shoulders of a new body, the Bray Township Commissioners.

Bray had twice had the opportunity to establish local government in 1840, but this had been missed, apparently because of an unwillingness by prominent residents to pay a municipal rate. Indeed it has been suggested that had there been local control in the early 1850s the railway might have been forced onto a different route and the shape of the town might have evolved differently. But in the event it was 1857 before Bray acquired town commissioners under the Towns Improvement (Ireland) Act of 1854. The area under their jurisdiction was at first quite limited; integral parts of the *shore a flag-staff was erected also, dressed in varied flags, and standing near three large marquees erected by Mr. P.J. Hynes, Blackhall-place. As the several yachts rendezvoused in front of the town, the view was almost pleasing, and when all was ready, at eleven o'clock, down came the rain, first in gentle, but soon heavy showers. A large number of persons who had come down by train and persons residing in the neighbourhood, who had collected on the esplanade, and on the points commanding a view of the sea, had to run for shelter to the marquees, to the railway terminus, and to the hotels.*

[various races took place, but hampered by too little breeze] ... *After six o'clock the evening was beautiful, and as the several yachts lay at their moorings with their after sails set the scene was most picturesque, and the exquisitely modelled S.S. Empress, R.S. Kane, Esq, R.I.Y.C. was much admired as she steamed about the numerous craft in front of the Esplanade. The bands of the 10th Regiment and of the County Dublin Militia were present, and played alternatively in excellent style. Those who had been driven to seek shelter from the rain during the day assembled in large numbers in the evening to witness the fireworks, and the attendance was most crowded when the pyrotechnic display commenced under the direction of Mr. Lawrence of Grafton-street. It was most brilliant and successful, and was loudly applauded by the numerous spectators.*

(*Freeman's Journal* 26.08.1863)

town such as Little Bray and the lands of the Loreto Convent, Bray Head House (with the southern end of the sea front) and much of Oldcourt were not included until the original area was more than doubled in 1866 under the Bray Township Act.

The first twelve commissioners — elected under a limited franchise based on property value — were drawn, not surprisingly, from the leading figures of the town. They included Lord Meath, who became chairman, John Quin junior as deputy chairman, Edward Breslin and Dr Waller, the last representing the significant interests of the railway company. William Dargan subsequently served briefly as commissioner, as did Alfred Sotheron from the mill and Charles Putland. Many of the same individuals were also local magistrates. The Bray Township Act of 1866 increased the number of commissioners to fifteen, representing three new wards: East, West and Little Bray. They still included the two hoteliers, although John Quin was to resign less than two years later on the grounds of ill health. (He died shortly afterwards, in 1869.)

At their first meeting, held in the board room of the courthouse on 1 September 1866, one of the first acts of the enlarged body was to regularise matters by setting up lighting, sewerage, finance, water and car committees. The indefatigable Edward Breslin was to play an active part on most of these. The commissioners were permitted to spend money on the provision of a range of services and to make bye-laws, but the amount of money that could be raised through rates was capped, and even after the 1866 act improved Bray's finances they were often hard-pressed to find adequate funding for the rapidly expanding town.

ACT FOR THE IMPROVEMENT OF BRAY, 1866

'... whereas the District of Bray *is a large, populous, and improving District, and the Population thereof has of late Years greatly increased and is increasing: And whereas the Extension of the Limits of the said Township, and the Formation of the District into One Township, would be of local and public advantage: And whereas it is expedient that further and better Provision should be made of the lighting, paving, sewering, draining, cleansing, supplying with Water, controlling Fairs and Markets, and otherwise improving and regulating the Township: and whereas it is desirable that the making and maintaining of Roads, Footways, and Bridges within the Township should be transferred from the Grand Juries of the Counties of* Dublin *and* Wicklow *to the Commissioners appointed under this Act: ... may it therefore please Your Majesty that* [this Act] *be enacted ... .*

The Number of the Commissioners shall be Fifteen, that is to say, Three Commissioners for Little Bray *Ward, Nine Commissioners for East Ward, and Three Commissioners for West Ward.'*

(*Act for the Improvement of the Town and District of Bray*, 23 July 1866, 29 & 30 Vict., c. 261)

We have to visualise the state of Bray in 1854 to understand the magnitude of the tasks to be faced. There was no public lighting supply of any kind; paraffin lamps and candles were still the order of the day, even though Dublin had had gas street lighting since 1825. There was no running water; many better-off households had their own wells or pumps, but many poor families would still have had to draw water laboriously from the Dargle or from minor streams — unlike the situation in many Irish towns of the time there seem to have been no public water pumps or fountains. There were no sewers. Although the main footpaths had been paved in 1859, the actual streets were neither paved nor cleaned — lack of a proper hard surface led to mud or to swirling dust, according to the weather, and without cleaning there were generous deposits of horse droppings and other detritus.

The Dublin & Wicklow Railway company made the first provision for lighting in 1856, even before the township came into being. (The company expressed its reluctance to be included in the new administrative area, which would require it to pay rates, on the grounds that it already had a lighting supply.) It built a small gas works in the railway yard, and this supplied the railway station and Breslin's hotel, reinforcing the image of these buildings as the epitome of the new Bray. After their election in 1857 the first town commissioners saw public lighting as a priority and in 1858–9 a gas works and gasometer were built on an exposed site on newly-made land north of the present Martello Terrace — far enough away from the fashionable parts of Bray but not, as it transpired, a wisely chosen spot. The foundation stone was laid on 4 October 1858 and the supply was in place for the opening of the Turkish Baths in 1859. Gas lamps shed their soft light on the main streets, though not at first on those of Little Bray which remained in darkness. Shopkeepers and householders took a supply and soon many premises were lighted by gas, the chore of filling and trimming paraffin lamps replaced by the simple striking of a match. But there were complaints over the years about the quality of the gas, about the cost, and about the limited hours during which the streets were lighted.

> *'OPENING OF BRAY GAS WORKS.*
> *This rising place now has the advantage of Gas for its shops, hotels, houses, and streets, which really gives it a very attractive appearance, and advances the town in the scale of importance 20 per cent. The works though opened on Thursday last are not yet quite complete, but are in rapid progress. The Directors of the Company were desirous to commence the supply of Gas to the inhabitants as early as possible, which has been duly appreciated by the trading part of the community, who have in every shop requiring light taken or ordered it.'*
> (*Freeman's Journal* 26 February 1859)

GAS LIGHTING

The earliest organised water supply came from a small reservoir at Killarney Wood on Herbert Road, which supplied the railway station (where a reliable supply was required for the steam locomotives), the Turkish Baths and a small number of nearby houses. This was soon found to be inadequate, and the difficulties were alleviated — if not wholly solved — when agreement was reached for Bray to draw its supply from Dublin Corporation's new reservoir on the Vartry River, twelve kilometres to the south. By the beginning of 1868 the laying of water mains was underway, although connection required a fee of five shillings, so the supply was taken up only by better-off households. To cater for the rest, public water pumps or fountains were erected in various places along the main streets: three each on Main Street, Vevay Road and Strand Road, and one each on Quinsborough Road, Killarney Road and Seapoint Road. For some decades there was only one pump in the whole of Little Bray. There were complaints from the first about the high cost of water to householders and about the less-than-generous supply and, as we shall see, these complaints were to become increasingly strident later in the century. The first sewers were laid in the late 1850s, with a new sewer planned for Strand Road in 1860, but it was not until the commissioners acquired more spending power in 1866 that the new sewerage committee was able to make a serious attempt to service the town at the same time as they tried to

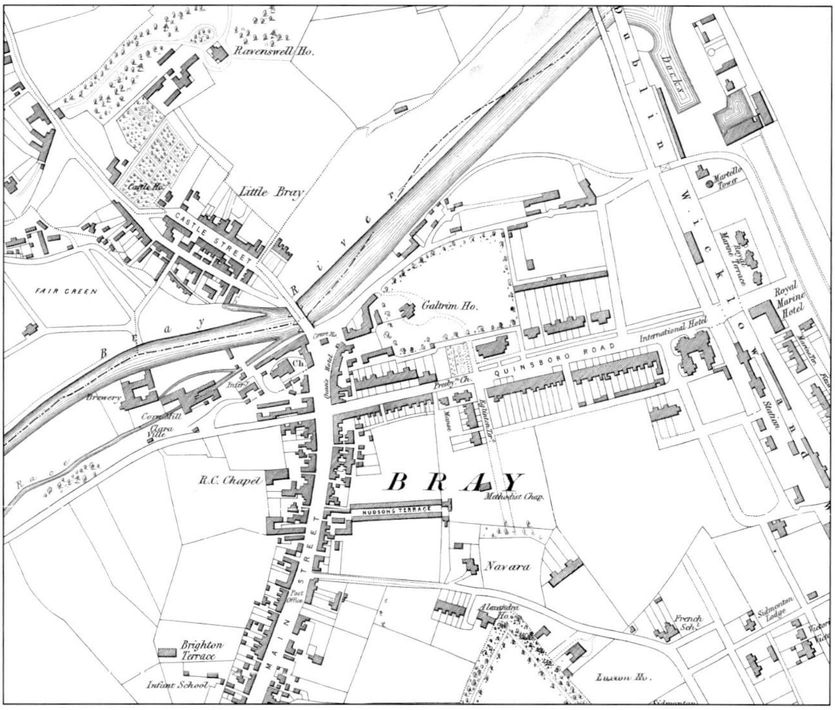

***7.22.** Bray in* c. *1870, part of* Heffernan's illustrated plan of Bray. *D.E. Heffernan, an engineer, added the new developments to the 1838 Ordnance Survey map.*

make private landlords provide 'privies and ashpits'. By 1870 work had been underway for two years, again mainly covering the more prosperous parts of Bray; the sewer pipes discharged directly into the sea or into the Dargle, following the common practice of the time. (The Liffey, for instance, receiving the outfall of the Dublin sewers, stank in the summer months.) This basic method of waste disposal was not finally dispensed with until the late twentieth century. The Herbert Road sewer was even allowed to discharge into the Dargle upstream of the mill race — the brewery manager refuted claims that the brew was affected, but admitted that he himself did not drink the water. Even so the sewerage system was costly, and the commissioners were forced to borrow heavily to finance it. In 1876 it was reported that although £3,000 had already been spent, large areas remained unconnected and another matching amount was needed.

The commissioners had another recurrent headache: the state of the Esplanade. Until the sea wall was built in the 1880s it was entirely unprotected from easterly gales and there was much damage each winter: sand and shingle piled up, erosion cut into the edges, the previous year's grass withered under the salt spray. The first task of the new season was to clear away the debris, mend breaches, top-dress and re-seed the grass areas. At the north end opposite Breslin's hotel, at least, an elaborate defence of wooden piling was erected at some stage in the 1860s. William Dargan had ensured that the Esplanade was maintained, but after it was transferred to the township in 1861 there were complaints about its state, despite the fact that the 1866 Bray Township Act specifically mentioned the requirement to keep it in good order. In November 1869 Lord Meath as lessor found it necessary to intervene. The commissioners received a solicitor's letter to inform them that unless the Esplanade was properly maintained, its fences repaired and trespass by animals prevented, the earl would resume possession and as a result new bye-laws were drawn up. Nonetheless the picture is not a cheerful one.

The commissioners had other related matters to exercise their minds. One of these was the need for an adequate harbour, an issue that was to arise again and again over the coming decades. The construction of the railway bridge had prevented boats of any size from entering the river mouth and Seymour's Dock. Following pressure from the Admiralty, the Dublin & Wicklow Railway Co. built a small new dock on the east side of the railway embankment, partly on the site of the present harbour but with its entrance facing northwards to the river mouth; the gas works and a coal yard lay on its seaward side.

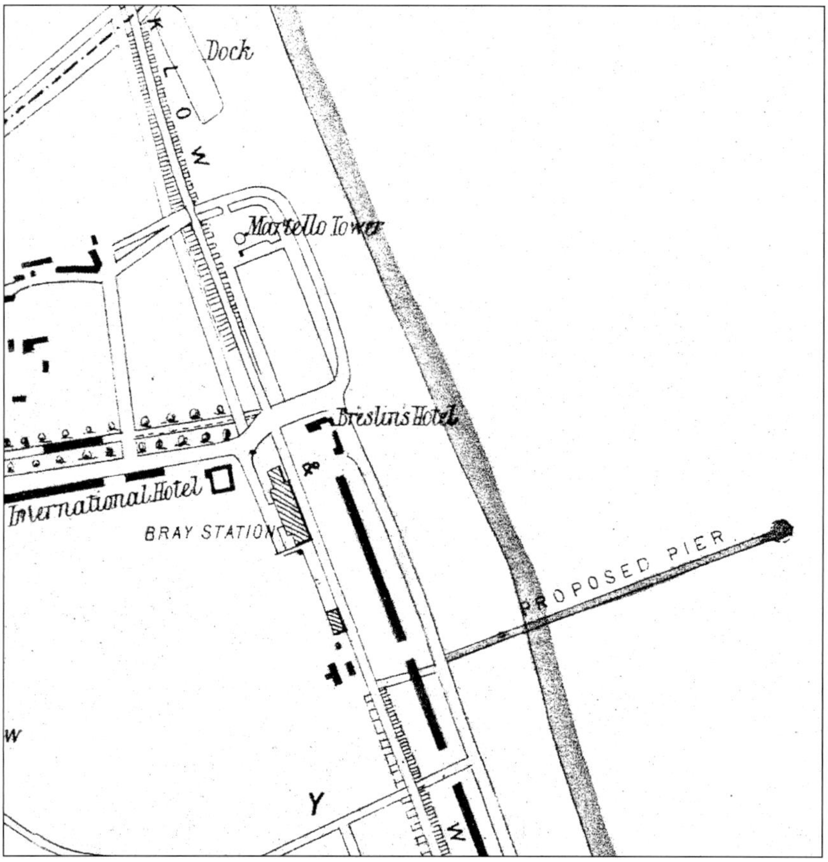

7.23. Part of the plan of c. *1866 showing the site of the proposed pier.*

While this dock provided shelter from easterly gales, at best it would only have accommodated small cargo boats. It was supposedly complete in early 1858, but two years later the state was obliged to take an action against the railway company, alleging that the dock, unprovided with mooring rings for boats or steps for passengers, had already fallen into disrepair. It was apparently soon more or less derelict and choked with sand and shingle, despite the fact that by the terms of the 1866 township act the commissioners undertook to keep it in 'good and efficient order and repair'.

The problem of the lack of a secure anchorage, whether for small cargo ships or for pleasure boats, was not solved, despite a cutting being made through the sandbar at the river mouth in 1860 and various proposals advanced in the following decades. The next question was the provision of a pier. Seaside piers, airy structures of cast iron and wood, had become highly desirable amenities at resorts in Britain after a pioneering one, the Chain Pier, was built at Brighton in 1823. Even minor British resorts were to aspire to a pier; major resorts built two or three. There was a boom in their provision in the 1850s and 1860s, as improved construction methods coincided with the growth of holiday resorts. By 1870 there were already some thirty in all, completed or building, including seven at Irish Sea resorts such as Blackpool (which already had two), Southport and Douglas, Isle of Man. Apart from the convenience of being able to embark and disembark from pleasure steamers in deep water whatever the state of the tide, a seaside pier provided an agreeable promenade, with health-giving sea air, an exciting sense of being high above the waves and an opportunity to look back at the beach from a distance. As one modern historian of piers has put it, there were 'all the advantages of going to sea with none of the attendant dangers or discomfort'.

Piers were commercial propositions and they were expensive to build — even in the 1820s Brighton's Chain Pier had cost £30,000. Landing dues from pleasure steamers made up an important part of the profits of British piers, particularly lucrative when a number of resorts were close enough together to encourage sea excursions between them, as in Lancashire and North Wales. Other income came from a fee for entry — in the early days the charge was twopence to stroll on the Chain Pier and later another Brighton pier charged the considerable sum of sixpence. The requirement for visitors to pay a fee meant that piers offered a degree of exclusiveness to their patrons, and so they were seen as adding 'tone' to a resort. They did, however, have a disadvantage in some eyes; in at least one English resort there was opposition on the grounds of morality, in that promenaders would be able to peek at bathers on the beach below.

> *'Several projects are at present under consideration at Bray for increasing the attractions of the place, but they have not, as yet, assumed a definite form. Amongst them is the erection of the proposed promenade pier, off the Esplanade and the association with it of an extensive and varied aquarium. A skating rink is also spoken of.'*
> (*The Irish Builder* 11 March 1876)

PLANS FOR IMPROVEMENT

The first proposal for an iron pier at Bray was made as early as 1863, followed by an enabling act of parliament in 1867. This pier would have jutted out to sea just north of Albert Avenue, more or less at the south wall of the present aquarium premises. A map shows it extending across the

Esplanade and some 1,200 feet long measured from Strand Road, which would have been a typical length for a pier of the period. Sufficient funding was not forthcoming, however, either in the 1860s or, as we shall see, later in the century. Perhaps there was just too little capital available, or perhaps potential investors, looking across the water, thought that Bray's pier would never generate sufficient income from landing dues. The lack of a pier can be regarded as one of the determining features of the status of Bray in comparison with other Irish Sea resorts.

While Bray was being actively promoted as an ideal place in which to spend time breathing 'the life and health-giving air', as Powell put it, the town was also being recommended as suitable for permanent residence, within easy reach of Dublin by rail. The earlier coach services, as we have seen, had enabled travellers to make day visits to Dublin, and from 1834 John Quin had run a service to connect with trains at Kingstown. Now, however, the entire journey could be made speedily and in comfort.

Many of the fine new houses were intended for well-to-do permanent residents, and by 1870 *Thom's Directory* was listing eighty or so members of the 'nobility, gentry, clergy, &c' living in or very close to Bray, including nine lawyers or barristers, seven doctors, eight clerics and five army officers. The rail service also encouraged Dublin professional people who fancied country life to move into the wider area, both north of Bray around Old Connaught and to the south and west. The diaries of one member of the gentry, Phineas Riall of Old Connaught, in this case from a family long established in the area, show that he thought nothing of making the train journey to Dublin twice a day. We have long since forgotten how liberating the arrival of the railways was a hundred and fifty years ago.

THE CHANGING STATUS OF QUIN'S HOTEL

'Pleasant recollections of "Quin's, Bray" have been carried to the Pyramids and the Ganges. Its former owner made for it a great and a hospitable name. Its breakfasts under the Quin regime *were dreams of luxury, its dinners feasts, its punch nectar. Such trout, such ham and chickens, and, above all, such appetite came to table, that nothing could surpass them but the moderation of the charges, Its visitors' book has often borne names now enrolled on the page of fame. The hotel offers excellent accommodation still, though in a quieter way than its more aristocratic sea-side rival, the Royal Marine Hotel.'*

(G.R. Powell, *The official railway handbook to Bray*, Dublin, 1860, p. 19)

Within a few years after 1854 the focus of the town shifted firmly from the north end of Main Street to the area around the railway station and the junction of Quinsborough Road with the sea front. One clear indication is the changing status of Quin's Hotel. Despite John Quin having rebuilt his premises, Breslin's Royal Marine Hotel seems quickly to have displaced it as the premier hotel in Bray. Breslin had the advantage of his pivotal site close to the station and his close connection with the railway company — the directors held dinners at his hotel twice in the summer of 1856. Breslin pulled off another coup in September 1857 when the infant British Association for the Advancement of Science held its annual meeting in Dublin. A party of 140 members visited Killiney beach, lunched at Breslin's, travelled onwards by train to Greystones where thirty jaunting cars took them on a grand tour, and then returned to Breslin's for dinner.

The Rathdown Union Farming Society's annual October cattle show had formerly been held in a field behind Quin's and the hotel had hosted its dinner, but by 1857 the show field was near the station, perhaps already on the site of the future Carlisle Grounds. Even Lord Eglinton, the lord lieutenant, and his wife were to desert Quin's Hotel in favour of Breslin's. There may have been a note of desperation when John Quin's annual advertisment of his reduced winter charges in December 1857 claimed that the railway station was 'within grounds attached to the hotel'. Quin not long afterwards gave up hotel-keeping, presumably amply supplied with income from ground rents, and his hotel was advertised to let in January 1862.

In the 1860s the opening of the International Hotel focused activity even more sharply within the 'new' Bray. Another hotel, Lacy's Bray Head Hotel, was opened by John Lacy in May 1860 at the south end of the beach. By 1870 there were more than 300 hotel bedrooms available on or close to the sea front. Fine new terraces and villas faced out to sea on Strand Road, the railway station hummed with activity and Main Street offered a wide choice of shops. The term 'the Brighton of Ireland' was in common usage. Optimism in Bray was, perhaps, at its peak and we can imagine that its businessmen and women, looking back on all that had been achieved in a decade and a half, must have hoped to sustain that dramatic growth in the years to come.

Chapter 8

'All the advantages': Bray in 1870

'It has some of the largest and finest hotels in the whole of Ireland, managed upon the most modern and enlightened system, and its numerous cleanly and comfortable private residences afford to those who wish to prolong their stay in the place all the advantages afforded by the most modern and fashionable English or Scottish watering-places or health resorts.'
([Craig], *A guide to Bray and the picturesque scenery in its vicinity, Co. Wicklow*, Dublin, 1884, p. 9)

Among the various moments in time when it is possible to pause and take an overall view of Bray, the year 1870 is one of the best. In that year the Ordnance Survey mapped the town at a scale of approximately ten feet to the mile as one of its new series of large-scale urban plans. The use of such a large scale — assigned to only about half the towns and cities mapped in the second half of the nineteenth century — has meant that the features of Bray in all their detail have been frozen in time. Not just the roads and pavements, buildings, letter boxes, lamp posts and water pumps, but also the front gardens and paths, the outhouses, greenhouses and cisterns, down to individual rockeries and trees, even rocks on the sea shore, are marked on the thirteen large sheets that cover the main parts of the town.

Outer parts of southern and south-western Bray, including Oldcourt, were also mapped, but at the smaller scale of five feet to the mile. Little Bray, though, was not included, and here the picture has to be pieced together from other sources such as *Thom's directory* and the valuation revision books. These yellowing pages of more than a century ago as well as drawings and early photographs can be used to breathe life into a portrait of Bray in its heyday as a Victorian seaside resort.

By 1870 the approach from Dublin was over a new three-arch bridge, the present one. This was built in 1855–6, using stone quarried in Loughlinstown, to replace the old four-arch bridge, by this time in bad condition and certainly not a fitting approach to a town newly conscious of its importance. Sir George

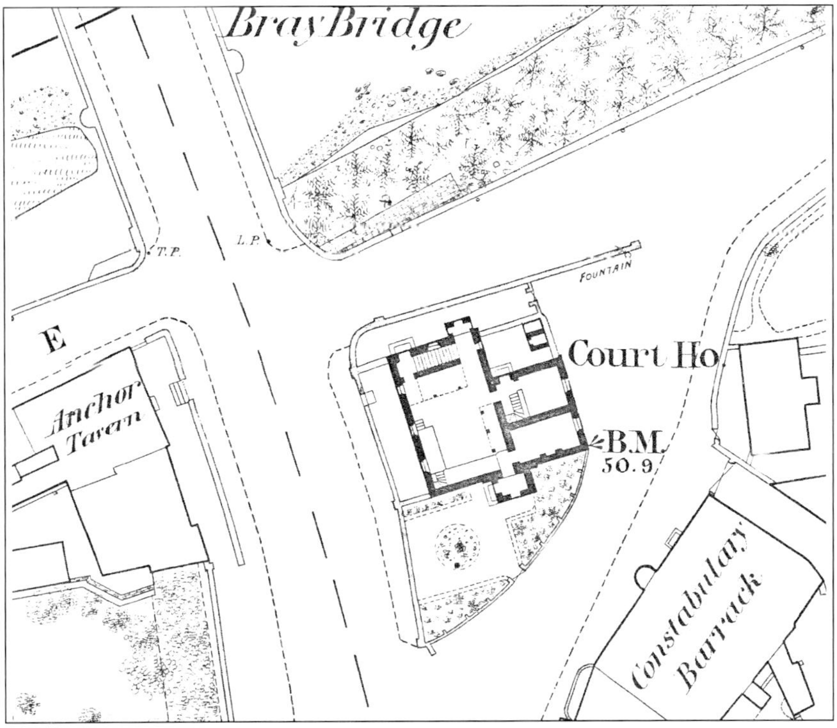

8.1. Bray was mapped in great detail by the Ordnance Survey in 1870. Above: internal detail was included for public buildings such as the courthouse. Below: the former bathing lodge Eden View, by now renamed, has its garden layout well recorded. Original scale 10 ft to the mile (1:500).

8.2. *Bray Bridge today. The courthouse is dwarfed by the modern Royal Hotel, the former Anchor Tavern (right), much rebuilt, now houses a building society.*

8.3. *Three-storey buildings on Main Street replaced the older fabric from the 1850s onwards.*

Hodson of Holybrooke had presided at the ceremony of laying the first stone of the new bridge on 24 July 1855, just as seven years later he was to preside over the opening of the International Hotel.

The corner building on the right, Mason's long-established public house, had by now been dignified with the name Anchor Tavern. Steps led up onto the pavement from the street outside. It and the adjoining building both remained, but the middle ones of the row had been removed, so that St Paul's Church had its present open frontage and small stepped pedestrian entrance to Main Street. Although it had just had a new extension on the east side and been officially dedicated to St Paul, the church was no longer the hub of the protestant community. It had been relegated to the status of a chapel of ease in 1863 when Christ Church, at the other end of the town, was consecrated.

The barracks building had come down in the world even more. The fever hospital was closed before 1853, and from the late 1850s the barracks was no more than a storehouse, with a coal yard in the grounds. It was soon to be nearly derelict. There was a weighing machine, presumably for the coal, on the street outside. Apart from the carriages of those still visiting St Paul's and its graveyard, Church Terrace must mainly have echoed to the rumble of coal trucks. The middle house of the terrace, no. 3, was a dispensary; earlier the township's first 'town constable, collector and inspector of nuisances' had lived at no. 1.

The Hibernian Bank already occupied the long, narrow premises squeezed between the Church Terrace roadway and the new Herbert Road, as it continued to do until, merged with the Bank of Ireland, it was converted to a mortgage store in the 1990s. Herbert Road had only one pair of houses, the present Clara and its neighbour, together with the substantial Mount Herbert; all three were built by 1868. Otherwise there were still fields on either side. The next section of Main Street, on both sides, by now had new business premises, some of them three-storey, many of them with impressive detailing, which had recently replaced the antiquated eighteenth-century, or older, buildings.

RENEWAL OF MAIN STREET BY SIDNEY HERBERT

> *'Mr. Sidney Herbert ... is also effecting great improvements, ... and many of the old houses and shops on his property in the town are in the course of removal, for the re-erection of improved and more commodious buildings. ... The old Parish Church stands on the high ground, surrounded by old and unsightly houses, near the bridge.'*
> (*Thom's directory*, 1861–3)

The Catholic church by 1870 had a fine railed frontage to Main Street; it had been extended an extra thirty-three feet at the front in 1850–54 with a bell tower at the east end, making it even more prominent in the centre of the town. A water fountain stood on the pavement immediately opposite, next to a lamp post — there were ten gas lamps in all between the bridge and the pound. A little further on, the first development had taken place behind the Main Street houses with the construction of terraced cottages in Purcell's Terrace. These twenty or so new dwellings with small back yards were built in about 1864 by butcher Thomas Purcell. They shared a single water pump. Hall's Court was still a cluster of five cottages off Main Street, by this time owned by Mary Hall.

The Methodist chapel was still in use in 1870; nearby four Brighton Terrace houses with Gothic touches had been one of the earliest post-1854 building projects in Bray, completed in May 1855. The roadway to the chapel and Brighton Terrace was a private one, closed at the Main Street end by double gates. There were fewer cabins in Pound Lane — all those on the south side had been demolished and not replaced. The surviving cabins were soon to be described as 'not fit for habitation', and they were compulsorily levelled in 1878. The grounds of Bray Cottage had been extended at the town end to their present size, but otherwise the northern end of Killarney Road was not greatly changed and small cottages still lined its eastern side as well as the northern end of the Vevay Road.

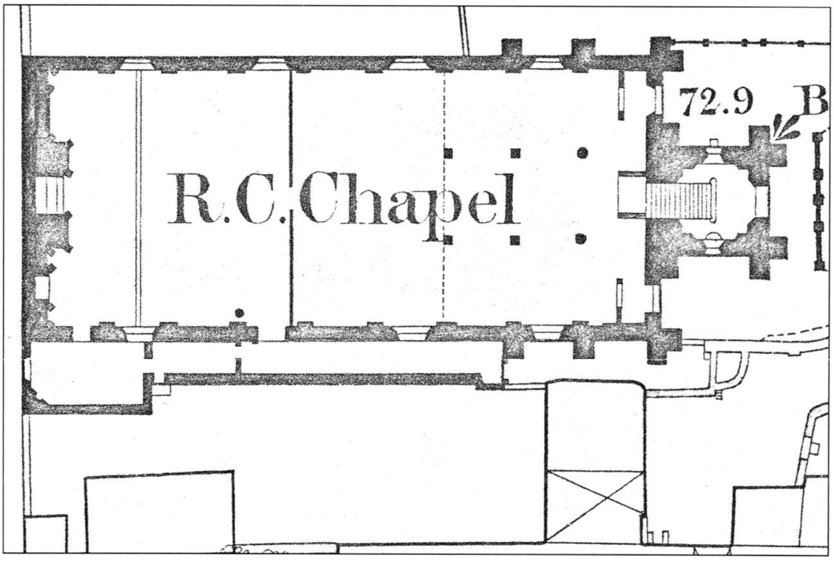

***8.4.** Bray Catholic church (now the Holy Redeemer) from the 1870 Ordnance Survey map, original scale 10 ft to the mile (1:500).*

By now the Loreto nuns had celebrated their first successful twenty years in what had been the Putland family's Sans Souci home. The grounds had groves of trees, winding paths, and the outcrop of rocky heath-covered ground onto which the front houses of Sans Souci Wood now face. The Putlands' walled garden had been maintained, with an elaborate herb garden and the convent's infirmary at the north-west corner. The nuns had added a large chapel at the side of the house and the unusual polygonal Spanish-style burial place, still there today, by the quarry at the northern end. Between the convent building and the Putlands' conservatory stood a massive bell, although, as one travel writer noted: 'its merits are comparatively unknown from the fact of its being hung too close to the ground'.

The Loreto Convent boarding and day school for girls, opened in 1851 soon after the Order's arrival, was flourishing; it had been extended in 1863. In 1864 the nuns had decided to open a new girls' national school and a schoolhouse was built by subscription close to the path that led down the hill towards the sea. By 1870 there were four classrooms for the nearly three hundred pupils, almost equally divided between girls and infants with a handful of boys. The pupils over the years included the children of fishermen from the strand and the children of railway workers, those drawn from the poorest parts of Bray such as Pound Lane, and a smaller number of those from more prosperous families whose fathers were sea captains, merchants or shopkeepers. The fee was a penny a week, with a few pupils admitted free.

If the Convent and its busy schools now provided a very different focal point at the top end of the town from that of the Putlands' time, by 1870 this end of Bray also had another important landmark, a building that drew in both locals and visitors. The old seventeenth-century church by the bridge had become inadequate for the growing Church of Ireland congregation — it was described as 'overflowing' for six months of the year — and the parishioners must have looked with some envy at the enlarged Catholic church making a strong statement in Main Street. There was some vigorous argument as to the respective merits of a town-centre site on Novara Avenue (where the Parochial Hall now stands) or a spacious and commanding site on the Rock of Bray with the newly laid out (but not yet named) Church Road to set the building off to advantage. The latter site had the support of Lord Meath, but was regarded as too far out of town by other influential parishioners such as Edward Breslin and Phineas Riall of Old Connaught. The supporters of the Rock of Bray site prevailed, however, and Christ Church was begun in 1861. The site was given by Sidney Herbert, by this

8.5. *Brighton Terrace houses, completed in May 1855 — some of the earliest houses near Main Street built after the arrival of the railway.*

time first Lord Herbert of Lea, while the eleventh earl and countess of Meath made a substantial donation to the cost of building.

Christ Church was built from Glencree granite to the design of the notable English architect William Slater, who had just completed the cathedral at Kilmore, Co. Cavan. It was consecrated on 25 July 1863 and the tower was added in 1865–6, although the fine peal of bells was not dedicated until 1881. (The bells were apparently the inspiration of the British politician William Gladstone on a visit to Killruddery and he headed the subscription list.)

Christ Church's massive tower crowned by a spire rises to 53 metres and dominates the southern end of Bray; from many directions it is still the most prominent feature of the town. The church has been described as being 'on a grand scale, verging on triumphalism', and certainly as a rare example of a Church of Ireland church built on a greenfield site in the nineteenth century it occupies the kind of dominant position more characteristic of Catholic churches of the period. As well as reflecting the strength of Bray's nineteenth-century protestant congregation, Christ Church also echoes the imposing Anglican churches that were springing up in the developing resorts across the Irish Sea. Church Road was to become one of the most fashionable parts of Bray, and already by 1870 had the first two of its substantial houses — Pelham Lodge (the present Lansdowne), which was lived in by the rector until the new rectory was built in 1878, and Pembroke Lodge.

8.6. *Bray Head House, built by Charles Putland in the 1840s and now part of Presentation College.*

Beyond Church Road there were a number of large houses, set into extensive grounds. Ardbrae, Killarney House and Ryecroft, all of which survive, and Glencourt, demolished in the 1970s to make way for new houses, were built in the late 1850s and 1860s. Newcourt, also demolished in the 1970s, and Vevay House were older, although the latter was largely rebuilt in about 1858 by John Brennan who briefly made it his home (he moved to Seapoint House in 1861 or 1862, after Robert Seymour's death and a few years before his own death in 1866). In 1870 Vevay House was sold to the earl of Meath; at the time it was let for the season at £50 a month and was valued at £8,000. Lord Meath had also acquired the nearby Oldcourt House four years earlier. Further to the south-west, Fairy Hill also predated the railway, while Ardmore and Violet Hill were built in the 1860s. All had elaborate gardens, with winding paths set among lawns landscaped with trees and formal walled areas. These considerable properties, among the best in Bray, were the homes of lawyers and the like with professional links to Dublin city.

There was also Bray Head House, the home of the Putland family since 1850. Its situation was not quite so fine, perhaps, as that of their old home San Souci, but it too had extensive uninterrupted views over the northern slopes of Bray Head and the Irish Sea. It had been built in a style rather similar to that of San Souci, with an enclosed porch and crenulations on the parapets, though it was not as elegant. Surviving members of the family would sell the property in 1917, and it passed to the Presentation Order in 1920.

Back at the junction of Killarney and Vevay Roads, the pound by 1870 occupied the whole space that it had formerly shared with the old courthouse. Its entrance was on the south side, facing the old cottages which still remained. No doubt it was often filled with stray horses and donkeys awaiting claim by their owners. The centre of the road, slightly further north than the present wyvern, had both a water fountain and pump, with a street lamp close by. In 1870 this cluster would have formed a focal point to viewers looking up Main Street, backed by the high wall of the pound. It was probably the main focus of activity, too, at the top end of the town, as carriers watered their horses and families from nearby cabins gossiped as they drew water. Otherwise the view up Main Street, lacking the town hall, had as yet none of its present distinction.

The post office was on Windsor Terrace, at today's no. 34 Main Street close to the junction with Novara Avenue, where it was a familiar sight until the 1990s. Novara Avenue still had something of a country air, its south side lined with trees surviving from its time as the driveway to Novara House. A few houses had been built, including those of Alexandra Terrace. Going northwards, the next side road was less salubrious — Hudson's Terrace, built by 1862, had two facing rows of cabins, more than thirty in all, crammed into a limited space. Despite their neat, regular appearance on the Ordnance Survey map, they were apparently of poor quality 'without privies or ashpits', and were quickly regarded as a liability. Nonetheless they were to survive until the twentieth century.

Given that Florence Road was not to break through to Main Street for more than another thirty years, the next turning on the seaward side was Quinsborough Road, with the new premises of Quin's Hotel, by now renamed the Royal Hotel, on its north-eastern corner. Looking back up Main Street from this point, it would have been possible, as it is today, to form some impression of the shops of Bray, the majority of which were still concentrated into this one street. *Thom's directory* listed exactly one hundred householders, mostly shopkeepers and tradespeople with some private residents, in Main Street in 1870, a total not very different from today. The two largest groups were the fifteen grocers and provision dealers, and the boot and shoe makers of whom there were a round dozen. Seven dairies, five butchers and three fruiterers, a poulterer, a baker and a confectioner all supplied the public's needs, as did four drapers, four milliners and a tailor. With the other assorted concerns, including auctioneers (who were presumably doing good business), building tradesmen and a pawnbroker, almost all the premises on both sides of the street must already have had commercial usage on the ground floors. The upper floors were the homes of the shopkeepers, and often of their apprentices and staff.

As for the Royal Hotel, images of its curving frontage into Quinsborough Road, like those of the Turkish Baths and the International Hotel, remain among the most enduring views of late Victorian Bray. John Quin's new hotel was three-storey, with very tall windows on the ground floor and small wrought-iron balconies on the first. Almost square in shape, the main entrance still faced onto the main street and there was a garden along Quinsborough Road, where the Bray Cineplex and other premises are today. In 1870 the building next door was vacant, but later it was incorporated into the hotel. As we have seen, despite its newness, the hotel had declined in importance after the building of the hotels closer to the railway station and sea front. Relinquished by Quin, it spent a short spell as The Quinsboro' Boarding House from 1863 before regaining its dignity under new ownership in 1866, briefly as the Bray Hotel and then from 1867 as the Royal Hotel.

'HOTELS.
BRAY — HAYES'S (Late Quin's Hotel).
WILLIAM HAYES begs to inform his Friends and the Public that he has re-opened the above Establishment under improved arrangements.
Families and Single Gentlemen Boarded by the Week or Month, as per agreement.
Bed and Breakfast, 17s 6d per week, including attendance.
All other charges equally moderate.'
(*Freeman's Journal* 23 October 1866)

REOPENING OF FORMER QUIN'S HOTEL

By 1870 the original Quin's hotel premises had been converted into a Royal Irish Constabulary barrack, conveniently facing onto the courthouse. Opened in about 1863, this police barrack was to serve Bray for nearly seventy years, until the Civic Guards (Garda Síochána) left at the end of 1929. The courthouse had a small walled garden in front where the forecourt is now.

Apart from the changing circumstances of Quin's Hotel, the opening up of Quinsborough Road had in any case detracted from the importance of the area around the courthouse. There was a tendency by 1870 to look seawards towards the railway station, down the broad new 'Forty Foot'. Quinsborough Road fell, as it still does, into two distinct halves with a contrast between the

8.7. Prince of Wales Terrace, built in 1860–61, remains Bray's most elegant and impressive terrace.

8.8. East-facing end of Prince of Wales Terrace. The end house was in use as the exclusive Bray Club from the 1860s until the first world war.

narrower part near Main Street and the wider seaward end. The more imposing half was the area nearer to the sea, where the avenue that had once formed part of Quin's Walk still provided a shady strollway on the northern side past the Turkish Baths.

Here three terraces of houses already faced onto the road. On the north side, Dargan Terrace, built by William Dargan in 1859, has survived as a row of grand if somewhat bleak, three-storey-over-basement houses arranged as a central block of six, with a semi-detached pair at each end. According to Powell's *Railway handbook*, each house cost £1,800 to build; with the Turkish Baths and the Carlisle Grounds William Dargan spent more than £20,000 on this side of Quinsborough Road alone. Dr Haslam of the Turkish Baths had been the first, brief occupant of no. 1, and some of the houses changed tenants frequently or, according to *Thom's directory*, lay vacant — they may have been rented only during the summer months. The houses were renamed Duncairn Terrace in 1870, after Dargan's death.

Two other grand terraces occupied most of the south side, next to the International Hotel. Prince of Wales Terrace, twelve Italianate houses three storeys over basement, was and is the finest terrace in Bray. It was built in 1860–61 and fortunately the houses have survived to the present with little alteration. The end house on the corner of Adelaide Road was home to the Bray Club, which flourished for fifty years from about 1865 to 1915. It provided the kind of genteel facilities enjoyed by the wealthier residents and visitors, with ample room for servants and coach houses at the rear. Prince of Wales Terrace has been described by a modern architectural writer as 'a splendid example of Victorian town development and a monument to nineteenth-century self-confidence', and so it remains.

THE BRAY CLUB

'There is also an excellent club at Bray, which, though particular as to its members, is open to visitors of good social position on temporary arrangements.'
([Craig], *A guide to Bray and the picturesque scenery in its vicinity, Co. Wicklow*, Dublin, 1884, p. 10)

The similar but less elaborate Goldsmith Terrace, another twelve three-storey houses built by 1863, has not survived the years unscathed. Unlike Prince of Wales Terrace, with its list of gentlemanly occupants, in 1870 it was already partly in commercial usage, with a chemist, a hairdresser, a 'fancy warehouse' and the 'Scotch House'. This difference in character, which has become more marked over the years, is symbolised by the absence, both in 1870 and today, of enclosed front gardens at most of the properties; from the first there was nothing here to compare with the imposing granite steps and cast-iron balustrades of its neighbour.

The views from the front windows of Goldsmith Terrace must have been somewhat blighted by the state of the Turkish Baths opposite. Evidently an almost immediate failure, the baths were described in a valuation record of April 1864 as 'not working' and 'about to be removed' and were indeed firmly closed by January 1865. Two summer seasons later, on 17 July 1867, a Grand Evening Concert marked the reopening of the central part as assembly rooms, perhaps welcome as a more widely useful asset to the resort. The new rooms began in style, with 'Grand Morning and Evening Concerts', a 'Grand Comic Concert', and other assorted entertainments. For a brief period Turkish baths continued to function under Dr Barter's direction in what was described as the 'north wing', but their fate is uncertain — his death in 1870 may have been responsible for their closure. The west wing was leased to the Society of Friends by Barter in 1869; the east wing was used for meetings of the Plymouth Brethern.

ASSEMBLY ROOMS

'ASSEMBLY ROOMS, BRAY — GRAND CONCERT.
A section of the beautiful structure erected by the late lamented William Dargan as a Turkish bath has been recently undergoing considerable internal alterations and embellishments. The northern wing has been exclusively set apart for a Turkish bath, which will be opened in a few days under the management of Dr. Barter, of Blarney. The remainder of the building has been fitted up as the Assembly Rooms, and the principal saloon, which is a magnificent apartment, is intended as a ball room and a place of general entertainment. It was inaugurated last evening with a grand concert, which, we are happy to say, was highly attractive and successful. The attendance was most numerous and distinguished, and the vocal and instrumental performances were in every way worthy of the cordial applause which they elicited.'
(*Freeman's Journal* 18 July 1867)

Goldsmith Terrace had a new and substantial edifice facing its west end, where in 1858 the present Presbyterian Church was built on the opposite

8.9. *Goldsmith Terrace housed commercial premises almost from the start.*

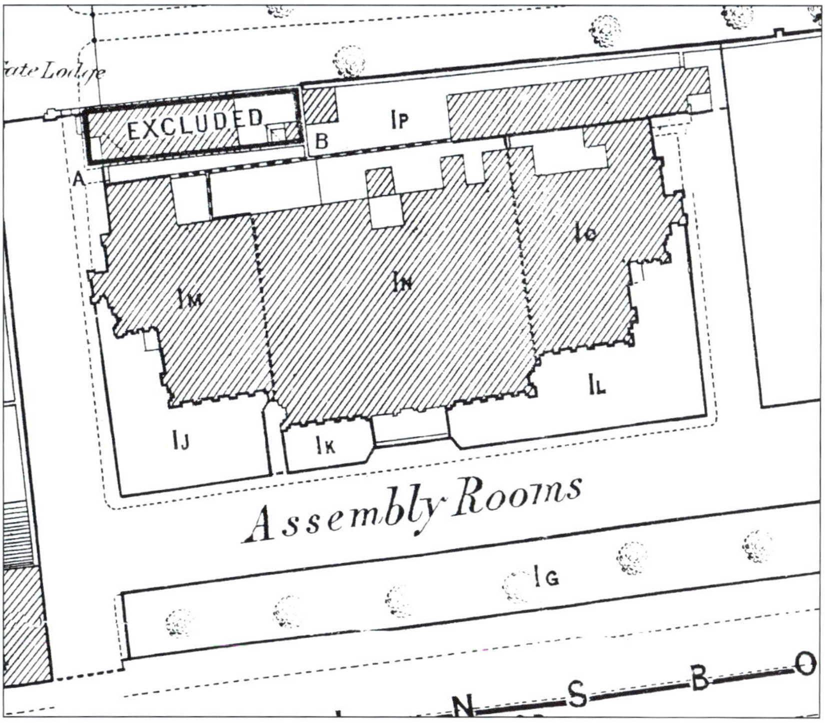

8.10. *Plan of the Turkish Baths from a 1922 rental, showing the division into three parts when the baths were closed. In 1922 the Society of Friends was still in the west wing (IM), where it held meetings until the 1940s, and the former Assembly Rooms (IN) were in use as a cinema. The caretaker's house is at the rear (IP).*

corner of Eglinton Road to replace the small chapel behind Main Street. A solid granite structure with a short tower and spire, it was designed by William Barre, a young Newry architect who was also responsible for the Church of Ireland church at Kilbride, two kilometres south-west of Bray. The church was to have north and south transepts added in the 1890s and a porch in 1929; it was formally named St Andrew's in 1925. It has stood the test of time well. The gothic-style manse was built at the same time as the church (despite the late twentieth-century plaque reading 'The Manse: built 1850' over its door) and in 1870 it shared the same grounds.

Eglinton Road was a cul-de-sac, with the first seven houses already in place and the new Wesleyan Chapel at the end. This Methodist church, also of granite and of plain design, was built in 1864. Its congregation was to increase in about 1878, when the Primitive Wesleyan Methodists from Brighton Terrace were reunited with the Wesleyan Methodists. There was still a field between the church and Main Street, with no access through to the latter.

Back on Quinsborough Road, from Eglinton Road to Main Street along the narrower part of the road, there was from the start a less gracious look than was deliberately created nearer the railway station. The newspaper reports and directories are silent on when exactly Quinsborough Road was broken through to connect with Main Street. What is certain is that this western part was not developed as early as the eastern part. It was not until February 1860 that John Quin held a meeting in his hotel to let the unoccupied frontage. There were twenty-nine lots, fifteen of which, not a very impressive total, were let at the meeting.

The first mention in *Thom's directory* of the properties along the south-west part of Quinsborough Road was in 1863; two were not yet occupied. By 1870, though, nearly all had shops on their ground floor, with Mrs M'Donald's 'silk mercer, millinery and dress warerooms, and fancy shoe warehouse' as the first tenant of a long, narrow property, since divided, on the corner at nos 1 and 2. Leverett & Frye, the grocers and wine merchants whose premises at this site are a familiar image, replaced M'Donald by 1880. It is conceivable that it was Frederick Leverett and Charles Frye who, with some poetic licence, embellished the corner with the date plaque 'Quinsborough Road 1854'.

Next to the Royal Hotel, on the north side of Quinsborough Road, Westbourne Terrace was built by 1870. The houses here were set back from the road, with front gardens that have in the twentieth century been built over to provide new street-front commercial premises. In 1870 they were private houses. The lane between the terrace and another block of four new houses led to the yard and stables of the Royal Hotel. What survives of this yard is now the rear car park of the Westbourne Hotel, with a row of the old buildings still on the seaward side. The property facing the Presbyterian Church was a private garden, with the entrance to Galtrim House, by now again a private residence, where Galtrim Park is today.

A view of 1865 taken from close to this point shows the wide vista down to the International and Royal Marine Hotels (see fig. 7.13). Quinsborough Road would have been busy, with visitors strolling between the sea front and the tempting Main Street shops, and jaunting cars setting off to the mountains from the cab stands by the railway station and in Duncairn Terrace and Seapoint Road. The station, still with a single platform (the second passenger platform on the seaward side of the track was not built until 1927) had ornamental flower beds facing the International Hotel. The station refreshment rooms had not flourished. They were closed for a time in 1863, in the 1870s they were described as 'not a very renumerative speculation to the tenant' and they were to go bankrupt at the end of the century. (In this they were in company with other railway refreshment rooms on the same line at Rathdrum and Woodenbridge, both of which closed.) If the Carlisle Grounds were hosting a performance, there would have been a buzz and the sound of band music.

'CARLISLE GROUNDS, BRAY, A FASHIONABLE PROMENADE,
BALLOON ASCENT AND GRAND DISPLAY OF FIREWORKS.
Will take place in the above Grounds,
On MONDAY EVENING NEXT, the 28th Instant,
Commencing at Half-past Six o'Clock.

By permission of Lieutenant Colonel Hillier of the Band of the Constabulary of Ireland, under the direction of Mr. Harry Hardy, will attend. To conclude with a magnificient display of Fireworks, supplied by Mr. John Lawrence, 39 Grafton street.

Admission — One Shilling. Holders of Railway Return Tickets for that day. Half price. Children Sixpence.'
(*Freeman's Journal* 23 August 1865)

'GRAND DISPLAY' AT CARLISLE GROUNDS

Passing over the level crossing, with the signal box on the left and a watch house on the right, the entrance to the Royal Marine Hotel now faced across to the five large brick houses of Royal Marine Terrace. Popularly known as the Red Houses and built by 1862, these still overlook the north end of the Esplanade. Close to Seapoint Road, martello tower no. 2 and its associated buildings was by now in private ownership. Edward Breslin acquired it and used the officers' quarters as livery stables for his hotel. (The quarters were converted to a private dwelling in the 1920s and the tower itself was converted during the late 1960s.)

8.11. *Royal Marine Terrace, built in* c. *1860 — five of the earliest and grandest houses built facing the sea.*

8.12. *Martello Terrace and the former Kelly's Baths today. The cars are those of commuters, rather than holiday makers. Inset: Martello Terrace before the verandas were added.*

The northern end of the Esplanade had in 1860 been given a prominent end-stop when Joseph Kelly built the eight houses of Martello Terrace, the most westerly of which, no. 1, was later to achieve some notability as a childhood home of James Joyce whose family lived there from 1887 to 1892. Facing southwards next to Kelly's baths, their appearance in 1870 was more severe than it is today; the distinctive cast-iron and timber fretwork veranda that runs the length of the block was a later addition. Their position was an exposed one, and they were very vulnerable to flooding.

From here the whole mile-long extent of the Esplanade would in 1870 have been a stirring sight, with the light glittering off the windows and fresh paintwork of the many and varied new buildings that lined Strand Road. The Royal Marine Hotel in the foreground was at its most impressive. Early drawings show it as three-storey over basement, its five-bay frontage onto Quinsborough Road with a central main porched entrance. In the drawing that accompanies D.E. Heffernan's *Illustrated plan of Bray* there appears to be a crest over the porch, perhaps indicating its 'royal' status. The garden at the side between the hotel and the railway crossing had been elaborately laid out with statuary, and was overlooked by the colonnaded ground floor at the rear.

'Breslin's Marine Hotel. … A colonnade opens upon an Italian garden from a noble reception-room, close to the Strand, where, in the season (on Mondays) a fine military band attends. Groups of statuary, tastefully placed, give a classic grace to the grounds, setting off the verdant and sunny gardens to advantage. … Entering the hotel by a portico and flight of steps, we find ourselves in a tastefully-arranged corridor, terminating in the large room already mentioned as opening into the grounds. On our left is the coffee-room, a luxurious apartment, commanding a magnifient view northward along the four-mile strand to Killiney, and eastward, the level sweep of the Esplanade and the sea beyond. The private sitting-rooms upstairs open on balconies commanding, on every side, extensive views of sea and mountain … .'

(G.R. Powell, *The official railway handbook to Bray*, Dublin, 1860, pp 13–14)

BRESLIN'S MARINE HOTEL

Breslin's early success allowed him to extend his hotel within four years of its opening, with a new wing of twenty bedrooms and four sitting rooms extending across his gardens almost to the level crossing. The L-shaped plan

8.13. *Brennan's Terrace, built by John Brennan. On the sea front and convenient for the railway station, most of the houses would always have boarded holiday makers.*

gave it an appearance of substantial bulk, almost comparable to that of the International Hotel. It now had a total of ninety bedrooms and twelve sitting rooms. On the seaward front there was a wide balustraded terrace set over the basement from which guests could enjoy the view of the sea and Esplanade while stylishly sipping their afternoon tea. The hotel was to come to a sad end in 1916, with its two top floors burnt out in an accidental fire, but this terrace and its ground floor area has by a quirk of fate survived as a ghostly reminder of Edward Breslin and his hotel.

The Royal Marine Hotel's gardens, no longer with a frontage to Quinsborough Road, extended as a long narrow strip alongside the railway station, with the stables, coach house and laundry rooms for the hotel added in 1863 next to Albert Avenue. By 1870, however, the gardens were almost entirely cut off from views of the sea by the houses of Marine, Fitzwilliam and Claddagh Terraces, built by Breslin in the 1860s. The houses of Fitzwilliam Terrace had and have reasonably imposing frontages, but were laid out with minimal gardens both front and rear; certainly their paying guests had to set out onto the Esplanade for their breaths of fresh sea air.

The last of the old cottages formed a lozenge-shaped island on Strand Road opposite Marine Terrace. Their low-lying position was an unhappy one, defenceless in times of storm; nonetheless they survived until the 1960s. Two, at least, of the women who made a living by looking after bathers lived here, and their bathing boxes must have been on the shore nearby.

Across Quin's Passage (the present Albert Avenue), John Brennan had in 1859 built the terrace of twelve houses that bears his name, another terrace that has survived remarkably intact to the present. This terrace, and the other houses southwards along Strand Road, have the benefit of being set further back from the road than is Fitzwilliam Terrace, with front gardens some ten metres long. When built they were at the very edge of the fields, with their flights of front steps touching the divide between pasture and strand. The front gardens, previously part of the foreshore, were leased separately from the eleventh earl of Meath in 1860 or, in the case of those south of Victoria Avenue, in 1867. Although they had good front gardens, the houses of Brennan's Terrace had only modest yards at the rear, given that Brennan's Parade with its small terraced dwellings had been fitted in behind next to the railway track and engine house. (Not all of Brennan's speculative building had been immediately successful: the sixteen houses of Brennan's Parade, built by 1862, were only very gradually occupied — eight in the centre of the row were still vacant in 1870.)

South of Brennan's Terrace the houses had greater pretensions. Detached or semi-detached villas and two terraces of four houses, all built between 1859 and 1865 in varying styles, extended all the way to Convent Avenue. Their names were as varied as their architecture: Eglinton Ville (more recently Tullyra), Dunalan, Tros-yr-afon Terrace (presumably its first owner, Dr Morgan, was a Welshman), the paired houses of Wave Crest (the Porter

8.14. *Original houses of* c. *1860 face the sea on Strand Road.*

8.15. *The former Eglinton Ville, on Strand Road.*

House), Elsinore and Holyrood House (the present Strand and Heather House Hotels). The four elaborate houses of Esplanade Terrace were built by Sir William Wilde, the distinguished doctor and antiquarian, father of Oscar Wilde, and were later briefly the property of Oscar Wilde himself before they were sold in 1878. Many of these houses kept their original names and retained much of their original appearance, at least until recently. Only one of the two pairs of Montebello Terrace, however, has survived, while Grosvenor Terrace has been replaced by late twentieth-century apartments. Seafield House on the corner of Victoria Avenue has also been demolished.

One small detail behind Esplanade Terrace, almost obliterated today, was a last remnant of the private path to the sea front from the Loreto Convent, a successor to the long driveway of the Putlands' time. A pedestrian tunnel ran under the railway embankment. It was extant in 1870 even though the path on the inland side had vanished; on the seaward side it led to a gated laneway that exited onto Convent Avenue.

Beyond Convent Avenue, Mariemount House, also built in the early 1860s, marked the end of the nearly continuous line of new properties. Next to it three of the old cottages, Rose Cottage, Clareville Cottage and Martello Cottage, occupied the space next to the coast guard station, by now reaching the end of its life — it was to be closed in 1877.

All the houses to this point overlooked Dargan's esplanade. Although Gaskin's view (fig. 7.12) published in 1869 gives the Esplanade a very rough appearance on the seaward side, with rocks and shingle reaching right into the grass strip, the Ordnance Survey map of 1870 shows a much more orderly arrangement, with long paths on either side and cross paths at intervals, much as today. The bandstand was opposite Wave Crest and martello tower no. 1 still stood, disused, its outer side jutting out onto the actual shore. There was one ominous sign — the 1870 Ordnance Survey map is of sufficiently large scale to show part of the outer path near the tower already worn away by the sea (see fig. 7.11); over the next decade the tower's foundations would be seriously undermined. The continued encroachments by the sea were soon to involve Bray's ratepayers in massive expenditure.

The most southerly stretch of Strand Road, the part that lay within Charles Putland's property rather than that of the earl of Meath, had retained a somewhat different character from the rest. There was a more intimate mix of old and new, and the South Esplanade was comparatively recent, having been laid out only after the township was enlarged in 1866. The granite coast-guard boat house, still a feature of the Esplanade, marked its southern end. This sturdy boat house, able to withstand the worse storms, was built in the mid 1860s to replace the old boat house up at the Dargle mouth; disused by 1902, it was transferred from the Admiralty to the town in 1904.

LACY'S BRAY HEAD HOTEL

> *'J. Lacys' Bray Head hotel, on the Sea Shore. Strangers visiting this delightful locality will find it to their advantage to call to the above Hotel. Dinners supplied at the shortest notice. A Table d'Hote on Sundays and Mondays at Four o'Clock. Bed and Breakfast 3/-. Picnic parties supplied with a coffee room capable of containing forty persons. Refreshments of the best quality.'* (*Freeman's Journal* 4 August 1860)

The new houses included Elsinore (the present Strand Hotel), and the semi-detached pairs of Merville and Dunluce (Dunluice House), Northcote (Neptune House) and Altona, again all built in the 1860s and with Mount Norris Villas, built in about 1863, tucked in behind close to the railway embankment. Then came modest villas and rows of cottages, a few of which have survived, including Railway Terrace at the rear, extending to the Bray Head Hotel. John Lacy had opened his hotel (today's The Bray Head) in 1860, although it was not extended to its present size until the early 1900s. The hotel had tea houses on a 'view bank' rented from Charles Putland. At the very end, tucked in under Bray Head and with only a narrow roadway separating their front gardens from high water mark, the six houses of Fontenoy Terrace were built by 1859. They were destined to pay for their delightful situation by suffering exposure to the full force of north-easterly gales, as their owners were quickly to discover.

While the sea front had by 1870 taken on its long-term appearance, the new roads behind were still very much in a transitional phase. There were more plots vacant than built upon, despite a slow but steady increase in the number of occupied houses right through the 1860s. The southern ends of Meath and Sidmonton Roads and most of the eastern part of Putland Road were to remain green fields into the twentieth century. Nearer to Main Street and Quinsborough Road the development was very haphazard and there were even two large gravel pits on the inland side of the railway line.

There were no houses on the present Adelaide Road, although the first four houses at the east end of Florence Terrace, owned by Edward Breslin, had just been built. Meath Road had scattered groups of houses of which the three large detached houses that form Meath Terrace, built in 1858, were the oldest by some years. The others — Aravon House, Belvidere Villa, Meath House, Somerset House, Victoria Terrace, the first four houses in Milward Terrace with a datestone 1864 — were all completed in the mid 1860s. Aravon House ('Novara' in reverse) had by 1870 given its name to Aravon School, a 'school for the sons of gentlemen' which occupied the house from about 1866 until shortly before it was demolished in the mid 1980s. Roger Casement was at school there in 1875; another pupil was the playwright John Millington Synge.

Sidmonton Square had its ornamental plantings around the margins of the park, but only two pairs of villas and Sidmonton House faced onto it; all five, together with Sidmonton Villa (demolished in the early twentieth century) across the road, had been built in about 1860. Further south on Sidmonton Road there was already in 1870 a block of development that was both very recent and comparatively complete, from Winsen (the present Kylemore House) to the semi-detached Daphne (Caragh) and Glenbervie, a fine pair of double-fronted, three-storey houses. Fort View, soon to be renamed New Grange Lodge (the present Garda Station), surrounded on all sides by large gardens, had been built on the east side by 1858, making it one of the earliest of the large post-railway houses. Between 1862 and about 1866 it had served as Bray School, forerunner of Aravon School.

There were three houses in Sidmonton Place, already converted to the French School, a private girls' school that flourished until 1966 and whose 'crocodiles' of pupils might have been seen wending their way to Christ

Church or the seafront. The picturesque Sidmonton with its datestone 1855 nearby was very different from its more substantial new neighbours. Like Florence and Milward Terraces, Novara Terrace was partly complete, with four houses built by 1862 — the three nearest to Novara Avenue were not added until the mid 1880s. But from here it was still possible to look across to the bulk of the International Hotel and watch the trains getting up steam in Bray railway station, with only pasture land in between.

The area alongside the Dargle had also had its changes in the two decades since 1850. The biggest change, of course, had taken place around the river mouth, an area that in 1870 presented a very different view to the visitor from the one of twenty years before. East of the new embankment that linked the railway bridge with the higher land at the martello tower, all the land was essentially newly-made, founded on the old shingle ridge. The customs boat house, once perched far out on the shingle, now had the gasworks and gasometer on one side and Richard Cuthbert's coal yard on the other. It had been sold to the Gas Company in about 1864.

Between these structures and the railway lay the much-criticized dock and, just below the embankment with the second gasometer at its north end, a terrace of twenty very small 'working-men's' cottages built in the 1860s, at first called Dargan Cottages — they were built by William Dargan — but by 1870 renamed Dock Terrace. As Harbour Terrace they were to survive as one of the humblest areas of Bray housing until 1952 when they were purchased for demolition by Bray Urban District Council. Although they had tiny rear yards, they had no sanitation in 1870. Not all were occupied.

The railway bridge was accompanied on its west side by a wooden foot bridge, built by Dargan and linking the two banks of the river. Briefly a favourite view point for artists sketching the town, it was clearly of dubious construction, for it was pronounced unsafe in 1866 and the town commissioners closed it in 1870. It was later pulled down. Seymour's dock was still visible cut into the bank below his house, but by 1870 it was disused and largely inaccessible by water. Although not visible to passers-by, the Seymours' Cherry Garden was at its finest in 1870; an elaborate, rather formal, garden, it was laid out with straight paths, a summer house, a well and rows of ornamental trees. There was already a cluster of commercial premises next to the river, with two lime kilns, a coal yard, and a large timber yard. But the older portion of Seapoint Road from Seapoint House to Main Street was one of the parts of Bray least affected by development.

Standing on Bray Bridge and looking upstream, on the left bank the mill complex with its flour mill and brewery was flourishing, with a new

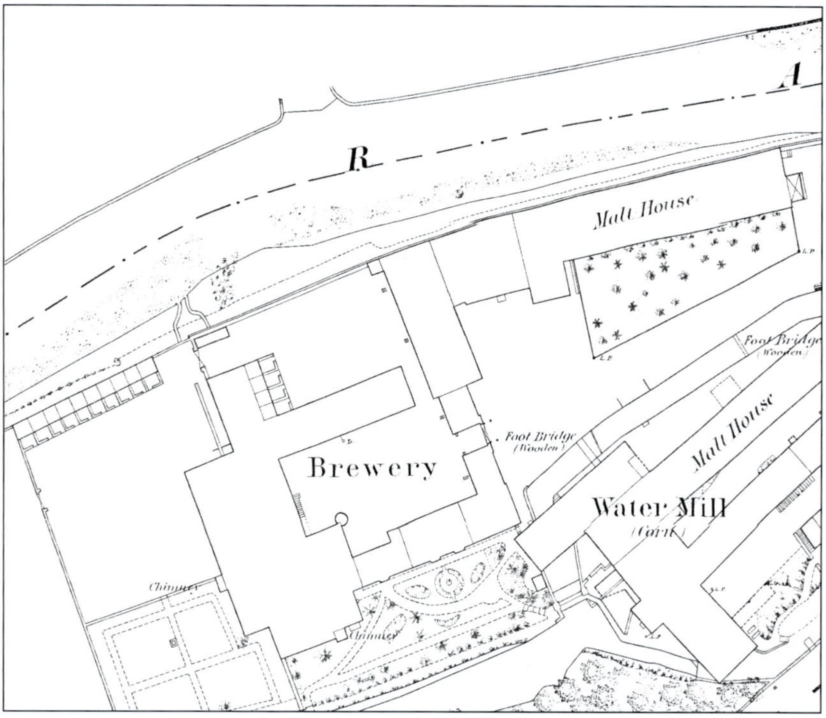

8.16. The mill and brewery in 1870. Original scale 10 ft to the mile (1:500).

8.17. Looking up Castle Street in the Dublin direction from Bray Bridge. The shopping centre car park at the left was in 1870 a busy island of cottages and small businesses between Castle Street and Back Street.

malthouse by the river; there were two water wheels and the tail race ran beside Mill Lane to merge into the Dargle under Bray Bridge. On the opposite bank lay the People's Park, still no more than a grassy stretch running alongside the river — it was to be another decade before it was landscaped and planted with trees. The fair green was conspicuous, occupying the whole rectangle between the Lower Dargle and Green Park Roads, Fair View and Fairgreen Road; it was opened in January 1870, with fairs on the first Monday of every month. Traders must have heaved a sigh of relief at no longer having animals penned on the street in front of their businesses, with the attendant nuisances. Beyond lay the grid pattern of new roads laid out on the commons — a grid that would have been very visible from the bridge given that most of the plots were still vacant; they would remain so for almost another twenty years until the present distinctive artisan cottages were built. But there were some new houses — Parkview Terrace already had four and Dunn's Terrace had eight. The four houses of Bruce's Terrace had been built on the uphill side of the Upper Dargle Road.

BRAY ALE

'Bray ale is a celebrity. It is neither a bitter nor a sweet ale, but a combination of both, which makes it exceedingly pleasant; slightly tonic in its effects, it is at the same time palatable and nutritious. The malting-floors, cooling-rooms, and vats are extensive, and the greatest care is exercised in the mysteries of production.'
(G.R. Powell, *The official railway handbook to Bray*, Dublin, 1860, p. 20)

Castle Street was lined with an assortment of enterprises, ranging from shoemakers, of whom there were three, through a variety of grocers, victuallers and vintners to a pawnbroker, a gunsmith, a cigar and tobacco dealer and a china shop. The Cuthbert family, long established as Bray coal merchants, had a coal and iron business on the street at least from the early 1860s, and were to trade there into the twentieth century; the property is today as Heiton Buckley's still in similar usage. But most of Little Bray other than the commons had been little affected by the boom years in Bray south of the river, and in 1870 Back Street and the Dublin Road probably looked much as they had done twenty years before. Little Bray remained a largely working-class area, with poor street lighting and lacking a good water supply or adequate sewerage facilities.

Chapter 9

'This delightful locality': Bray 1870–1910

'... the delightful and now fashionable watering place of Bray, with its handsome hotels, wide streets and magnificent marine promenade. We put up at the 'International' considered by many to be the finest hotel in Ireland. A better centre for doing Wicklow cannot be imagined. We are amazed at the number and elegance of the jaunting cars ... .'
(G.A. Philip, *Holiday fortnights at home and abroad*, Paisley, 1896, p. 74)

Despite the eulogies of the travel writers, Bray's early promise was not to be fulfilled, and by the 1870s the town's growth was slowing down. Although the population continued to increase during the rest of the century, the rise was no longer a dramatic one. Bray township had a population of some 6,000 in 1870 and by the 1911 census the population was 7,700, a respectable increase of 28 per cent over forty years compared with the heady 90 per cent increase in the twenty years from 1850 to 1870. Unlike many of the English and Welsh resorts, which were by now competing against each other, Bray as an expanding seaside resort had few rivals within Ireland — only Bangor and Portrush in Ulster and the much smaller Bundoran, Co. Sligo, came close in percentage population increase. It was factors such as the Irish economic and political problems of the late nineteenth century that were to act against it.

In the late 1870s there was an agricultural recession with plunging prices for cattle and crops, which led to much hardship once again for small farmers and which was accompanied by agrarian unrest in many parts of Ireland. For a resort such as Bray, there was insufficient investment money available matched by too few Irish holiday-makers with high spending power. And although visitors were still tempted across the Irish Sea, some must have been deterred by reports of Fenian activity and by widely publicised acts of terrorism such as the Phoenix Park murders of 1882. At the end of the century the Boer War, too, was to interfere with the flow of funding and visitors from Britain.

Another problem may have come from within the town. Three of the energetic early players had departed the scene — William Dargan, John Quin and John Brennan had all died by 1870 and only Edward Breslin provided continuity as a powerful force in the business world until his death in 1897. (Breslin's influence extended well beyond Bray, as shown by his presidency of the Conference of Hotel Proprietors held in Dublin in April 1894.) It is possible that the lack of a new generation of equally dynamic entrepreneurs contributed to Bray's failure to realise its full potential. The failure of imaginative schemes by Edward Breslin and John Brennan's son-in-law Charles Dufresne suggests, however, that in the last part of the nineteenth century more than dynamism was necessary and that Bray's entrepreneurs were swimming against the economic tide.

With the start of the 1870s the town commissioners were still trying to balance the needs of the resort against the desire of the ratepayers to keep charges upon themselves to a minimum. The commissioners were soon to be faced with the need for massive expenditure to contain Bray's greatest friend and enemy, the Irish Sea, and the building of the new sea wall and promenade was to be the town's finest nineteenth-century achievement. Meanwhile the empty plots along the new roads were taken up little by little. And as the century wore on the character of Bray, as of all seaside resorts, changed gradually as the emphasis on the medicinal and health-giving

9.1. The sea wall and promenade — Bray's finest nineteenth-century achievement. The holiday-makers in this postcard have an air of prim respectability with their hats and parasols; sun-tanned faces were not yet fashionable.

BRAY REGATTA.

Thursday & Friday, 19th & 20th August, 1897.

Yacht Races, Sailing & Rowing Matches,
Swimming Contests, &c.

Grand · Aquatic · Carnival,
INCLUDING:
POLO MATCHES, TILTING TOURNAMENT,
DUCK HUNTS.
TUGS OF WAR & VARIOUS OTHER INSHORE SPORTS.

BAND PROMENADE.
SWITCHBACK AND HOBBY HORSES.

Open-Air Concerts by Operatic Artistes.
GRAND DISPLAY OF FIREWORKS EACH EVENING
SPECIAL CHEAP RAILWAY EXCURSIONS.

Admission to Enclosure—Day, 1s; Evening, for Fireworks, 6d.

FOR PRIZE LIST, ETC., APPLY TO
J. J. FULLERTON, Hon. Sec., Bray.

9.2. Poster for Bray regatta, 1897, with a wide range of entertainments.

benefits gave way slowly to the idea of a stay as being purely for pleasure, a pleasure, moreover, that was available to all levels of society rather than just the well-to-do.

Visitors were becoming more discriminating, and more was expected of a resort than sea bathing and the occasional concert or band performance. There were complaints that visitors to Bray were not being provided with a level of entertainment 'such as in England'. As a result, a meeting was held in the International Hotel in May 1875, and the Bray Improvement Committee, later the Bray Amusements Committee, was set up to organise events. The founding members included Edward Breslin, Charles Dufresne, by this time proprietor of the International Hotel, and pharmacist Alexander Doran, who would later write a standard guide book on Bray for the

Committee. The Dublin, Wicklow, & Wexford Railway Company subscribed £50, and offered to carry all military and other bands free of charge.

The Bray Improvement Committee was to play its part until well into the twentieth century. It organised polo matches, flower shows and fireworks displays in the Carlisle Grounds — Edward Breslin provided free use of the Grounds — and rowing regattas. It also organised twice-weekly military band performances on the Esplanade; the first month of these, June 1875, featured the bands of the 5th Dragoon Guards, the 50th and 61st regiments and the R.I.C. (Some years later, in 1889, the Amusements Committee was to spend over £500 on the season's bands, a considerable sum, compared with £20 on fireworks, while by 1910 the figure had risen to £765.) It even paid for the flags that added gaiety to the Esplanade. The Committee was, however, a voluntary organisation dependent upon local goodwill and with limited funds raised by local subscription; in some years it overstretched its resources and was faced with a deficit. More substantial, permanent recreational facilities required commercial backing. This was not always forthcoming and, when it was, success did not always follow.

FIREWORKS TO END THE SEASON

> *'THE SEASON AT BRAY.–The programme of amusements laid out by the Bray Improvement Committee for the enjoyment of visitors to this charming watering place was brought to a close last night by a magnificient display of fireworks given by Mr. Lawrence on the Esplanade. The band of the 90th Regiment also attended and played a choice selection of music during the evening.'*
> (*Freeman's Journal* 2 October 1875)

One scheme that, had it been carried to completion, would have foreshadowed the present aquarium/restaurant building on the Esplanade was that for an elaborate pavilion complex. In February 1878 the town commissioners approved a plan put forward by the Bray Improvement Committee for the erection of ladies' baths on the north side of martello tower no. 1 at a cost of £1,000, together with a further plan for a new concert hall and floral promenade near the bandstand; the commissioners granted sites for both buildings, subject to the approval of Lord Meath as 'lord of the soil'. By the following month matters had moved on. The Bray Pavilion Company was launched in March 1878; its pavilion was to comprise a large saloon with promenades, refreshment areas, reading and writing rooms, a

9.3. *Concert poster, c. 1900. By this time the Bray Amusements Committee was spending a considerable part of its budget on the season's bands.*

9.4. *In the late twentieth century Bray Esplanade finally acquired a pavilion-type structure, the aquarium/restaurant, on the site proposed in 1878.*

pleasure garden and the ladies' baths. Edward Breslin spent £1,000 on taking up nearly half of the shares in the company and with the addition of a small shareholding by Charles Dufresne, the two formed a shareholding majority. It could be deduced that the scheme was very much Breslin's own from the first.

The first site chosen had to be abandoned when it emerged that it was in front of building ground on Strand Road granted by Lord Meath on condition that no structures more than four feet in height be erected between the houses and the sea. The town commissioners dutifully leased a nearby site on the Esplanade opposite Claddagh Terrace, where the present aquarium/restaurant building stands, permission was obtained from Lord Meath, the foundation stone was laid on 30 May 1878 and work began. Matters did not go smoothly, however, and after legal objections by a sea-front resident that the structure on the Esplanade would interfere with the 'reasonable use of the Esplanade by people of the town' and that it would be 'a public eyesore' the scheme had to be scaled down.

NEW BATHS

'BRAY IMPROVEMENT COMPANY.– The new baths about to be erected by the above company, on a site granted to them on the Esplanade by the Earl of Meath, have been commenced, and it is purposed having them ready for use before the close of the season. The foundation stone was laid today in presence of a large number of the inhabitants. Sir George Ribton, Bart., laid the first corner-stone of the new building, which it is hoped will prove as prosperous as it will be useful in replacing the antiquated and dingy machines that now disfigure the strand.'
(*Freeman's Journal* 31 May 1878)

'BRAY PAVILION COMPANY (LIMITED). LADIES' OPEN SEA-BATHING ESTABLISHMENT. These beautiful and commodious Baths, replete with every convenience will be opened on MONDAY NEXT the 9th June 1879. CHARGES Tickets, for a dozen Baths, 2s 6d. Ticket for Single Bath, 3d. Children under 12 years of age, 2d each.'
(*Freeman's Journal* 5 June 1879)

Only the ladies' baths were built; they were opened to the public in June 1879. Later the property of the township, they were to remain open, a prominent feature of the sea front, until their demolition in the 1960s.

When mixed bathing became the norm in the twentieth century, they were available to men as well as women. Breslin and Dufresne revived the pavilion idea in the 1880s, but this second time round were refused a site on the Esplanade, although they were told that the use of any other site would receive support. Unlike Kingstown/Dún Laoghaire, which in the early 1900s acquired an elegant pavilion with tea-rooms, reading-rooms and smoking-rooms overlooking the harbour, Bray was not to have an entertainment centre on the Esplanade to compare with those in British resorts.

The continued failure to build a pier also exacerbated the problem of the lack of all-weather facilities on the Esplanade. As they became more elaborate features of the seaside scene, piers frequently incorporated concert rooms, theatres, and entertainment booths, precisely what Bray needed to satisfy its visitors. After the abortive effort to fund a pier in the 1860s, another attempt was made in 1876 to provide a pier 1000 yards long and 45 yards wide 'similar to that of Brighton'. But neither this, nor further attempts made in 1884, in 1890, in 1893 and in 1899 were successful and the idea was finally abandoned in 1906. The proposal in 1893 had been to move an existing pier from Douglas, Isle of Man; the 1899 plans failed through lack of the necessary funding from England during the Boer War. Bray never managed to offer a maritime stroll to match a walk on the harbour walls at Dún

9.5. *The Carlisle Grounds, now home to Bray Wanderers Football Club, were laid out for cricket and archery in 1862; a roller skating rink operated briefly in the 1870s but other ambitious plans for development came to nothing. Prince of Wales Terrace is in the background; the end house of Duncairn (Dargan) Terrace is at the far right.*

Laoghaire, or along the shallow-water — and rather flimsy — Merrion Promenade Pier at Sandymount which was opened in 1882.

Ambitious plans were also made for the Carlisle Grounds. The first modest development there was in 1876, with the opening of a roller-skating rink, built by subscription as the brainchild of the Bray Improvement Committee. Roller skating had become a popular pastime from early in the nineteenth century, and it had a place in many seaside resorts. The Bray rink with 'as near as possible a perfect floor' was 120 yards long by 75 yards wide; after the inaugural day it was open for three two-hour periods daily with the bonus of a string band in attendance at some evening sessions. More wide-ranging proposals were made with the launch in November 1877 of the Bray Aquarium Company. The Carlisle Grounds were to embrace not only a marine aquarium and concert hall, with lecture, exhibition, reading and refreshment rooms, but were also to find space for the rink, croquet and archery grounds, and walks. The capital to be raised was £20,000. The scheme came to nothing, however, and the skating rink itself disappeared after 1880, presumably for lack of patrons.

BRAY SKATING RINK

'BRAY SKATING RINK, CARLISLE GROUNDS.
INAUGURAL OPENING DAY.
The First Skating Assemblies on the above Rink will Open on WEDNESDAY, the 30th instant, from 3 p.m. to 6 p.m., and 7 p.m. to 9 p.m. When, by kind permission of the Colonel and Officers, the splendid Band of the 6th Inniskilling Dragoons will be in attendance.
The Proprietors have much pleasure in stating that they have succeeded in obtaining, as near as possible, a perfect floor, and feel assured it will be thoroughly appreciated by lovers of this pleasant pastime.
There will be a magnificent display of Fireworks by Mr. Lawrence at 9 p.m.
Admission, 1s; use of skates, 6d.'
(*Freeman's Journal* 28 August 1876)

The proposal for a switchback railway to be built on a site between the boat house and Lacy's Hotel — which would have been a forerunner of the amusements that came to dominate this end of the Esplanade — also came to nothing. The town commissioners rejected the scheme on the grounds that it would attract an undesirable class of visitor, driving away more acceptable visitors as, they claimed, had happened at Blackpool. There was an abortive effort in the 1880s to build a three-foot-gauge tramway, with its trams to travel at not more than six miles an hour, from the railway station to Lacy's Hotel. The chosen route was along Adelaide Road, Albert Avenue and Strand Road, and the tram would have provided a sea-front visitor attraction comparable to those operating in resorts such as Blackpool and Douglas. A rather different scheme was approved, but never implemented, in the 1890s for six tramlines of over two miles in total, serving the township as a whole. Another proposal for an electric tramway from Bray to Enniskerry fared no better in 1908.

Only one such project actually got off the drawing board, and even so it was not completed. The idea for a light railway from Bray to Enniskerry dated back to the 1860s and in 1886 it received sanction through the Bray & Enniskerry Light Railway Act. The line was to hug the south bank of the Dargle — an addition to the valuation map shows its planned route running under Bray Bridge and between the brewery buildings and the river. The work began in optimistic mood during April 1891 but the project seems to have run into difficulties almost immediately. By the following autumn the town commissioners were complaining of interference with Bray Bridge, and Lord Powerscourt was taking the company to arbitration on a claim for payment for land. In June 1893 the company was taken to court by the Wicklow Grand Jury for leaving a bridge half-completed. Despite extensions of the time limit for finishing the line amidst pleas of financial difficulties, no progress was made and the company was wound up in 1901. The tracks are long gone, but the railway works are still visible in places, notably approaching Enniskerry, as a discreet memorial to an imaginative but unsuccessful business venture.

These various private schemes had they been carried through would have provided only small advantages to Bray; the greatest improvement of the second half of the nineteenth century was achieved by the town commissioners. As we saw in an earlier chapter the Esplanade was always a problem, it was never safe from incursions by the sea and matters did not improve during the 1870s. In 1870 the commissioners ordered it to be protected with an edging of timber posts, except where 'parties on the strand were accustomed to pull up their boats in stormy weather'. Timber piling was still being purchased ten years later. A view of the Royal Marine Hotel showing elaborate wooden defences along the shore edge probably dates from this time. There were complaints not only about sand and gravel, but also about rotting seaweed on the roads.

In the winters of both 1872 and 1873 high tides and gales flooded the sea front and severely damaged the gas works on its exposed site; Bray was temporarily forced to depend again on paraffin lamps. One report in the *Irish Builder* suggested that the Dargle was 'working its way back into its ancient south channel', the last traces of which had only been obliterated when the railway was built. In January 1874 the commissioners had to authorise a supply of timber to repair breaches, and in the following December they tried to protect the road alongside Fontenoy Terrace with larch piling. They also at other times received timber or railway sleepers from the railway company and even the debris from a landslip at Bray Head. By 1878 the condition of martello tower no. 1 was causing serious concern, with the foundation undermined and a long crack up the side; an engineer from the Board of Works recommended its demolition. Its derelict appearance may have been picturesque, but neither it nor the timber piling can have enhanced the look of the Esplanade.

There was an acute problem at the very southern end in the mid 1870s, when the roadway in front of Lacy's Bray Head Hotel and Fontenoy Terrace was destroyed by storm waves, piping was swept away leaving residents without either light or water, and access became difficult to say the least. In 1876 the township was sued by a resident who claimed that the road was impassable and the houses unsaleable; it was the end of the decade before a new roadway was built but, as today, without a footpath for those strolling towards Bray Head. In January 1877 another exceptional tide flooded the Esplanade right to the doors of the seafront houses and turned Martello

9.6. Wooden piling in front of the Royal Marine Hotel — an attempt to keep back the waves before the construction of the sea wall (collection of the late Joe Loughman).

9.7. Close to Bray Head, Fontenoy Terrace was cut off by storms in the 1870s.

Terrace into an island; bathing boxes were thrown onto Strand Road, parts of the promenade were demolished and the unfortunate fishermen at Bray Head once again had their cottages inundated.

EXCEPTIONALLY HIGH TIDE

'HIGH TIDE — The tide last night rose to an unusual height, and in many instances covered the low ground along the coast, particularly at Bray, where it covered the Esplanade, and flooded the premises in connection with the gas works, when the furnaces were extinguished and the supply was suspended for some time. But little inconvenience, however, ensued, as most of the inhabitants had retired to rest, and a bright moon illuminated the streets.'
(*Freeman's Journal* 8 October 1873)

The town commissioners first contemplated solutions to the problem at the beginning of 1880, perhaps inspired by the start of a new decade. At the February meeting of the commissioners, Charles Dufresne gave notice of a proposal to apply for a further loan on the rates in order to construct 'a substantial concrete wall along such portions of the Esplanade as is necessary to secure same in the places injured by action of the tide'. Coincidentally, within days the *Freeman's Journal* reported that a storm had damaged the piling works that Joseph Kelly was undertaking to protect his houses on Martello Terrace.

> *'The engineer (Mr. Comber) presented plans and specifications for the proposed sea wall to be erected on the Esplanade to prevent the encroachment of the sea. The wall was to be twelve feet in height and eight feet wide at the bottom, sloping gradually upwards to three feet, and composed of concrete blocks, tongued together with same material and similar to works carried out on the North-Wall by Mr. Stoney. It is also proposed to have an asphalte walk eighteen feet wide, running the whole length of the protecting wall.'*
> (*Freeman's Journal* 22 November 1881)

PROPOSED SEA WALL

The plans took a while to mature; it was 1881 before the work was sanctioned through the Bray Township Act of that year and the town engineer placed a comprehensive scheme before the commissioners. More time passed while the commissioners waited for the necessary loan to come through — in October 1882 they still were worrying about 'the great loss likely to be sustained during the winter owing to the encroachment of the sea'. It must have been a relief not only to the commissioners but to sea-front residents when work finally began by McAlpine of Glasgow in 1884.

Progress was rapid. The commissioners chose the name 'Grand Marine Promenade', almost forgotten today ('Esplanade' remained in common usage), and invited the lord lieutenant, Lord Caernarvon, to perform the opening ceremony in October 1885. They made elaborate plans for a déjeuner in a marquee on the promenade, with the vice-regal party, the town commissioners, local gentry and their wives. But this was apparently seen as a misuse of ratepayers' money, the plans were quickly cut back, and Lord Caernarvon was merely presented with a 'non-political address' at the sea wall. The wall was extended as far south as the boat house by 1890, but the south end of the sea front remains to this day faced by only a low wall.

Even though the prime aim was protection against the sea — an aim that was not entirely realised — the new combination of promenade and sea wall was of immense benefit as an amenity. Visitors during the several summers of building work must have found the shore a far from restful place and hardly an inducement to visit Bray, but the long-term reward has been

9.8. The new sea wall with fixed concrete seating and ornamental ironwork, in a postcard of the early 1900s.

9.9. The seating and ironwork are still extant today.

considerable. The promenade with its edging of iron railings immediately gave dignity and substance to the sea front, as it still does. There was now an ideal walkway along which to stroll, and a place to lean over the railings and contemplate the waves, bathers, pleasure boats and, in the distance, the many ships sailing in and out of Dublin Bay. The fixed concrete seating added along the inner side was an additional bonus; previously there had only been moveable iron seats that had to be taken into storage each winter. As a disadvantage, though, the wall of necessity formed a barrier between the beach and the promenade; access to the shore at the north end was quite limited and involved negotiating steep flights of steps. This constraint has given Bray's sea front a greater separation between promenade and beach than is found in many resorts elsewhere.

Apart from the major headache of raising and repaying the necessary funds, some £20,000 in all, a considerable sum at the time, the sea-front changes gave the commissioners various minor problems to grapple with. The removal of the martello tower was not a cause of contention given its dangerous condition and it was demolished in 1884. Any possible dispute over the Ladies' Baths was circumvented by purchasing the property from Edward Breslin and thirty new bathing boxes were built on the seaward side at a cost of £192, two reserved for the Loreto nuns. But there were vigorous disputes with the owners of the old bathing boxes over their loss of livelihood. Three women from the seafront cottages were eventually given compensation: two received £75 each, while Mrs Elizabeth Byrne, from a family that had been in the business for many years, received £200. The commissioners also decreed that no boats were to be allowed on the sea wall, but were subsequently forced to relent somewhat and permit storage north of Kelly's Baths and south of the boat house.

The new look of the sea front also gave opportunities for small improvements. A second bandstand was added, and in 1892 the commissioners decided to erect shelters, one slightly north of Montebello Terrace and the other near Marine Terrace. They also provided urinals near two of the railway bridges and the boat house. A line was drawn, however, at the idea of erecting tennis courts; presumably they were seen as likely to 'lower the tone'.

The ambitious plans for the Esplanade were hardly brought to fruition before the commissioners embarked on a fresh scheme — that for a new harbour. Hopes of building a fishing pier had been raised and then dashed in the mid 1880s, with Edward Breslin again to the fore in offering funding. But the main part of the cost would have come under the Sea Fisheries (Ireland) Act of 1883 and state funding was refused on the grounds that fishing was of little importance in Bray. There were only a score of fishermen, and in summer, at least, they had an alternative livelihood. Instead, and at much greater cost, Bray acquired a harbour, one that proved to be of very little long-term value.

The harbour with its twin encircling piers and small cast-iron lighthouse with a revolving white light was built between 1891 (the first block was laid on 13 July that year) and 1897 at a cost of some £46,000 — the township had

9.10. On the promenade; a postcard sent in 1906.

9.11. One of the pair of shelters erected by the Town Commissioners in 1892.

to borrow heavily at a time when it still owed £19,000 for the sea wall, a massive burden on the ratepayers for years afterwards. The modest return from harbour fees never recouped the cost of construction. Partly intended to make the importation of coal easier, the harbour was too shallow from the first and even with dredging could allow ships in only at high water. Where sailing boats were concerned, it was optimistically described as providing 'accommodation for boats of fair size that do not mind taking the sand between tides'. The Ordnance Survey in 1909 shows it largely choked with mud. It also quickly suffered from storm damage, which involved extra expense; fifty feet of the piling of the north pier was broken off in north-easterly gales as early as 1905 and this pier remained in bad condition during the following years. The small lighthouse was spectacularly demolished during a storm of 1957 and not replaced.

Although it did shelter colliers and employ dock workers in the winter months, it totally failed where its other possible usage was concerned — as a calling point for pleasure steamers, i.e. a substitute for a pier. In 1893, while the harbour was under construction, there was a proposal that steamers would cross the Irish Sea directly to Bray — a ship, the 'Kelvin Grove', was supposedly to be built by a Liverpool firm to run a service as soon as the harbour was finished. But for that service, or for the Liffey pleasure steamers to carry visitors from Dublin, a berth reliable at all states of the tide was required. Pleasure steamers travelled from Dublin to Wicklow harbour, sometimes with several hundred passengers, but none of these were able to call at Bray.

Tucked away out of sight of the Esplanade, the harbour has added little to the amenities of Bray's sea front and has lain largely derelict for the last fifty years. Ironically — and most unfortunately — the building of the harbour piers apparently interfered with the north–south movement of shingle along the coast. By the end of the 1930s the level of the beach at the north end of the Esplanade had fallen by some three metres due to this interference, and the sea wall, undermined, was described as being 'in such a serious danger to call for an expenditure equal to its original cost'. There was considerable damage to the wall opposite the level crossing in the winter of 1941–2 before extensive — and expensive — repairs were carried out.

While the sea front was undergoing drastic changes, the south end of Main Street was also transformed by the building of the town hall, provided for Bray by the Meath family. The family's role as ground landlords and lords of the manor was changing, but it was far from over. In some respects their role had diminished. There was less involvement in local government as the town's ratepayers sought greater powers for themselves and as the town commissioners became less traditionally minded — manorial rights were

9.12. Bray's notable Town Hall, built in English-revival style in 1882–3, is even more impressive from the side.

increasingly questioned in a more radical and nationalist society. The eleventh earl had been re-appointed chairman of the commissioners in 1870, replacing Edward Breslin, but he was one of the targets of the 1874 ratepayers' revolt and he resigned at the beginning of 1875. At the same time the family continued to show its traditional interest in the town, partly benevolent, partly in pursuit of its own concerns, and it was through this continued interest that Bray acquired a remarkable building.

The moves to build a new town hall and market house began under difficult circumstances. Lord Meath's heir, Reginald, Lord Brabazon, had returned to Ireland in 1875 after spending much of his life abroad. His father bought Ravenswell House for him in 1875, and the estate included the new Ravenswell Road alongside the Dargle, the route to the north shore, which had become neglected and a dumping place for gravel and stones. (Given that there were complaints that inhabitants of Little Bray with no sanitary facilities of their own had taken to using the lands of Ravenswell as a 'common place of convenience' after the commons were enclosed, no doubt there was the same problem in Ravenswell Road.) In 1878 Lord Brabazon took the extreme step of putting gates across Ravenswell Road, but after a public outcry the gates were forcibly removed a year later; he had little choice but to give in with as much grace as he could muster.

Lord Brabazon was not, therefore, the most popular of landowners when he wrote to the town commissioners in August 1879 to announce that he wished to erect at his own expense a covered market house at a cost not exceeding £4,000. The idea of replacing the utilitarian but uninteresting pound with a handsome structure was an inspired one. The site was in a commanding position, at the junction of three main roads and closing the view up Main Street. At the same time that part of Bray was still one of the poorer areas, not greatly touched by the urban renewal further down the street and much in need of rejuvenation.

The design for the building was equally inspired. It was entrusted to Thomas Newenham Deane and Son, leading architects of the day, and it was Thomas Manly Deane who produced the plans, with a considerable input from a fledgling architect, Edward Guy Dawber, who later had a distinguished career back in his native England. The Tudor or Old English style was fashionable, and the creation of a building of such size and with such elaborate decoration attracted much attention — in a way it was the 1880s equivalent of the Turkish Baths. Built of red brick, with black-and-white half-timbering and mullioned windows, the lower floor was at first left open for use as a market house, with a weigh house and a 'large and commodious coffee-stall'. The upper floor, reached by a stone staircase at the east side and with an open timber roof and oak chimney-pieces with carved panels, was designed to serve as Bray's council chamber and is still a familiar venue in the town.

INSCRIPTION AT MARKET HOUSE

'Who traffic here beware no strife ensue
In all your dealings be ye just and true
Let [justice] *strictly in the scale be weighed*
So shall ye call God's blessing on your trade.'
(mock Tudor inscription on the porch wall of the market house.)

Although the new town hall was presented as a gift to Bray, it came both with a layer of symbolism and with strings attached — and the strings were to be the cause of more bitter friction. Symbolism lay in the thirty stained-glass panels proudly displaying the arms of the Brabazons and their wives from Norman times onwards incorporated in the windows of the council chamber — a constant reminder to the deliberating town commissioners of the earls of Meath's long proprietorial relationship with Bray. And the highly visible new drinking fountain and water troughs at the front were given extra prominence by the crowning wyvern, a mythological winged dragon that forms part of the Brabazon coat of arms. The wyvern on the fountain has never been popular, not for the obvious reason as an emblem of the landlord, but rather because it has commonly been regarded as a 'devil'; this is still true today — blue paint was thrown over it, apparently for this reason, in 2003.

Friction broke out quickly between Lord Brabazon and the town commissioners. The gift of the town hall was used as a weapon by the eleventh earl and his son in opposing some of the draft provisions that

9.13. *Wyvern drinking fountain in front of the Town Hall. The wyvern is a replica of the original; four water troughs for horses around the base have been covered over.*

would have affected the manorial rights over the market, the Esplanade and the foreshore in the Bray Township Act of 1881 — the one that authorised the building of the sea wall. Compromises were reached over the provisions of the act, and again later after acrimonious disputes on restrictive terms that the Meath family sought to include in the lease, which divided the whole town into 'for' and 'against' camps. Although the work was completed by 1883, the first meeting of the town commissioners in their comfortable new council chamber was not held until 19 May 1884 and the market opened only in December of that year. The town hall cost Lord and Lady Brabazon £6,359, more than half as much again as was intended. But Bray acquired a public building to be proud of.

Before the century was out, an existing Main Street building was to undergo massive renovation, when £18,000 was spent on the extension of the Catholic church in 1895–7. The reconstructed church was built of granite to a design by W.H. Byrne, a prominent church architect of the day; his work includes Loughrea Cathedral, Co. Galway, and the Holy Rosary Church at Greystones. With a handsome new interior and given its present name of the Church of Our Most Holy Redeemer, it has continued to dominate the centre of Main Street. The new organ was inaugurated on 24 August 1913 with an organ recital and a choir of fifty.

Within a short space of time the Holy Redeemer's position was further enhanced by the long-awaited opening of Florence Road. Whether it had always been intended that this east–west street would reach Main Street directly opposite the church is not clear. The earliest projected lines suggest that it would have broken through some way to the south. The final line, dependent upon the purchase of two properties numbered nos 13 and 14 Main Street (the numbers are still missing from the sequence) involved slight changes of direction which takes Florence Road out of a straight course. At any rate, even if the positioning is largely fortuitous, it is a happy one, giving an impressive view of the church from the east. After some years of vacillation, the necessary properties were purchased and both they and six cottages in McCormack's Avenue were demolished. Florence Road was opened in May 1902. A plaque dated 1903 marks the completion of the building on its south-west corner.

During all this period the day-to-day role of the town commissioners was to remedy problems and to maintain standards, a role continued into the twentieth century after Bray became an urban district in 1899. In the early 1870s there were complaints about the way in which the town was run by the commissioners, including accusations that the rates were too high and that too much was being spent on improvements that benefited only certain individuals. After what has been described as a 'ratepayers' revolt', a number of new representatives intent on reform were elected in 1874.

'RATEPAYERS' REVOLT': CONCERNS ABOUT LOCAL GOVERNMENT

> *'We have received a copy of a circular which has been issued to the ratepayers of Bray inviting their attention to the manner in which the affairs of that township have been administered by the local governing body. The circular begins with a reference to the "enormous increase in the taxation", which now amounts to 3s. 6d., the heaviest impost, we are told, laid upon any town in Ireland. The bad lighting and watering of the streets is the next subject of comment. We are told the constant blowing of dust injures the goods of the traders and annoys visitors, while the lamps, "by a curious arrangement," are totally extinguished during the entire Bray season, when the town is full of strangers and it is most important that it should be made bright and attractive.'*
> (*Freeman's Journal* 7 October 1874)

The existing problems were not easy to solve, however, and deficiencies in the water supply continued to exercise the commissioners' minds as the ratepayers protested loudly about high costs and a supply inadequate for the seasonal needs of a resort town. The International Hotel and the Loreto Convent were already suffering water shortages, and in desperation the township engineer was ordered in 1877 to organise a house-to-house inspection of water taps to check waste. The supply was described as falling short by 30,000 gallons a day and in one summer season the water was turned off from 5 to 11 p.m. 'almost daily', while later it was turned off overnight — situations that neither hoteliers and landladies nor their guests can have found easy to cope with. In desperation the commissioners even contemplated drawing water from the mill race. It took almost thirty years from the time water first flowed in the taps until Dublin Corporation was able to announce in January 1894 that, since the Roundwood reservoir had been improved, 'Bray would be placed on a continuous supply'.

NOTICE.

The Bray Township Commissioners hereby give Notice that in the event of persons using this Fountain, causing or permitting a Waste of Water, the Supply will be cut off.

Persons found leaving the Water turned on after using the Fountain, washing carts, or otherwise causing waste, will be prosecuted for recovery of legal Penalty, £5, as in such cases provided.

BY ORDER,

P. M'DONNELL,

Town Clerk.

Town Hall, Bray

24th June, 1893.

9.14. *Water shortage poster, 1898.*

In the early 1870s the main sewerage system was not yet complete and there were no sewers in Little Bray; even a decade later Bray's sanitary officer was to report that many properties north of the river remained without 'the necessary sanitary accommodation'. In the town centre Church Terrace, Hudson's Terrace, Pound Lane and Purcell's Field were particularly singled out for condemnation (Hudson's Terrace was supplied with 'privies and ash pits' in 1877). In 1879 the commissioners received a strong letter complaining about the insanitary state of the south end of the beach, while Dock Terrace was still without a sewer in 1888 when Edward Breslin, as owner, finally agreed to provide one. There were still houses near the Town Hall without any sanitation in 1901 when their owner, pressed to take action, tried to persuade the commissioners that an earth closet for each house would be sufficient.

Bray's gas supply was still insecure given that the gas works was vulnerable to easterly gales, and again there were many complaints about the cost and quality of the gas. There were also complaints about the limited times of public lighting, and that some of the street lamps were on occasion left unlighted. One request was for the lamps to remain on until midnight and the arrival of the last train and until 'late' for major events — evidently Bray at night was a rather dark and dismal place. The gas works met its end in 1877, when it was finally destroyed in a storm. The Alliance Gas Company opened a new works on the landward side of the railway in 1880 and this at least secured and improved the supply — a supply that was soon, however, to have a rival.

ELECTRICITY ARRIVES IN BRAY

> *'ELECTRIC LIGHT IN BRAY*
> *The electric lighting of Bray has become* un fait accompli, *and the Brighton of Ireland has taken the lead of the townships in the matter of improved illuminants. The other night the dynamos were set to work, and a current was sent through the vast network of connecting wires and cables that underlie the roads, and for the first time since its formation Bray was seen in the glare of the mysterious illuminating agent. Some of the lamps did not light on account possibly of defects in the connections, but the majority of them burned with considerable brilliancy. The four main roads surrounded the township are supplied with arc lamps, and the back portions are illuminated by means of the ordinary Edison Swan incandescent lamps, which are a decided improvement on the gas lamp method of street-lighting. The electric system will be turned over to the Township Commissioners in the course of a few days.'*
> (*Wicklow Newsletter* 23 July 1892)

The first electric lights blazed on the Esplanade in 1886, when electricity was generated in the gas works and sixteen of the street lights were converted. The rest of Bray had to wait until 1892, when an electricity works was opened in the former corn mill, and all the street lights were switched over. The Carlisle Grounds were soon able to boast of 'coloured electric lights' at evening band and fireworks performances. The electricity works was originally a commercial venture by the Bray Electric Light Company, but it quickly proved unsuccessful and the town commissioners reluctantly bought it from liquidators in 1896. This was, of course, a sound move; the demand rose steadily, and although there were only 66 consumers when the commissioners took over there were 230 a decade later. Money was immediately spent on putting the works into good order and a new chimney shaft was added.

The commissioners were also responsible for lesser improvements, such as the street name plates that were erected for the first time in the autumn of 1885. They continued to look across the Irish Sea for guidance on the necessary standards to set, for example by obtaining copies of the byelaws for Brighton and for Llandudno in North Wales. And small details of seaside life in Bray in the last decades of the nineteenth century emerge from the record of their deliberations. The Bray car men, of whom there were by this time more than a hundred, were constantly taking up more spaces than they were allowed at the various car stands. They were liable to charge more than the official fares, and unlicenced cabbies from Kingstown came and 'poached' passengers on bank holiday weekends — which at least suggests that Bray was the more popular venue on such dates. The numbers involved could be large; there were an extra thirty-seven car owners, unlicensed, on Whit Monday 1880. The drivers also had to be discouraged from washing their vehicles, and no doubt their horses, at the public fountains, causing both an inconvenience and a waste of the precious water supply.

CAR DRIVERS: 'DISORDERLY MEN'

'A letter was received from a hackney car driver, of Bray, named Doyle, who complained that in consequence of the regulations of the commissioners in reference to car-drivers not being sufficiently enforced, the disorderly men who never kept their places on the hazards could make as much money as they liked, and the orderly men were starving. The Chairman said they ought to be obliged to Mr. Doyle for his letter. From his own observation he would characterise the conduct of the Bray carmen as a disgrace to any civilised country. On last Sunday there were about twenty of them during the hours of public worship playing pitch-and-toss on the Esplanade or riding donkeys with their faces to the tails, he supposed practising for the new game of polo. Such a state of things should be put an end to. The board inspector, having been summoned, stated that he was preparing summonses against all the men mentioned in Mr Doyle's letter. He was directed to issue the summonses, and to call on Mr. Doyle as a witness.'
(*Freeman's Journal* 21.7.1874)

The owners of bathing boxes and fishing boats also disregarded regulations and operated wherever they pleased along the Esplanade. The decrepit state of the bathing boxes came in for frequent criticism — their condition was hardly improved by exposure on the Esplanade through the winter, since all efforts of the commissioners to have them stored elsewhere were stoutly resisted. There were regular problems with the unauthorised removal of sand and gravel from the beach — one of the causes of the erosion that had made the Esplanade so vulnerable — and both the town commissioners and the railway company had to take measures from time to time. The 'filthy state' of the portion of the beach south of the Esplanade was also a problem, with blame laid on the cottages opposite.

BATHING BOXES: NEED FOR STORAGE

> *'With reference to the bathing boxes lying on the Esplanade, Mr Breslin offered a place for their storage on the private roadway at the east side of the Carlisle Grounds. The secretary was directed to write to the owners of the boxes requesting their removal to this place.'*
> (*Freeman's Journal* 22 November 1881)

EDWARD BRESLIN PRAISED

> *'BRAY AMUSEMENTS COMMITTEE*
> *The annual meeting of the Amusements Committee was held on Thursday evening in the Town Hall. ... Mr Dufresne proposed a vote of thanks to Mr Edward Breslin, J.P., for his generosity in lending the Carlisle Grounds for their amusement during the last year. Without Mr Breslin's assistance it would be very hard for the committee to so successfully cater for the amusement of the townspeople and visitors. Mr Langton seconded the motion, which was passed unanimously. Mr Breslin, in returning thanks, said he had been 40 years working for beautiful Bray, and he was glad to see it improving every day, and when he was dead Bray would be a prosperous town and he would like above all things that the name of Breslin would live in Bray after his death (hear, hear, and applause).'*
> (*Wicklow Newsletter* 7 May 1892)

Obstruction was a theme in Main Street: shop owners were liable to spill out their wares, including clothes and furniture, onto the pavements; men congregated in numbers at the 'hiring corners' at the junction of Main Street and Quinsborough Road, and along Bray Bridge, as they did well into the twentieth century. By the end of the century pedestrians faced a new hazard as cyclists chose footpaths rather than the gravelled and no doubt pot-holed road surfaces. The first motor cars arrived and required regulating — little could the commissioners foresee that some seventy years later this new means of transport was to contribute to the demise of the seaside resort as they knew it.

All the while Bray was putting a brave face on its underlying difficulties. The season was comparatively short, from June to September, and typical wet summer weather did not help — small attendances at events such as flower shows were often blamed on the weather.

THE WEATHER

> *BAND AT BRAY. - Last evening the band of the Dublin Metropolitan Police performed on the Esplanade from 7.30 to 9.30. The evenings are now getting late for an open air band after 8.30, and in consequence the attendances are growing small by degrees and beautifully less."*
> (*Freeman's Journal* 23 August 1884)
>
> *'It was a damp, dark December, with rain and wind nearly every day. Bray Head was rarely without a cap of grey cloud, and a restless pack of waves mouthing and leaping at its foot. The Esplanade was a mile-long vista of soaked grass and glistening asphalt, whereon the foot of man apparently never trod; once or twice a storm had charged it from the south-east, and had hurled sheets of spray and big stones onto it, and pounded holes in the concrete of its sea-wall. There had been such a storm the week before Christmas. The breakers had rushed upon the long beach with a "broad-flung, shipwrecking roar,' and the windows of the houses along the Esplanade were dimmed with salt and sand.'*
> (E. Œ. Somerville and Martin Ross, *The real Charlotte*. London, 1894, p. 365)

Attempts were made to extend the season and promote the town as a health-giving winter resort, comparing it to English south-coast resorts such as Brighton and Torquay. But this was not a valid comparison. Brighton and Torquay, particularly the latter, had a milder climate than London and caught the best of the winter sunshine — they were desirable places in which to escape the 'pea-souper' winter fogs of the English capital. Bray's east-coast climate was little warmer and drier than that of Dublin and there were disadvantages, as we have already seen, in having a sea front facing into easterly gales.

The International Hotel was constantly struggling to stay in business. It was for sale or to let a number of times and its rateable valuation was reduced

9.15. *Bray Railway Station on a quiet evening* c. *1900, as seen from the International Hotel. Note the cab shelter facing the station entrance.*

9.16. *The impressive bulk of the International Hotel belied its many financial problems. Jaunting cars and a vis-à-vis (bottom right) wait for passengers. (Lawrence Collection, courtesy National Library of Ireland)*

by stages from £455 in 1863 to £260 twenty-five years later. Taken over by Charles Dufresne in 1875, it was under the control of several English hotel managers, including one from Margate and another from London, but it remained a white elephant, expensive to run, and with too few 'up-market' visitors. (The prices seem to have been high — 4s. 6d for dinner in the 1870s, compared with Dublin prices of 4s. at the Shelbourne Hotel or 3s 6d at the

Gresham.) *Thom's directory* for 1900 listed it as vacant and, although it managed to reopen for the season, that August there were only forty-three guests spread through its original two hundred bedrooms.

> *'INTERNATIONAL HOTEL, BRAY.–The manager begs to inform tourists and visitors to Bray that there is a table d'hote dinner at 6.30 o'clock p.m. on each day in this first-class hotel; price 4s 6d, inclusive of attendance.'*
> (*Freeman's Journal* 28 July 1876)

INTERNATIONAL HOTEL

> *'BRAY ASSEMBLY ROOMS. — The visitor to Bray is not likely to be impressed with any favourable opinion of the town if his first impressions are taken from the building bearing the above name. It seems to be devoted to ruin and neglect. Standing in one of the leading thoroughfares, it is a perfect eye-sore. The stunted trees surrounding the building are united by cords, on which are displayed a variety of household linen for the purpose of attracting the attention of the passer-by to the building. A number of fowl are also busy in obliterating all signs of regularity or order that might remain. The several divisions of the building are let to three or four religious sects, but the idea of cleanliness being akin to anything good seems to be beyond their teachings. The worshippers attending at the different wings are quite independent of one another, as each has effected a separate entrance through the dilapidated hedge which runs in front, and the wire fencing may be regarded as a trap to the unwary passer-by. It is to be hoped that the Town Commissioners will take measures for the protection of the public and the cleanliness and appearance of the township.'*
> (*Freeman's Journal* 16 February 1877)

STATE OF ASSEMBLY ROOMS

Breslin's Royal Marine Hotel also had its valuation reduced in the 1870s, and although Lacy's Bray Head Hotel was extended several times the Lacy family, too, seem to have overreached themselves and their hotel went bankrupt in 1897. Findlaters' grocery chain acquired the Royal Hotel at the turn of the century but apparently had no better luck; in 1910 its hotel businesses were declared in the *Investor's Guardian* to be 'a total loss to the company'.

The former Turkish Baths, now the Assembly Rooms, provided a valuable facility for both visitors and locals, with concerts, operatic

9.17. *Lacy's Bray Head Hotel (centre) and Fontenoy Terrace (left), with surviving fishermen's cottages at the extreme right, c. 1910. The message on the back of this postcard, written in July 1912, reads: 'We are at Bray now, this is a lovely place, very lively, we have had a splendid holiday, sorry the time is passing so quick.'*

9.18. *Edwardian style inside Lacy's hotel.*

performances and balls; by the early 1900s they were also used for boxing matches. Both Percy French and the cockney singer Albert Chevalier performed there in the summer of 1902. During the winter months the premises were home to the Bray Philharmonic Society's concerts, with special late trains back to Dublin. There was said to be seating for 750. But there were complaints at least once about the neglected state of the grounds, a 'perfect eyesore' with a dilapidated hedge out over the pavement and roving fowl. There were complaints, too, about the poorly-kept state of

THE BETHELL HOTELS, Ltd.

International Hotel, Bray.

100 Rooms. Splendid Situation. Re-decorated
30 minutes by rail from Dublin. and
15 ,, ,, ,, Kingstown. Re-furnished.

EXCELLENT CUISINE AND WINES.

Terms from 7/6 per day.

Bray Head Hotel, Bray.

60 Rooms. Facing Sea. Situated under Bray Head, and commanding magnificent views of Dublin Bay. 15 minutes by rail from Kingstown.

RE-MODELLED, RE-DECORATED & RE-FURNISHED.
SANITARY ARRANGEMENTS NEW.

Terms from 7/6 per day.
TARIFF AND FURTHER PARTICULARS SENT ON APPLICATION.

Marine Station Hotel, Bray.

50 Rooms. Facing the Sea.

Up-to-date in every respect.

Terms from 9/- per day.
TARIFF ON APPLICATION.

9.19. Three prominent Bray hotels in 1910 as advertised in Porter's directory. *Although the smallest, the former Royal Marine Hotel was the most expensive.*

the station forecourt and at one point Edward Breslin was forced to take a legal action against the lessee of the Carlisle Grounds for 'dilapidation'.

A creditable number of good houses were added on the new suburban roads between 1870 and 1910, but many of their residents would have returned to Dublin during the winter. Other houses remained summer lets only and the static state of the properties on Strand Road is an indication of the lack of Bray's evolution as a resort. There was little or no renewal and only a limited number of commercial premises to cater for the wants of the visitor. In many British resorts by the end of the nineteenth century the sea front was lined with four- and five-storey hotels and boarding houses, those nearest to the town centre often with shops on the ground floor.

The sea front at Douglas presented, as it still does, an unbroken sweeping curve of tall terraced properties mostly built after 1880; by 1900 Douglas had over a thousand hotels and boarding houses and catered for over 300,000 visitors a year, mainly from northern England and Scotland. Bray businessmen could only look across the water with envy.

While the sea wall and Esplanade stand as a permanent memorial to the achievements against the odds of late nineteenth-century Bray, the image of

9.20. Will C. Pepper's White Coons performing on the small bandstand.

life in the resort before the first world war is more fragmentary. Despite its difficulties, at the height of summer Bray was a busy place. As crossing the Irish Sea became speedier and more comfortable, so more holiday-makers came from Britain. Crowds of day trippers spilled out of the trains and looked for diversion. Many visitors, the men wearing jackets and hats or caps, the ladies also hatted, with long sleeves and carrying sunshades, sat on the sea wall or the grass, while others strolled along the front. On bank holidays the Esplanade could be 'black with people'.

Early photographs and postcards give an aura of prim respectability to these holiday-makers, different from the cheerful seaside cards of the mid-twentieth century. Exposure to the sun's rays was still not part of the pleasures of the seaside; for that, another revolution in thinking would be necessary. Brown skins were regarded as a sign of manual work in the open air and as such distinctly lower class; a pale complexion was a sign of social superiority and was essential for ladies. In any case hat wearing out-of-doors was de rigueur at all levels of society and the custom could not be frivolously put aside.

GOOD FRIDAY ON THE COAST

'KINGSTOWN AND BRAY INTELLIGENCE.
GOOD FRIDAY ON THE COAST. — The fineness of the weather yesterday attracted unusually large numbers of excursionists from the city to the places of interest in Bray and its neighbourhood. The bay between Killiney and Bray was dotted with boating parties, and crowds betook themselves to those favourite trysting places — The Dargle, the Glen of the Downs, Powerscourt Waterfall, and Deerpark. A large party of the members of the Cyclists' Touring Club came en masse *on their machines to spend the day at Bray. The fields on Bray Head were covered with pic-nic parties, and the Esplanade was thronged with people. Kingstown detained many pleasure-seekers, and the picturesque Dalkey Sound was crossed by large numbers. A roulette man set up a table at Bray and was soon doing a flourishing trade. One young man laid on the colours to the amount of seven and six pence, and lost, then laid a half sovereign, and the ball falling on his colour won. On his claiming the money, a friend of the table-keeper came up and argued the point, while the latter bundled up his table and decamped. He, however, was arrested and taken before a magistrate. By way of compromise the money was refunded, and the roulette men agreed to leave the locality.'*
(*Freeman's Journal* 12 April 1884)

On the Esplanade the military and police bands in their smart uniforms set the tone and drew the crowds; by the 1880s there were three band performances a week; Monday afternoon in the bandstand at the north end, Wednesday and Friday in the one in the centre. There were no band performances on Sundays — the idea was turned down by the commissioners at least once.

Other kinds of musical entertainment became widespread on seaside promenades by the end of the century, with the advent of concert parties and pierrot shows performing the popular songs of the day. Pierrots, in their distinctive white suits decorated with pom-poms, became all the rage in the 1890s. (According to some sources visitors to Bray in the summer of 1891 were the very first in Ireland and Britain to be entertained by a pierrot troupe, that of Clifford Essex, a singer and banjo player still commemorated in a make of banjo that bears his name; it seems more certain, however, that his troupe's performance was at Henley-on-Thames.) In some resorts performers used a portable stage, or, if wet, they retreated under the pier. In Bray performances took place on one or another of the Esplanade's bandstands; old photographs show an audience largely standing, rather than seated in deckchairs as might have been expected.

LETTER FROM THE TROUBADOURS

'To the town Commissioners, Bray. Gentlemen,

We respectfully beg to make application to give our morning concerts at the south end of the Ladies Baths, as so many Ladies find it such a distance to walk to our present pavilion, which is almost at the extreme end of the Esplanade.

In order to protect the pathways, we would have proper bridge-covers made, to use when crossing, or with your kind permission we would with pleasure pay the expense of having a gateway fixed which would then not necessitate us crossing any of the pathways. Our reason for trespassing on your valuable time is simply a desire to do our best to please all the visitiors to Bray and at the same time benefit ourselves.

We should also be grateful if you would allow us to sing alternatively with the Band on Wednesdays and Fridays, as in the Carlisle Grounds. We should in no way interfere with the Band, but simply sing during their ordinary intervals.

We remain, Gentlemen, your obedient servants, "The Troubadours"'

(Letter 3 August 1895, courtesy Bray Heritage Centre)

SUNDAY EXCURSIONS AND SEASIDE SINGERS

'KINGSTOWN SUNDAY EXCURSIONS.–The Kingstown Sunday season, which has for some time back been in full swing, exhibits no symptoms of decline. To-day the greater part of the inhabitants of Dublin seemed to precipitate themselves into Westland-row, thence to be poured out in a never-ending stream along the coast. Every station from Booterstown to Bray had its crowd of visitors. All day the pleasant plash of waters was heard at the various bathing places along the line, as bather after bather plunged into the inviting waves. Gay parties strolled over the smooth sands of Sandymount, and through the shady avenues of Blackrock. At Kingstown the snowy-sailed yachts flitted in and out of harbour like cheerful ghosts ; while all day long the brilliant tide of fashion slowly ebbed and flowed upon the pier. At Dalkey, the boatman's sterotyped inquiry–"Going out for an hour, sir?" met with a ready affirmative, and white oars dipped harmoniously into the gleaming water, and crabs were caught and Sunday toilettes damaged, according to the nautical proficiency of the pleasure seekers. The Esplanade at Bray was crowded, and even the dark and silent old Head was gay with fluttering muslin and ribbons, and noisy with cheerful laughter.'
(*Freeman's Journal* 3.8.1874)

'The proposal to boycott seaside singers, which has been strenuously adovated in some quarters seems undignified. To revenge ourselves on these poor strolling musicians for our inability to arrange affairs to our liking, reminds one of the fable of the dog in the manger. Take Bray, for instance. In the fashionable quarters alluded to a dead set has been made on the White Coons, a clever and harmless troupe, who have sucessfully entertained hundreds of people for several successive seasons. By all means have the artistic element purified and elevated … it is another matter to attempt to injure unoffending persons in the pursuit of their professions. The only result hitherto is that the Bray UDC have raised their rent charge on the White Coons and the Crescendos to a degree which is almost prohibitive. I hope the council will see their way to reduce their charges, which are simply preposterous.'
(*Irish Tourist*, vol. viii, no. 5, 1901, p. 3)

The Troubadours performed in Bray in the 1890s, and there were three concert parties on the Esplanade in 1900. One of these, 'Will C. Pepper's White Coons', came to Bray for the season every year from about 1899. (The term 'coon' did not have a particularly racial connotation; one meaning was 'a sly, knowing fellow'. The popular 'black-faced minstrels' were a distinct group.) An English concert party of four men and at different times one or more women, dressed all in white as was typical, they sang on the south bandstand by the Esplanade Hotel on Wednesday and Saturday afternoons, apparently moved to this minor bandstand because of their act was considered to be in dubious taste. There were also apparently attempts to banish them altogether by raising the rent that they paid to Bray Urban District Council for use of the Esplanade; the *Irish Tourist* commented in 1901 that the White Coons were a 'clever and harmless troupe' and the rent charged was 'simply preposterous'.

By 1909 the Coons had moved to the Assembly Rooms, where their performances were put on four nights a week, despite one censure that they were 'considered by many as ridiculous, uninteresting, and in some cases not edifying'. This was their last year; in 1910 they said that the Bray season was not sufficiently profitable, and apparently moved to Clacton pier in south-east England. Will Knott's troupe of pierrots served to fill the gap; there were also at different times, among others, the Harcourt and Gilbert Troupe, the George Rapley's Troupe, the Crescendos and Maddock's Merrie Men. In twentieth-century Bray popular entertainment, rather than stately military bands and operatic singers, would take centre stage. To some these would seem no more than the pastimes of a 'vulgar seaside resort'.

A boat trip was a popular amusement, at least in calm weather, and the boat races and regattas provided excitement and vicarious pleasure in the waves. The two-day regattas held each August involved more than water events. A typical example included on the one hand 'Yacht Races, Sailing & Rowing Matches, Swimming Contests, &c.' with a 'Grand Aquatic Carnival' and on the other tugs of war, bands, switchback and hobby horses, open-air concerts by 'operatic artists' and a fireworks display each evening, all subsidised by the Amusements Committee — in 1910 the event had a budget of £400. An enclosure was set up on the Esplanade, so that for a shilling it was possible to watch in relative comfort and without having to lean on the seawall railings with the rest of the spectators.

Donkey rides were introduced to Bray at some time before 1874, a classic seaside experience and a key part of a childhood holiday until within living memory. Their arrival marks part of the change to the idea of the seaside as a place for frivolous pleasures as much as for worthy ones. In 1878 the organisers of Bray horse racing leased a course at Coolagad near Greystones, and a race meeting was held there in August of that year, although it had to be briefly postponed because of bad weather which would not have helped attendance. There were dog shows and flower shows and Bray Industrial Exhibition was held annually in the late 1880s and 1890s either in the Town Hall or in Ravenswell House. By the end of the century visitors — of the right sort — could play nine holes of golf at Bray Golf Club or cricket and lawn tennis in the County Club in Newtown Vevay. There was badminton in winter in the International Hotel, the Bray Harriers to follow, and fishing in the Dargle River. Access to Bray Head for walkers was improved with the opening of the imposingly named Grand Marine Park (later known as Bray Head Park) in 1896; the railway company had repaired the roadways and paths, built new fences and added seats before handing their property over to the town commissioners.

There were occasional unexpected excitements. In September 1872 a train boiler exploded in Bray station, killing the driver and fireman and causing some damage. As disasters tend to do, this drew crowds. Three years later there was an even more spectacular accident. The 1st Reserve Squadron of the British Fleet was cruising off the east coast and dropped anchor in Dublin Bay; when it set sail on 1 September there was a collision in dense fog eleven miles off Bray Head between the battleships HMS Iron Duke and HMS Vanguard. The Vanguard, built only five years before, sank in nineteen fathoms of water with her top mastheads protruding at an angle above the waves. The pleasure steamers that circled the site in September 1875 enjoyed the excitement of the salvage operations, with naval vessels and Admiralty divers sent over from England. The masts and rigging were removed, the hull remains offshore to this day. And it was not only the British fleet that sailed into Dublin Bay, in May 1902 Bray holidaymakers must have gazed in awe at the visiting German Naval Squadron as it sailed by.

> *'The Vanguard lies at this moment fathoms deep under the waves off Bray Head, on the coast of Ireland, sunk with all her stores, great guns, munitions, equipment, tackle and gear. ... we have here lost from the strength of our national fleet, at a time too, when we can ill afford it, one of the grandest and finest warships which her majesty owned. Indeed the Vanguard was one of the 11 best ships we had for foreign naval warfare.'*
> (*Daily Telegraph* 3 September 1875)

THE VANGUARD

Ladies, of course, had their baths, conveniently close to the railway station; bathing for men remained more haphazard. Naylor's Cove at Bray

Head, with conveniently deep water and still fondly remembered, was the men's preserve in the nineteenth century, although even there problems of modesty could arise from the presence of women. For several summers a temporary gentlemen's bathing place was set up on the Esplanade, but this ran at a loss and was not continued; even after 1900 the 'inadequate bathing facilities' for men exercised the minds of the authorities.

Bathing. 'I can well remember a time when the men would have thought it strange to don a bathing suit for their dip, and they were kept a very considerable distance from women bathers. A tall pole separated the two areas, and a no-man's land of a hundred and fifty yards stretched to either side of the pole.

The women's attire for swimming was not very practical, being upon the whole more voluminous than is now adjudged necessary for ordinary attire. The colour was generally a kind of red, and amorphous masses of what looked like old red sandstone cleft the waves. Nor did the wearers venture far out of their depth. For the most part, the shore was shriekingly fringed with what might well have been boiled lobsters engaged in a Lewis Carroll dance.'

(letter, *The Irish Times* 11 June 1931; reprinted 11 June 2001)

BATHING AT BRAY

'BATHING AT BRAY: TO THE EDITOR, August 25.

Sir, — The hot weather we now enjoy naturally increases the number of bathers, and bring into prominence the great indecency with which this healthful and refreshing practice is indulged in this country. At Bray, for instance, the public pathway around the head goes within 50 or 60 yards of the men's bathing place, the bathers are unclothed, and all day long women of every age and degree are passing backwards and forwards along the path. At Killiney, within 60 yards of the railway, men are to be seen in the same unclothed condition bathing in numbers up to nine o'clock in the morning, and occasionally during the day, when the beach is covered with women and children; they bathe in close proximity to them. Youths of 12 to 15 years of age actually bathe among the women. … In the absence of any regulations, the bathing and beach frequenting public are accustoming themselves to a brutal disregard of ordinary decency. [signed] MODEST.'

(*Freeman's Journal* 27 August 1883)

But by this time the debate was becoming an academic one — bathing mores were changing in the freer spirit of Edwardian times. By 1904 there were complaints that ladies were 'bathing off the promenade' and by late summer 1906 the tenant of the Ladies' Baths was asking Bray Urban District Council for a rebate on her year's rent because she was losing money now that 'free bathing [was] being sanctioned along the foreshore for a portion of the season'; she was allowed a 40% reduction. One councillor expressed strong opposition to mixed bathing on moral grounds, a local expression of a view that was held more generally by church authorities.

Visitors met inconveniences. On Sundays they had to contend with open-air preachers, sometimes accompanied by brass bands. There were peddlers and organ grinders, popular with some, anathema to others. If they elected to take a drive into the country, they were liable to be mobbed by jarvies touting for custom outside the railway station. Fine weather — when it came — meant that clouds of dust swirled into the air, particularly on the Esplanade and Quinsborough Road, while to reach the sea by any route other than Quinsborough Road involved risking a splashing by oily water dripping off the underside of the railway bridges.

'... parties causing annoyance by singing hymns or preaching on the Esplanade to be removed or summoned.'
(Bray Township Commissioners minutes 21 July 1884)

INCONVENIENCES: OPEN-AIR PREACHERS

'TOURIST INVASION. — Tourists still continue to arrive at Kingstown and Bray in numbers that are continually increasing. All the hotels, Royal Marine, Breslin's and International are crowded. Wearied American tourists arriving late at night and being unable to procure a bed, are incidents of almost daily occurrence.'
(*Freeman's Journal* 23 August 1884)

TOURIST INVASION

These were only minor problems. Bray offered a good day's outing, one that as the nineteenth century came to an end could increasingly be taken advantage of as bank holidays and subsequently annual holidays for the workers became the norm. On Whit Monday 1894, for instance, the *Wicklow Newsletter* reported that there were 20,000 day trippers in Bray — an

9.21. Bicycles added a new means of reaching Bray and in this postcard the rack is fully occupied, c. 1910.

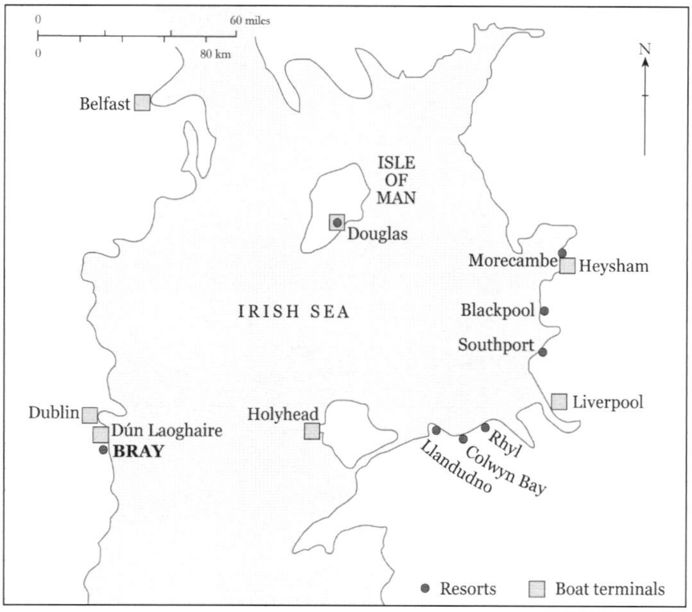

9.22. Main seaside resorts around the Irish Sea; Liverpool and Holyhead were the ferry terminals for Dublin and Kingstown (Dún Laoghaire).

astonishing figure if correct — and that 1,200 pints of stout were sold by early evening in one establishment alone. (In 1904 there were forty-nine licensed houses in Bray, including twenty-eight 7-day premises.) The arrival of the bicycle added a new kind of visitor, out for healthy exercise in Wicklow but not adverse to refreshment stops; there were even cycle polo matches and fancy-dress cycle parades in the Carlisle Grounds. In May 1901 a patient newspaper reporter counted 182 bicycles outside the Royal Hotel and a contemporary postcard shows a rack fully occupied on the Esplanade.

Bray was so busy at the Whit weekend of 1904 that supplies of bread were said to be at a premium.

The social mix of the visitors was changing; inexpensive amusements and public houses flourished rather than luxury hotels; there were complaints that the 'trippers' were noisy and in the early 1900s extra R.I.C. men were being drafted in on bank holidays — though at Whitsun 1902, at least, their presence was 'wholly needless'.

Four miles down the coast, Greystones was emerging even before the end of the nineteenth century as a small but fashionable seaside resort, drawing away some of the visitors who were looking for peace and quiet. A satirical magazine of the time, *The Leader*, somewhat unkindly described Bray as full of trippers putting on 'airs' in an atmosphere of 'real waves and imitation quality'. And whereas in 1870 only the comfortably off could manage a fortnight or a month at the seaside — a mark of their prosperity — increasingly, too, this became open to a wider market, both from Ireland and from Britain. In the early years of the twentieth century the numbers of Scottish and English workers spending their holidays in Bray swelled, in an annual invasion that presaged the role that the resort was to play between and after the two world wars.

9.23. *Bray and its surroundings, 1898 (Ordnance Survey of Ireland, original scale 1:63360).*

9.24. *Main Street looking south, c. 1880.*

QUEEN VICTORIA'S JUBILEE

'THE NATIONS LOYALTY.
THE CELEBRATIONS IN THE COUNTRY.
BRAY The Royal Marine Hotel (Breslin's) displayed a magnificent Royal Standard and a Danish flag. On the International Hotel, Mr Dufresne ran up the Red Ensign, and at Mouillot's Hotel, Mrs Tickell hung out the Union Jack. On the highest peak at Bray Head was another Royal Standard, erected by Mr W G Morris, whose flagstaff on the hill above his house was also dressed with bunting. Many thousands of people took advantage of the general holiday to enjoy the true Queen's weather of this brilliant day at Kingstown, Bray, and other places along the coast, and were rewarded, as they returned late in the evening, by a view as splendid as could possibly be conceived, for, at a given signal, a semi-circle of bonfires, extending from every peak of Bray Head, over both the Sugar-loaf mountains by Charleville and Powerscourt and ending on the summit at Katty Gallagher, burst forth with a glow which proclaimed in unmistakeable terms the fervour of the loyalty which exists in Wicklow and Dublin.
(*Wicklow Newsletter* 25 June 1887)

'As the summer time draws on, the higher families of Rathmines go down to Greystones, a seaside resort, which they have made so specially their own, that it is sometimes called Rathmines-by-the-sea. Greystones lies some miles south of Bray, another watering place, once indeed supposed to have been fashionable, but now sadly desecrated by Dubliners, Irishry in general, and even English tourists. The superior classes of Rathmines consider that Greystones is to Bray what Rathmines itself is to Dublin... .'
(*The Leader* 11 May 1901)

'... we notice that many showed themselves off on the grass between the road and the Esplanade. They, perhaps, were the "Real McCoy" of Bray, just too good for the Esplanade, and not yet feeling fit to venture on the sacred soil of Rathmines-super-Mare [Greystones] *further south. The air at Bray on Sunday was very good, and we could not feel sorry that we spent a few hours looking at real waves and imitation quality.'*
(*The Leader* 17 August 1901)

'REAL WAVES AND IMITATION QUALITY': THE SOCIAL MIX

9.25. *Bray,* c. *1910; the message on the postcard back reads 'We are having a lovely time, have just returned after a refreshing swim'.*

ENGLISH WORKERS HOLIDAY IN BRAY

> Postcard to Staffordshire address
> *'Just a line to say we are having nice weather and enjoying ourselves first rate. We had a ride today on a jaunting car, about 24 mls. Grand scenery through the Dargle Glen, and Lord Powerscourt's estate. Saw a waterfall 300 feet high. We went to the church on the left (Presbyterian). There are plenty of churches and lots of parsons here. We had a walk round Bray Head to Greystones, road about 200 ft above sea.'*
> (Bray, August 1907)

Bray residents had good cause to be proud of the town's development between 1850 and 1910. But despite early hopes the resort was not in the long run to be another Brighton, patronised by the wealthy, rather was it to join the company of the smaller seaside resorts around the Irish Sea: Morecambe on the Lancashire coast; Rhyl, Colwyn Bay and Llandudno in North Wales. And for all the British resorts and for Bray the era of the bucket and spade holiday, with more freedom and more emphasis on keeping the children happy, was just around the corner.

Chapter 10

'Bray, beautiful Bray': Bray in 1910

> *'Bray, beautiful Bray, is a remarkably well-built town, health and pleasure resort and fashionable watering place … . The chief industry consists in the attendance on visitors during the season in the hotels, furnished houses, boarding and lodging houses. It is computed that at least 350 people are engaged in this occupation, and at least 150 car drivers are employed in the summer.'*
>
> (Frank Porter, *Porter's post office guide and directory of the County Wicklow 1910*, Dublin [1910], pp 2–3)

By 1910 Bray had passed through almost sixty years of post-railway development, some rapid, some less so, and physically it had become recognisable as the town we know today. It was, of course, much smaller, with green fields close to Main Street and many vacant lots along the new roads, but it had already taken on the general outline that it was to retain until the explosive suburban expansion of the last part of the twentieth century. Again, it was captured at a moment in time by the Ordnance Survey in 1909, in a map published at twenty-five inches to the mile two years later. And in the space of a decade there were three new books that prominently featured Bray: local pharmacist Arthur L. Doran's *Bray and environs*, Frank Porter's *Porter's post office guide and directory of the County Wicklow*, and best known, Canon G.D. Scott's erudite and imaginative story of its early history in *The stones of Bray*.

Porter's guide, the most factual, lists a hundred and thirty Bray residents, the majority of them women, who let 'apartments' — i.e. rooms — to visitors. This was a widely popular kind of seaside holiday and many of the houses concerned were small ones that could take only one family at a time: twelve of the sixteen houses in Brennan's Parade, three houses in Church Terrace, some of the cottages on Strand Road near Bray Head. But houses of varying sizes all across Bray offered rooms to rent, although there were only a handful in Little Bray.

10.1. Bray sea front from a postcard sent in about 1905.

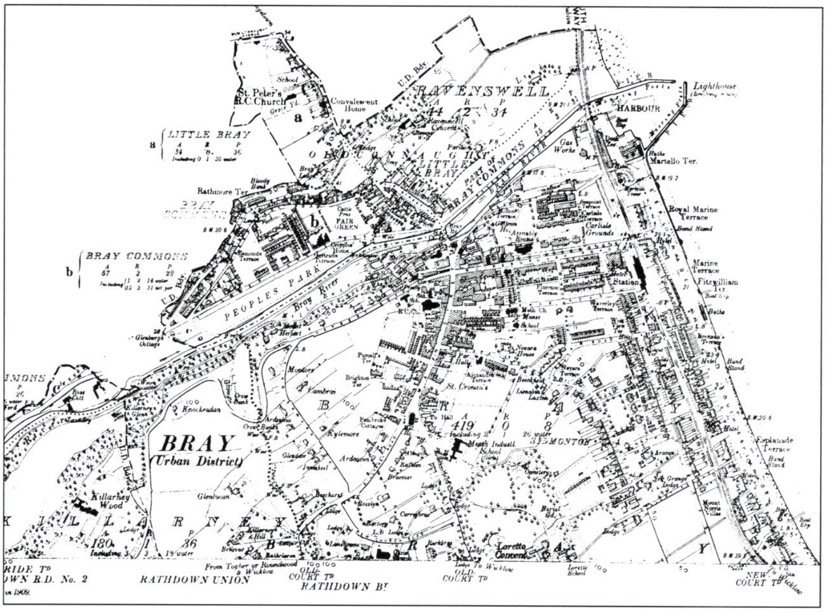

10.2. Bray and Little Bray in 1909 (Ordnance Survey of Ireland, original scale 1:63360).

The next level of accommodation was in a boarding house, able to house a number of families and supplying an evening meal, usually at a fixed hour. The figure of seven for Bray seems very low compared with what would be expected in resorts elsewhere; there were four on the Esplanade and three on Meath Road. There were eight private hotels, all listed under female proprietresses and mostly on the Esplanade, and at the top, four hotels. Three of these — the Marine Station Hotel (Breslin's Royal Marine Hotel, renamed when sold after his death), the International Hotel and the Bray Head Hotel — by 1910 belonged to Frank Bethell's Bethell Hotels chain.

Bray railway station saw almost a hundred trains a day to and from Dublin and although the automobile had begun its rise to prominence, in 1910 the old and new forms of road transport operated side by side. Several Bray firms advertised themselves as motor engineers, the well-established Denehey's of Little Bray claiming to be 'open day and night for accessories, oils, spirits and greases'. But these advertisements were matched by those for livery stables, offering horses for hire, 'driving for pic-nic or pleasure parties' and 'special brakes and wagonettes from Bray railway station'. There were 'hackney carriages, chars-a-banc, coaching and motoring services' available for touring. The sixteen 'car proprietors' listed by Porter were presumably still offering horse-drawn vehicles, and employing the many drivers available during the summer season.

'Coaching.–A four-in-hand, "The Shamrock," Coach runs regularly during the season from Dublin to Bray and Greystones. Chars-a-banc to Dargle, Glendalough, the Waterfall, Bride's Glen, Rocky Valley, The Scalp, Glen of the Downs, and other beauty spots.'
(Frank Porter, *Porter's post office guide and directory of the County Wicklow 1910*, Dublin, [1910], p. 7)

CHARABANCS

'THIS FOUNTAIN IS ERECTED
TO THE MEMORY OF CHRISTOPHER THOMPSON M.D. F.R.C.S.I.
WHO DIED DEC. 16TH 1876
IN TESTIMONY OF HIS WORTH'
(inscription on monument)

'Before it [the courthouse], *on the south side, stands one of the most deplorably inartistic memorials to the memory of one of the best of physicians (the late Dr. Thompson), a concrete obelisk placed over a drinking foundation, of which only the water is praiseworthy.'*
(A.L. Doran, *Bray and environs*. Bray, [c. 1905], p. 42)

MEMORIAL TO DR CHRISTOPHER THOMPSON

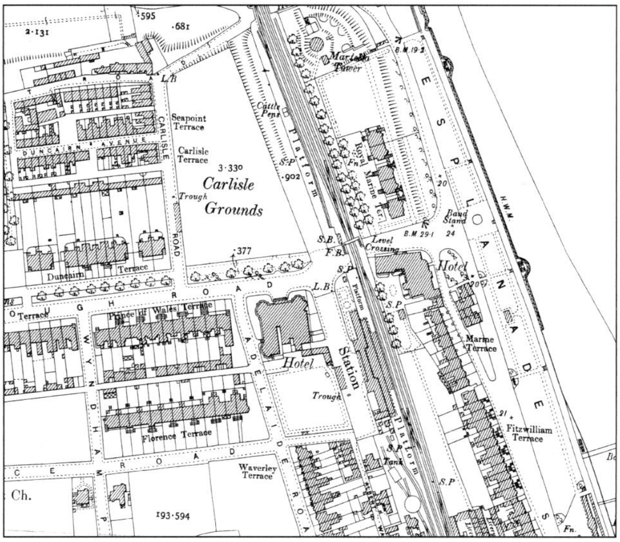

10.3. *Station area in 1909; the International and Marine Station hotels are still prominent features (Ordnance Survey of Ireland, original scale 1:2500).*

10.4. *One of the charabancs operated by the Irish Motor Service Company between Bray, Dalkey and Kingstown (Dún Laoghaire) from 1905. (courtesy Royal Irish Automobile Club Guinness Segrave Archive).*

Main Street and Quinsborough Road, then, still echoed to the sound of horses' hooves as visitors set off through the town. Granite slabs set into the streets at crossing points and kept free of mud and horse droppings by crossing sweepers still survive. The visitors would have found that the area around the junction of Main Street, Quinsborough Road and Herbert Road had a settled look, not very different from forty years before. The only

***10.5.** Main Street in the early twentieth century, looking northwards; the tower of Holy Redeemer is at left.*

addition was the sandstone obelisk erected in front of the courthouse in 1877 to Dr Christopher Thompson, a Bray resident who died of typhoid while treating patients during an outbreak in 1876. The police barracks behind had a force of eighteen. Opposite, the overcrowded graveyard of St Paul's Church had been closed in 1888, while in 1910 the church itself was undergoing major repairs and reconstruction. The Royal Hotel, the fourth of Bray's hotels, had a fine new pavilion, opened in 1908 for concerts and other entertainments; in 1910 it claimed to have a skating rink.

Herbert Road had acquired a few new houses, substantial ones, together with the presbytery built in 1895, and the new St Paul's Schools, on the site of the present car park, that in June 1904 had replaced the Church of Ireland national schools in Little Bray. A little further up Main Street a big change had taken place with the completion of Florence Road in 1902, offering a new route to the sea front, and terraces of new houses facing the road had already sprung up. Nearby was the Presbyterian St Andrew's National School at the end of Eglinton Road, opened in 1888 and with a hundred or so pupils. The original buildings were destroyed by fire in 1942; the present larger premises, now part of Coláiste Ráithín, date from soon afterwards. The Carnegie Library, now Bray Public Library, was built during 1910 on a site given by the Quin estate and with a grant of £2,000 from Andrew Carnegie, although plans for a two-storey building had been turned down by the council. The library was formally opened on 20 May 1911.

Florence Road was in the process of acquiring another building of interest that survives to the present, although one of undistinguished appearance. A corrugated iron building, today in use as commercial premises, was opened as the workshops of the Bray Art Furniture Industry in 1911. This woodcarving industry originated in a class for Christ Church choirboys, begun in 1887, which had later been converted into an evening class for men. When Bray's technical school was opened in 1902, the class was affiliated to the school under the direction of its formidable teacher and manager, Miss Sophia St John Whitty. The class evolved into the fully-fledged Bray Art Furniture Industry, based in the technical school until the workshop was opened together with a showroom at 81 Main Street. The business flourished, winning many prizes, until it closed on the outbreak of the first world war and there are examples of its elaborate carvings in Christ Church and in the Parochial Hall, Novara Avenue; the choir seats and organ loft carved for the Holy Redeemer Church have not, however, survived. The red-brick Parochial Hall on the south side of Novara Avenue had been built in 1886, with beside it a lodge built in the 'old English' style with a red tiled roof. The hall contained a subscription library which, before the opening of the public library, had several hundred subscribers.

On the other side of Main Street there were newly-occupied rows of houses in St Kevin's Square, Aberdeen Street (now the east part of James

10.6. *Kilmantain Place replaced the old cabins of Pound Lane opposite the Town Hall.*

Connolly Square) and Kilmantain Place where Bray Urban District Council had purchased land from the twelfth earl of Meath in 1904. The Council was active from its establishment in 1899 in building new dwellings in accordance with the Housing of the Working Classes Act of 1890 and the results were visible both here and in Little Bray. But Brighton Terrace was still a cul-de-sac with a pillared entrance, divided from Herbert Road by a wide extent of fields. The Methodist Chapel had been closed in about 1878; after standing empty for a decade it had served as a Union Hall and by 1910 it was in use by various small religious groups. Across the road the old infant school with an extra wooden building had in 1902 been converted to Bray's technical school, which taught art, commercial subjects and domestic economy as well as the obvious trade subjects. The technical school was to remain on this site until 1993, when the students moved to the present Coláiste Ráithín building on Florence Road.

At the top end of Main Street, in addition to the new Town Hall, there were major changes. The last of the old cabins in Pound Lane had gone, replaced in 1877 by the neat two-storey houses of Kilmantain Place. Ten other new houses, also with a Kilmantain Place address, had been built by the Council in 1905. The cabins behind the Town Hall had been swept away and the end of Killarney Road had been transformed by the construction of the present four large houses, Ardara, Abingdon, Braemar and Rathlin (in 1910 the home of Canon Scott), set in wide, tree-shaded gardens.

There were another half dozen fine new houses on King Edward Road, one of which, Ard Soluis, an Arts and Crafts Movement house built in 1904, was designed by the same Thomas Manly Deane, by this time Sir Thomas Deane, who was responsible for the Town Hall. King Edward Road, laid out in 1900–1, neatly marks the transition from Victorian to Edwardian Bray. It was originally to have been named Victoria Road, apparently at the insistence of Lord Pembroke on whose land it lay, but on the death of the old queen in January 1901 the provisional name was replaced by that of the new monarch. Despite changing political allegiances, Bray still clung to some of the old snobberies.

Further out, Oldcourt Castle and its grounds were by now open to the public. The eleventh earl of Meath had acquired the property from the Edwards family in the 1850s, and in 1897 Reginald Brabazon, who had in 1887 succeeded as twelfth earl, followed his previous work on behalf of Bray by restoring the tower and renovating the grounds. There were seats and a summer house, and bathing was permitted in the small lake. The charge for admission was 6d, with 3d extra for entry to the castle and a fee for fishing. It would be interesting to know whether many visitors ever penetrated to this inland part of Bray.

OLDCOURT CASTLE GROUNDS

> Oldcourt Castle. *'In 1897, Reginald, the present Earl, restored the keep, the best portion of the old ruins, exceptional care being taken to preserve as much as possible of the ancient masonry, and to thoroughly respect the* genius loci. *At the same time the grounds were put in order, and liberally provided with seats, while the little lake received most artistic treatment, was re-stocked with fish, and provided with a cool grot[to]-like summer-house, not forgetting an altar to Prometheus, for the benefit of picnickers. A pair of swans regularly inhabit the lakelet, and as, between certain hours, bathing is permitted, lifebuoys are in evidence where necessary, to meet an emergency.'*
> (A.L. Doran, *Bray and environs*, Bray, [c. 1905], p. 71)

The Main Street end of Vevay Road had a large new building, one familiar to the present day. The Meath Industrial School, now St Patrick's National School, had begun in 1872 as a school for fifty protestant girls at Oldcourt, but the building had been found 'insanitary' and there had been a temporary move out to Templecarrig. With the support of Lord Meath, the extensive premises, intended for a hundred girls, were built in 1892. It was said in 1903 to be the only Irish protestant industrial school outside of Ulster; apparently girls had recently been transferred from the former industrial school in Cork. There were six staff members teaching the usual subjects plus needlework, cookery and laundry work, and on leaving at sixteen the girls were placed in employment, mostly in domestic work.

MEATH INDUSTRIAL SCHOOL FOR GIRLS

> *'Meath Industrial School for Girls was founded by William, the 11th Earl of Meath, and a wing was recently erected to his memory by his daughter, Lady Kathleen Brabazon. It is supported by a Government Grant of 5s. per week for each child, supplemented by subscriptions and donations from the public. The present Earl of Meath takes a great interest in the school, which is managed by a committee of ladies and gentlemen. It was built in 1892, and is licensed to accommodate 100 girls, who leave the school at the age of 16, but are provided with situations, having been carefully trained in all branches of domestic science.'*
> (Frank Porter, *Porter's post office guide and directory of the County Wicklow 1910*, Dublin [1910], p. 3)

10.7. Meath Industrial School for Girls, built in 1892.

10.8. Substantial Edwardian houses on Galtrim Road.

Between Main Street and Strand Road more than 150 new houses had been built since 1870 — not a very large number, perhaps, for a period of forty years. These included the remaining houses of Florence, Milward and Novara Terraces, the houses on Adelaide Road (the road had been renamed by the council in 1907 as a posthumous tribute to John Brennan, 'who built so much of Bray'), many of the houses on Meath Road. The long terrace of typically Edwardian houses on the north side of Galtrim Road was almost

10.9. *Postcard of Quinsborough Road in c. 1907, with message '... we are enjoying ourselves first rate. We had a ride to-day in a jaunting car, about 24 mls, grand scenery ...' (see p. 252).*

complete, though only half of the houses were as yet occupied, and the first two houses had been built on Kingsmill Road.

Some parts of Bray, such as Eglinton Road, Westview Terrace on Adelaide Road, and Sloan Terrace and Belgrave Villas on Meath Road, had a high proportion of rooms to let to visitors; other areas, clearly the preserve of professional families, had none. Meath Road had the Trafalgar Private Hotel on the corner site at nos 1 and 2, with the three Meath Road boarding houses in Belgrave and Claremont Terraces. Two Misses Haughton ran a convalescent home and private hospital in Killisk House, a forebear of the many nursing homes that were to take over substantial Bray houses in the late twentieth century. The biggest change on the seafront was the replacement of the old coastguard station by a commanding structure — the combined Esplanade and Lacy's Hotels, built in about 1897. With its turrets and seaward-facing timber balconies the hotel building was an impressive addition to the vista along Strand Road. Mrs Mills, proprietress of the Esplanade Hotel in 1910, advertised herself as late of the Russell Square area of London. The Esplanade Hotel was unlicensed, and therefore despite its bulk it was a private hotel. The five other private hotels on Strand Road were the adjoining Lacy's Hotel, run by Mrs Lacy; the Eagle Hotel, opened in 1907 the Holyrood Hotel in the former Holyrood House (Heather House Hotel); the Victoria Hotel (Strand Hotel); and Holywood.

The new coastguard station close to the railway line on Putland Road had been completed in 1877 — the ground was leased from George Putland in

1874. Its terraced row of six two-storey coastguards' houses and watch tower, fronted with Wicklow granite, had a wide view across the Irish Sea, today obscured by the entertainment buildings in front. There was also a rocket cart house. The coastguard station was closed and used as an army barracks by the Free State army in 1922; after a brief spell as a police barracks it was converted to private houses, as it is today, some three years later. The boat house still stands as an unmarked memorial to Bray coastguards on Putland Road.

'EVERY VARIETY OF HOLIDAY PURSUIT'

> *'Bray provides a rich fund of Entertainment, Sport, Pastime, and every variety of holiday pursuit, so that visitiors to "the Brighton of Ireland" need never be bored by lack of incident or bewail a moment's* ennui.*'*
> (Frank Porter, *Porter's post office guide and directory of the County Wicklow 1910*, Dublin, [1910], p. 6)

The Bray Head Hotel, formerly Lacy's, by now formed an impressive end to the sea front. It had been enlarged over the years into an extensive four-storey building with long verandas on the ground and first floors. It was closer to the water with better sea views than any of its competitors — it was advertised as having 'the finest situation in Bray' — but was perhaps a little isolated from the main activities of the resort. (A local carman was banned from offering a 2d ride from Lacy's to the Station Hotel, either because there was no permission to wait at the former or because this was seen as overcharging.) Sold by the Lacy family in 1899, there were seventy-five rooms with two dining rooms capable of seating two hundred and fifty guests.

The thatched fishermen's cottages at this south end of the Esplanade still had their boats drawn up in front on the foreshore. Various attempts had been made by the Putland family as ground landlords to displace the occupants and to tidy up the area to match the rest of Strand Road. In 1894 the town commissioners had waxed indignant about the cottage that had 'ten people living with donkeys and other animals'. But the cottages and their residents remained, providing a picturesque 'quarter' under Bray Head.

Beyond the end of the Esplanade part of Bray Head was by now a park, officially named Grand Marine Park on its opening in 1896, with tea rooms at its foot. There was a railway halt at a half-platform, built in 1906, to cater for visitors to the open-air baths at Naylor's Cove, later Bray Cove Baths. The cliff walk ran all the way to Greystones, firstly on D.W.W.R. land and then past an isolated gate lodge, now in ruins, where an admission charge was collected from those wishing to continue through the Killruddery estate. Visitors wandering over Bray Head would have come to the obelisk placed there in 1887 by a local landowner to commemorate Queen Victoria's golden jubilee. It was to be blown up in 1933; the present thirty-foot-high cross was erected at the summit in 1950 to commemorate the Holy Year.

The Esplanade had just acquired an elegant bandstand on the site of a temporary wooden one put up in the 1880s. This new bandstand, still a feature today and recently restored, was acquired by Bray Urban District Council from the 1907 Irish International Exhibition in Herbert Park, Dublin, and placed on its sea-front site in June 1908. It was formally opened with bands and singers on 15 July, before, it was reported, an audience of 4,000 people. Another bandstand opposite the Esplanade Hotel was the one used for variety shows such as the White Coons, while a third bandstand still stood opposite the level crossing, where guests in the Marine Station Hotel could enjoy the band performances without leaving the hotel terrace. Breslin's former hotel was, in fact, enjoying its last few years of predominance. It had been sold to the railway company in 1900, three years after Edward Breslin's

***10.10.** The bandstand acquired by Bray UDC from the 1907 Irish International Exhibition, and still a prominent feature today; the paving has been added in 2006.*

death, and appropriately renamed; it was the most expensive hotel in Bray, charging more than the International Hotel around the corner. But its days were numbered, for the upper floors were to be destroyed in an accidental fire in 1916 and after that its doors never again opened to resident guests.

The Marine Station Hotel was advertised as having fifty rooms in 1910, while the International Hotel was down to a hundred, so presumably large parts were closed off. The International's role as a hotel, shaky as it already was, would also soon come to an end, albeit a temporary one — it would close with the outbreak of the 1914–18 war and not reopen as a hotel for another thirty years. The Arcadia Ballroom had been built in the International's gardens. Taking the role of the seafront pavilion Bray never had, the Arcadia replaced the Assembly Rooms as a venue for entertainments such as dances, concerts and boxing matches. The old-style entertainments were already under threat from the new, however, the first 'animated pictures' had been shown in Bray soon after the turn of the century, and within three years more there were plans for a 500-seater picture house on Florence Road.

Quinsborough Road also had a private hotel, the Imperial, at no. 5 Goldsmith Terrace, and the new main post office, built in 1904–5, on the north side of the road, where fourteen postmen were employed. The Northern Bank, Bray's second bank — the Hibernian Bank on the corner of Herbert Road was the oldest — lay on the north side of the road where it had been opened in 1890 in purpose-built premises, still in use as the National Irish Bank.

The Assembly Rooms had undergone a change in appearance; the red and white bricks were obliterated under a coating of plaster in about 1900, presumably because of their decrepit appearance. What Arthur Doran neatly called the 'speckled elephant' was now a pale brown one. The only saving grace was that the entire building, including the minarets, was plastered, unlike at least one English Turkish baths where the minarets were removed. The Quakers and the Plymouth Brethren both still held meetings there.

RENOVATION OF ASSEMBLY ROOMS

'Of late years the present proprietor has had the building thoroughly renovated, and has decently shrouded the vestiges of its once gay exterior under a dun but servicable coat of cement, reserving the work of decoration for the interior … .'

(A.L. Doran, *Bray and environs*, Bray, [c. 1905], p. 45)

Rows of houses facing onto Seymour Road and Duncairn Avenue had been built by 1910, backing onto Duncairn Terrace and with the grounds of Galtrim House still intact over the boundary wall. The 1880 gas works, protected from Irish Sea storms by the railway embankment, were in full use, as they were to be until their closure in 1934 when the gas supply was piped in from Dublin, leaving only a gas holder on the site; the remains were demolished in 1981 on the building of the present sewage works.

Bray by now, of course, had both gas and electricity, with the electricity works operating in the old mill. The residents were still in the process of slowly adopting the supply; although the street lights had been converted, the great majority of households were still using gas and the need for power for more than lighting and cooking was still in the future. The electricity works served Bray until 1928 when the town went onto the national network.

Little Bray had been part of County Wicklow since the establishment of Bray Urban District Council in 1899; it had undergone a radical change by 1910. The old commons area had taken on something of its present appearance with the construction of the link, originally called New Bridge Road, between Castle Street and Lower Dargle Road in 1873 and with the building of houses on its new roads. Sixty-two single-storey two- and three-roomed cottages were built by the Dublin Artisans' Dwellings Co. in 1888 on the block of property owned by Lord Meath and comprising Ardee Street and Maitland Street, both named after members of the Meath family, with five

10.11. *Little Bray, looking towards the former Upper Commons from across the Dargle,* c. *1910.*

'of superior class' later added facing the Lower Dargle Road. (The Dublin Artisans' Dwellings Co. was a philanthropic enterprise, set up in 1876, devoted to the improvement of housing conditions; the Little Bray houses were its only major scheme outside of central Dublin.) The cottages had been welcomed by the town commissioners, as a 'boon to the town and particularly Little Bray, where the poor were so badly housed'. Nearby the

10.12. Houses built by the Artisans' Dwellings Co., Little Bray. The exterior of the one at the left is in near original condition.

10.13. Home for Crippled Children as it looks today; founded in 1874, it provided a home and training for forty disabled children.

Council built forty-four two-storey 'worksmen's dwelling houses' on Dargan Street in 1905.

The Bray Laundry, a major concern, had been opened on Green Park Road, between Ardee Street and the present Pearse Road. The Fair Green was in full use, with cattle pens and a central drinking fountain for the cattle; fairs were held monthly. Close by was one of Little Bray's most attractive terraces — Brabazon Cottages, built in 1882; the end house was one of the few in Little Bray offering visitors' accommodation.

The most interesting establishment in Little Bray was the Home for Crippled Children. This had been founded in 1874 by Mrs Lucinda Sullivan as a residential school for training disabled children so that as adults they could support themselves. The building the home occupied, now in commercial use, was itself of interest. It had been built as a workmen's hall in 1866, using the stones of martello tower no. 3 — a rare instance where we know the fate of dressed stone from a notable structure. Six years later it served briefly as the Bray Auxiliary Hospital for Incurables before its new role as the Cripples' Home. A new wing with thirteen rooms was added in 1878 and there were forty children in residence. Many of the children would have been in poor health, and it is perhaps not surprising that twenty were buried in St Paul's graveyard in the last decades of the century. The Home was renamed Sunbeam House by 1930; it moved from Little Bray in 1962.

HOME FOR CRIPPLED CHILDREN

'Home for destitute crippled children founded by Lucinda Sullivan 1874 as a thanks offering to Almighty God for deliverance from peril of shipwreck on the Lake of Zurich August 19th 1872'
(plaque in Home)

'The conditions of admission are non-sectarian, and depend simply upon indigence and the current capacity of the Home, no votes or fees of any kind being required.
Each child on entering is enrolled in the Band of Hope. Boys are eligible for admission from 3 to 8 years old, girls from 3 to 12 years.
AN ANNUAL SUBSCRIPTION OF £10 MAINTAINS A CRIPPLE IN FOOD.
A DONATION OF £250 FOUNDS A BED IN THE HOME.
Basket-work and needlework are carried on as industries, and an annual sale is held about the month of September.'
(A.L. Doran, *Bray and environs*, Bray, [c. 1905], pp 116–7)

Just down the road from the Cripples' Home, there had been for twenty years another medical establishment, the Meath Hospital Convalescent Home. Lord Brabazon had taken the initiative on behalf of the Meath Hospital in Dublin. He offered the use of five bedrooms and a sitting room on the first floor of Dargle View House, the present Park Court, built in 1880 on the corner of Bray Bridge Road and Sheridan's Lane and overlooking the green space of the People's Park. The convalescent home opened in 1882 with the first four patients and a nurse; at first the Dargle Coffee Shop had the ground floor but the home quickly took over the entire premises. In 1899, seeking more space, it moved to the pair of houses on the Dublin Road in front of Arbutus Lodge, where it was to remain until it was closed in the early 1970s (Arbutus Lodge, the once fashionable 'bathing lodge', was apparently used as the matron's house). It depended upon voluntary subscriptions. By 1910 Dargle View House had been divided into three separate dwellings.

The People's Park had been railed in and planted with trees and shrubs, again at the expense of Lord and Lady Brabazon. This had been done in 1881–3, at the same time as its elegant caretaker's lodge was built and given to the town. Like the Town Hall, the lodge was designed by Newenham Deane & Son, and was in the same English-revival style — its destruction by fire a hundred years later deprived Little Bray of a small gem. The People's Park, like the Esplanade, was the source of problems for the council. Horses were exercised there, and it was decreed that permission was necessary; pitch and toss was played, presumably attracting huddles of spectators; and there were complaints about bad language.

> *This lodge was erected and the park ornamentally laid out at the cost of Lord and Lady Brabazon and presented as a free gift to the Bray Town Commissioners to be maintained by that body in good repair and trust for the perpetual enjoyment of the public. A.D. 1881.*
> (Plaque on People's Park lodge, prior to fire of 1983)

PEOPLE'S PARK LODGE

In 1910, however, the event still uppermost in the minds of the inhabitants of Bray Commons was the flood of 1905. This was not the first flood to strike Little Bray since the Commons had been enclosed. There were floods in January 1877, and in October 1881 another combination of exceptionally high tide and heavy rainfall had again caused flooding on the

10.14. *People's Park, Little Bray.*

10.15. *Caretaker's Lodge, People's Park, as designed in English-revival style by the architects of the Town Hall.*

Commons as well as along the sea front. Little Bray residents were on that occasion driven out of their houses by two to three feet of water, and the Assembly Rooms were made available as temporary accommodation, although apparently only four families took up the offer. Less than fifty years after the floods that had destroyed the racecourse, there were already uncomfortable reminders that the Commons was indeed part of a river flood plain.

The flood of the night of Friday/Saturday, 25/26 August 1905 was far worse than the previous ones, not least because there were now many more houses on the Commons. (Coincidentally the most recent major flood, that caused by Hurricane Charlie in 1986, also took place on 25/26 August; the floods of 1931 and 1965 were in September and November respectively.) As the Dublin doctor and meteorologist Sir John Moore wrote in his detailed account, after a wet August, 'a pitiless and incessant rain' over a day and a half brought three to four inches of rain to the Dublin area — as much as 4.45 inches were recorded at Fasseroe and even more in the mountains. Great quantities of water poured down the Dargle, the river burst its banks upstream of Little Bray and within hours around midnight the water rose in the streets to a height of four feet. It was fast-flowing water, many walls, several old cabins and the railings of the People's Park were demolished, and furniture, domestic animals and fowl were swept away.

The electricity works on the opposite bank of the Dargle were also flooded, the generators failed and all the lights in Bray went out. Darkness, the rapid current, and floating debris, including vehicles, made rescue work difficult. 'Next morning the surface of the sea of Bray was seen to be thickly studded with floating articles of furniture, barrels, and trees, which had been carried out to sea by the resistless flood.' Four hundred families and two thousand people were said to be affected — though this would seem a high figure — and at least one person died. With limited means of drying out their

Hely's, Limited] THE DISASTROUS FLOODS AT LITTLE BRAY, AUGUST 25th, 1905. *[Dublin*

10.16. *Little Bray the morning after the great flood of 1905; one of a number of postcards issued to mark the disaster.*

houses and possessions, the effects of the inundation must have plagued the unfortunate residents for months if not years to come.

The longer-established Castle Street and Back Street area was also affected by the floods, though to a lesser extent. Unlike the Upper Commons, this part of Little Bray had changed little in the forty years since 1870. Dublin Road had the Meath Convalescent Home and, in Rack Rent or Abbeyview House, the William Henry Elliott Home for Little Children — it would be converted to St Peter's presbytery in 1921. (There was also the Father Healy Nursing Association, founded in 1896 in memory of a much-loved parish priest of Little Bray, famous for his wit, but this did not have premises other than the nurse's house at no. 2 Bay View Terrace.) The overcrowded graveyard at St Peter's Church had been extended in 1905 while the nearby national school had been rebuilt in 1874 and taken over by the Sisters of Charity in 1899.

The Sisters first lived in Rack Rent House, but by 1910 they were established in Ravenswell House, which they had purchased in 1901 and where they had opened new schools in the stables; the pupils had moved there from the girls' national school in Seapoint Road. There were some four hundred pupils. Little Bray had thus gained a primary school at the same time as it lost one — the ninety-year-old protestant Bray Bridge Schools were closed in 1904 when the pupils moved to Herbert Road. Lord Meath bought back the property leased by his forebear, and in 1906 converted the buildings to the present Belton Terrace houses.

THE GOLF CLUB

'The [Golf] *Course is designed to give a golfer scope for every kind of shot. It is very prettily situated and as it borders the sea, the cool refreshing breezes always prevent it from being too hot. There is a large, commodious Club House, with capital accommodation for ladies; Tennis and Croquet Grounds. ... Visitors have the use of the Club House, Links, Croquet and Tennis Grounds for 2/6 a day, 7/6 a week, £1 a month, or, if staying at the Bethell Hotels, 1/6 a day, or 6/- a week ... .'*
(Frank Porter, *Porter's post office guide and directory of the County Wicklow 1910*, Dublin [1910], p. 6)

Part of Lord Meath's lands of Ravenswell behind Castle Street had been leased to Bray Golf Club, founded in 1897, and a nine-hole course had been laid out complete with a red-painted galvanised iron pavilion. By a covenant in the lease, golf was not permitted on Sundays before 1.30 p.m. The club was to lose land at the seaward end of the links when in 1912 the railway company, by now renamed the Dublin & South Eastern Railway Co., was forced through coastal erosion to relay its track further inland. The railway around Bray Head was also diverted inland at the same time, which involved boring a new tunnel some 1,000 metres long.

Little Bray still remained the least prosperous part of the Bray urban district. The occupations of its inhabitants in 1910 included many with regular jobs such as railway workers and postmen, but also large numbers of building workers, labourers, drivers and gardeners whose employment would have been seasonal or casual — Little Bray supplied most of the men who waited daily at the 'hiring place' on Bray Bridge. Women took in washing and worked on farms in the general area at harvest time. Bray penny dinners were given out from a depot at the forge in Castle Street at the rate of some 5,000–6,000 dinners a year. In a survey of 1912, fifty-nine houses in Little Bray were found unfit for habitation — the total for the whole of the rest of Bray was only thirty-six. Presumably the unfit houses were mainly those dating back to before 1800 that clustered around Back Street and neighbouring lanes, none of which rated having their inhabitants listed in Porter's guide. Bray's sanitary officer had drawn attention to their unhealthy state as far back as the 1870s, while the 11th earl of Meath, in a strongly worded letter to the chairman of the Urban District Council after the 1905 floods, had urged the demolition of 'the worst hovels in Little Bray ... which are a constant danger and a disgrace to the town'. This was undoubtedly the most extensive impoverished part of Bray and the part that had undergone least renewal in the nineteenth century. It was all to be swept away in the twentieth.

Chapter 11

Buckets and spades: Bray 1910–70

'From its unrivalled situation between mountains and sea, its exhilarating air, its mild and equable climate, its abundance of sunshine, its splendid promenade, its highly-organised facilities for holiday-making, and its charming surroundings, Bray claims for itself the distinction of being the premier seaside resort in the Irish Free State.'
(*Pictorial and descriptive guide to Dublin and its environs,* Ward Lock & Co., London, 1935–6, pp 145–6)

The six decades between 1850 and 1910 saw Bray transformed; the following six, extending from 1910 to 1970, link the height of the Edwardian era and the point at which seaside resorts in Ireland and Britain began their slow decline. These were eventful years in the twentieth century, both nationally and internationally, and Bray could not escape the effects of wider happenings — two world wars, the struggle for Irish independence, the depression of the inter-war years all left their mark. In the decades after the second world war the seaside resort was to have a last flowering, one that is within living memory today. And Bray was to be fortunate, for the town was to find other roles just as its seaside role was fading.

Both the first world war and the upsurge in nationalist agitation seem to have taken Bray's entrepreneurs by surprise. The season of 1913 was noted as a particularly good one, with 1,200 Bray guide books sent out, and Whitsun 1914 saw big crowds; it was reported proudly in June that there had already been 700 enquiries from Britain. There were the customary military bands and seaside acts on the Esplanade, charabanc (open-topped motor coach) trips to the countryside and, of course, the new film shows. The Bray regatta, which had lapsed, was revived that August. On the surface Bray seemed set for a good year and a continuation of the town's modest prosperity.

The situation changed rapidly, however. National events had always, of course, had their echo in the town. Charles Stewart Parnell was a Wicklow man, and the release of Michael Davitt, the 'father of the land league', from prison in the 1880s had been marked by decorations in Main Street. Bray had a branch of the politically-active National League and later of the Gaelic League, and there was active support for home rule. At the same time there were those who were strongly loyal to the British crown, a reality manifested, for instance, in the public welcome given to the Duke and Duchess of York when they passed through Bray in 1897 or by the draping of Christ Church and St Paul's in mourning black on the death of Queen Victoria.

THE SEA FRONT, 1912

'The Sea-front.–The Esplanade is a mile in length, runs in a line with the beach, and is separated from the terraced houses with their pleasant gardens by broad stretches of turf. A specially noteworthy feature is the line of comfortable seats that runs from one end of the Esplanade to the other. A strong iron railing prevents the youngsters from falling off the sea-wall onto the beach. Stands have been provided for the benefit of cyclists — another example of the way in which the needs of strangers are anticipated at Bray.

On the grand Bandstand a Band gathers to discourse sweet music three or four evenings each week, and, at frequent intervals during the season, Fêtes, Fireworks, and Military Tattoos are arranged by the ever-active Amusements' Committee. At these times the foreshore looks particularly gay. First-rate concert troupes perform each morning and evening of the week on the north and south Bandstands.'

(M.J. Maguire, *Through the garden of Ireland: an illustrated guide … issued by the Dublin and South Eastern Railway Co.*, Dublin, 1912, p. 41)

Only a month after the hopeful report of large numbers of positive enquiries from England, the *Wicklow Newsletter* struck a different note with a mid-July report that the political disturbances were resulting in fewer visitors than usual and causing anxious questions to be received from England. The confidence of visitors from across the Irish Sea would not have been boosted by reports of the gun running at Kilcoole, seven miles to the south of Bray, on 1 August 1914; the guns and ammunition passed through Little Bray *en route* to Dublin. While Bray itself was for the most part pro-British or at least uncommitted, republican support was strong in Little Bray and there were a number of local volunteers.

Running parallel to this were the wider international events. War between Britain and Germany broke out on 4 August after Germany invaded

11.1. *The area around the Marine Station Hotel at the height of the Edwardian era (Lawrence Collection, National Library of Ireland).*

Belgium. British army reservists in Bray were called up and the bandstand on the Esplanade was the venue for recruiting meetings as well as for the usual concerts. Belgian refugees, some fifty-two in all, spent a year or so in Bray from late 1914 onwards and were given accommodation and employment. The men worked at cultivating the 'Belgian Field', the empty plot on Adelaide Road later known as Barry's Field when in the hands of the amusement proprietors Barry family and today partly occupied by the Fáilte Games Park and the Bray Bowling Club. They also worked land adjoining Putland Road. Whether there was the same degree of anti-German hysteria as in England is perhaps unlikely, but in September it was reported that the German chef at the Marine Station Hotel had been arrested, presumably as a possible spy.

The war dramatically, if temporarily, resulted in the utilisation of the International Hotel with its many rooms, which had until then continued its sad decline. In 1915 the hotel was converted into the Princess Patricia Military Hospital, staffed by the Red Cross and the St John's Ambulance Brigade. It was first used for amputees, but later for more general war-wounded. A surviving photograph shows the bay-windowed ballroom filled with iron bedsteads each with a uniformed soldier alongside; the flowery bedspreads, complementing the elaborate wallpaper, overmantle and chandelier, seem very frivolous to be those of military issue and may have belonged to the hotel. The convalescent soldiers, sent on from Dublin hospitals to recuperate, became one of the regular sights of Bray as they wandered through the town. In 1918 Bray's seaside influence showed when they formed the Princess Patricia Pierrot Party.

The Bray Arts Furniture Industry building on Florence Road became reading and recreation rooms for the soldiers, operated by the Y.M.C.A. The Meath Industrial School for Girls was also put to wartime use, and from 1916 to 1920 became the Duke of Connaught's Hospital, catering for amputees and blind veterans. The Carlisle Grounds was used as a parade ground for drilling British army volunteers and in 1914 there was a reservist military training camp on Bray Head, based in tents on the large, moderately level field on which the ruined Raheenacluig church stands. Presumably all these activities, with an influx of both the military and those in attendance upon them, compensated Bray to some extent for the loss of visitor revenue.

At the same time, a large number of young men from the Bray area — perhaps as many as nine hundred — enlisted, many in Irish regiments. Those who died, some hundred and fifty-five in all, were later given a public memorial on a prominent site provided by the railway company adjoining the Carlisle Grounds. When the war ended in November 1918 the military gradually withdrew. The Princess Patricia Hospital was closed in 1919 and the owner Frank Bethell resumed possession, although the International Hotel did not reopen — presumably it would have required a considerable outlay for renovations. Some of its contents were auctioned in 1922 and there was talk of converting it to apartments; in April of that year it was even proposed by the Urban District Council that it be taken over to relieve the housing shortage in Bray. The Meath Industrial School was reopened as the Royal Drummond Institution for the orphaned daughters of ex-servicemen and it was used in this way until its closure in 1944.

November 1918 did not, however, mean the end of problems in Ireland and events closer to home now left their mark on Bray. One was the great influenza epidemic of 1918–19, when schools were closed and those at Ravenswell were turned into a temporary hospital to cope with some of the six hundred cases in the town. Earlier the 1916 Easter Rising had been watched with anxiety and had briefly caused food shortages; the distant glow from the fires in Dublin had been visible in the night sky. In the last years of the decade 'the Troubles' brought military raids in Little Bray, where there was a Sinn Féin cumman, and troop movements in the town. The Royal Irish Constabulary in the barracks next door to the Royal Hotel had its personnel augmented by the infamous 'Black and Tans', and both it and the courthouse were surrounded by protective barbed wire.

The last year of the war of independence seems particularly to have affected Bray. In April 1921 republicans fired on the police barracks and courthouse, and a large number of bomb explosions on one night also damaged shop and bank premises nearby. Damage was also done at the railway station, where two motor ambulances were destroyed by fire; subsequently two railway wagons each carrying a Ford motor car — valuable commodities — were also burnt. In May the Royal Hotel was taken over by the army and its street front was reinforced with sandbags and barbed wire. There were overnight curfews, although the hours were relatively limited, from 10.30 p.m. to 4.00 a.m.

The ongoing warfare did not prevent Bray from trying to continue its normal resort activities. There was a two-day regatta in August, with the usual boating and swimming events, and seafront amusements. The summer months seem to have been relatively quiet. The signing of the Anglo-Irish Treaty in December 1921 was commemorated by a torchlight procession and bonfires in Little Bray when the republican internees from the area returned home. Sandbags and barbed wire were quickly removed from the Royal Hotel and the British military personnel left. The adjacent barracks was vacated by the Royal Irish Constabulary in March 1922 on its disbandment. The hotel was not yet to return to normality, however; still the property of the Findlaters' grocery chain, it was requisitioned first by the Free State Army in

11.2. *Bray bathers in 1915 (courtesy Kathleen Kinsella).*

11.3. *'Bray' seaside postcards — standard cards overprinted with the resort's name. The one above was posted to Switzerland in 1911.*

July 1922 (when it was used for the temporary detention of anti-treaty Wicklow Republicans) and then taken over in late October by the Civic Guard (Garda Síochána). The Guards moved into the refurbished R.I.C. barracks next door the following March (not without some alarms, as the Civil War was still in progress) and the hotel was then relinquished, although it needed extensive renovations before it could reopen.

In May 1920 Bray Urban District Council acknowledged the authority of Dáil Éireann as the duly elected parliament. In 1923 the council members decided to change the name of the town to what they called the 'old name of Bray' — Brí Chualann. This was not a success. Presumably potential visitors, particularly from Britain, were confused by the loss of the familiar name with its carefully cultivated resort image. One railway tourists' guide, for instance, dealt with the problem by referring awkwardly to 'Bré (Bray)' throughout, reserving 'Brí Chualann' for its map. Only four years later in 1927, after a poll in the town was in favour by a majority of nearly 4:1, the council agreed to restore the name Bray to general usage. If a satirical poem of the time is to be believed, this was seen by some as a retrograde move, favouring Bray's 'West British' past.

BRÍ CHUALANN CHANGED BACK TO BRAY

'BRAY AGAIN
'Tis Bray again' Brí Chualann is no more,
That frenzied nightmare — thank the Lord — is o'er.
The mad Republic lived its hectic hour,
But now West Britain has come back to power.
The menials of his Majesty are here.
To bid each loyal Briton have no fear. …
We'll put this Gaelic speech and all it means
Among John Bull's collection of Have Beens.
Hip, Hip, Hurrah The Rebels' Day in done –
And all West British Donkeys have begun
To Bray again.'
(Brian O'Higgins, quoted in Colbert Martin, *A drink from Broderick's well*, Dublin, 1980, pp 84–5)

In the 1920s Bray needed to recreate its pre-1914 ambience as a seaside resort, but it was operating under a number of disadvantages. The area around the railway station must have been particularly depressing. The first sight to greet visitors on alighting from the trains was the neglected bulk of the International Hotel, which stood vacant, its windows and façade grimy with soot, its gardens overgrown and filled with litter. The building was used only once a year, when it was opened up to serve as a grandstand for the Armistice Day ceremonies at the war memorial opposite; it was also used in 1931 to shelter some three hundred evacuees when the Dargle yet again burst its banks in Little Bray. The Marine Station Hotel, once Edward Breslin's pride and joy, was an even sadder sight; having lost its top two floors in an accidental fire of 1916, it stood derelict — not a cheering view on the way to the beach. These miserable first impressions for train passengers were to last right through the 1920s and until the mid 1930s.

The disappearance of two of Bray's four large hotels meant that only the Royal Hotel, which thus regained some of its lost importance, and the Bray Head Hotel remained from pre-war times. A more modest hotel, the Marine, later the Marine House or Royal Marine Hotel, opened in no. 1 Royal Marine Terrace in the mid 1920s and operated into the late 1970s; it faced across to the site of Breslin's more famous hotel of the same name. Accommodation in private houses remained important and was often fully taken up at the height of the season; many local families moved into chalets in their back gardens during June, July and August, thus freeing up the whole house for visitors. The income from these summer lets was a valuable supplement to the family earnings. Some houses were purely for letting, rented out in summer by the month or more to middle-class Dublin families whose menfolk commuted to their businesses in the city — this probably partly explains the frequency with which good houses are listed as 'vacant' in *Thom's Directory*.

BATHING PLACES

'At the Sea Wall are bathing places for ladies and gentlemen (mornings only); further north along the beach is the Strand; and at Naylor's Cove, under Bray Head, both sexes may bathe at all times. For those who dislike bathing in the open sea there are Municipal Sea Baths — open to both sexes — where facilities are provided for various kinds of baths, under the most hygienic conditions.'
(*Pictorial and descriptive guide to Dublin and its environs*, Ward Lock & Co., London, 1935–6, p. 146)

The Turkish Baths, still a remarkable building despite its drab coating of stucco, had undergone another transformation in the early 1900s when it was converted into McDermott's Picture House, one of Bray's first cinemas — there was another cinema on Florence Road on the site of the present toy supermarket, the Gaiety Picture House built in 1913, which was accidentally burnt down in 1918. In the 1930s there were three cinemas: the Picture House; the Royal, opened in 1935 in the grounds of the Royal Hotel and still in business today as Bray Cineplex; and the Star on Albert Avenue, later renamed the Roxy. The Arcadia Ballroom behind the International Hotel had room for five hundred dancers and provided a venue for an assortment of seaside entertainments; although it lacked the ambience of a sea-front premises, it was convenient for the railway station. For some years the nearby Barry's Field held a circus and amusement park; in 1931 it was described in the trade publication *The World's Fair* as 'all shuttered around and painted in attractive panels'.

The Esplanade still had its bandstands, and a light pavilion, giving welcome shelter from rain and perhaps the one proposed to the Council in 1929, stood on the grass opposite the Esplanade Hotel during the 1930s; it was used by concert troupes and for band performances. A roller-skating rink was opened on the Esplanade opposite the end of Quinsborough Road and there were also tennis courts. Six sales kiosks were added by the council in 1935 for those indispensable adjuncts to the seaside: ice cream, postcards, beach balls, buckets and spades. They still survive though not always in use. (Ice cream became generally available during the twentieth century with the spread of cheap refrigeration; ice cream cones had been invented in 1904, through the co-operation of a vendor with a waffle seller at the USA's St Louis

11.4. *Regatta crowds in the 1920s (courtesy Eddie Power).*

11.5. *Arcadia Ballroom poster — dancing was outside or inside depending on the weather.*

11.6. *In this aerial view the International Hotel dominates the foreground; the remaining floors of the Marine Station Hotel can be glimpsed at the extreme left (Bray Library).*

Fair.) The regattas were resumed — the programme for the Regatta and East Coast Carnival of August 1925 was the standard one, with rowing, swimming and diving events, band performances, hobby-horses and swing-boats, culminating in a firework display. The first amusement arcade — Funland, later the Fun Palace — was opened at the north end of Strand Road in the late 1920s by the Dawson family, who in 1941 added a wooden arcade building next to the Bray Head Hotel. Later there was a semi-permanent dodgem-car building on the Esplanade opposite the Fun Palace.

Up on Bray Head with panoramic views, the Eagle's Nest café was a popular venue from its opening in the mid 1920s. It was at first approached up a steep and slippery slope, but later whitewashed steps, popularly known as 'The Great White Way', were built near Raheenacluig church. The café offered a range of refreshments — lunch, teas, supper, wines — and also served as a dance hall. It was to have a new lease of life in post-war Bray when the chairlift was built and the journey to the Eagle's Nest became an entertainment in itself. In the mid 1930s there was also a large amusement park in the Bray Head Park run by the Barry family, including, as *The World's Fair* noted, a 'figure eight [that] can be seen for miles and is beautifully illuminated'. The park had apparently been leased by John McGurk, formerly a major amusement caterer in Tramore, who had left the Waterford resort after a poor season there in 1930 and moved to Bray with 'his many side shows'.

AMUSEMENTS

'I hear Mr Barry has sole rights of riding machines with Mr McGurk on Bray Head. Mr Barry has had a big offer to sell his own piece of freehold ground in Bray. He is putting up some fine machines, including water dodgem, electric dodgem, figure eight scenic railway, which will look a fine sight on the top of Bray Head, especially in view of the way Mr Barry lights his grounds.'
(*The World's Fair*, 24 March 1934, p. 37)

'The famous Bray Head Amusement Park is now open for the season and contains all the latest devices, side shows, games, ice cream saloons, pagoda tea rooms. Among them are Barry's dodgem cars, scenic railway, figure eight, thriller, motor boats, sea on land, etc., while the side shows include Buried Alive, Black Magic, Vanishing Lady and Marionettes.'
(*The World's Fair*, 7 July 1934, p. 10)

The crowds that came in the season had more relaxed pleasures than those their predecessors had enjoyed. One of the big changes in mores was the new emphasis on exposure to sunshine. The previous view of a pale complexion as a sign of membership of the leisured classes gave way to the opposite: a suntan became the badge of the possession of leisure and wealth enough for an extended stay in a sunny climate. Summers in Ireland and Britain were not so dependable, but the acquisition of a 'nice colour' became one of the requisites of a seaside holiday.

The old conventions of separate bathing areas for men and women were swept away — not without protest from the more puritanical minded — and just as women's clothing was transformed with the advent of short skirts and the removal of restricting corsets, bathing costumes for women also became looser and skimpier. Instead of voluminous and unwieldy garments, the costumes first became more like ordinary dresses with tiny sleeves and medium-length skirts and then were pared away to expose the arms, back and legs in figure-hugging suits. These, of course, allowed a greater area of skin to be exposed to sunshine and so to acquire a tan. Modesty played a part in dictating that there should be a short rim of skirt and the bikini was, of course, still in the future when it, too, would cause a shock to the conservative minded. Modesty also dictated that those who could afford it would hire one of the bathing tents on the beach in which to undress in comfort.

Men, paradoxically, tended to be more fully clad during bathing now that the beaches were mixed; nude bathing and the wearing of drawers only was superseded by the wearing of one-piece bathing costumes. The greater exposure to sun and wind on the beach had its unfortunate side — sunburn was a common torture and sunstroke was another hazard for the unwary, particularly children. Tanning lotions and sunblock creams gradually came into use only after world war two having been developed for wartime use by the military and that other seaside accessory we now find indispensable — sunglasses — only became commonplace from the 1960s onwards.

By now the beach was a place essentially for recreation. Besides swimming, serious or otherwise, there were the children's pleasures of paddling, building sandcastles and riding donkeys along the sand; rubber beach balls and flotation rings added to the fun. Deckchairs, first used on passenger liners in the late nineteenth century, could be hired for a small fee and made sitting on the beach comfortable. Bray with its comparatively limited shore area was at a disadvantage compared with British resorts such as Blackpool, Southport or Bournemouth, with their very extensive beaches of pure sand. There were also better Irish beaches within reach of Dublin, but here Bray had the advantage in that it provided the ambience of a bustling resort. If the tide was in, there was the promenade to stroll upon, and the various entertainments to visit.

MIXED BATHING: MORAL OUTRAGE IN 1913

'Notes and Queries: Mixed Bathing.
Rev. Dear Sir,–1. It is much to be deplored that this evil continental and English system is coming into vogue in the land (or the sea?) of St. Brigid. What should be our attitude regarding it?

2. Quite recently a young girl, who mentioned incidentally that she was a daily Communicant, told me she took part in mixed bathing. It did not appear to be a scandalum *to her. Whilst wholly reprobating the system, I did not feel justified in refusing absolution. Ought I have done so?*

Mixed bathing is extensively practiced, and judging from some photos I have seen, the costumes leave something to be desired.
[signed] Confessor.
[Replies]

1. The morality of mixed bathing is mainly a question of custom and of costume.

In our Irish social and religious atmosphere many things are out of place which in other parts of the world are not objectionable; the modesty which has been the hall-mark of Irish virtue does not fit in harmoniously with some of the practices that have been creeping into Irish life; and many admirers of our customs regard with disfavour the practice of mixed bathing which has gained prevalence at some of our seaside resorts.

If the undesirable practice is to be continued it ought to be safeguarded from the taint of indecency. It ought to be regulated by vigorous byelaws, especially in regard to the costumes of the bathers. We have been told that there is room for considerable improvement in this direction. Not only the material and form of costumes demand better management, but also the perambulations of the bathers on their way to and from the baths. ...

2. In the case mentioned by 'Confessor' it would have been wrong to refuse absolution, since, whatever is to be said of the system of mixed bathing, the penitent was not in the occasion of sin and is not stated to have been the occasion of sin to others.'
[Prof.] J.M. Harty [DD.]
(*Irish Ecclesiastical Record*, vol. I, 5th series, January June, 1913, pp 71–2)

11.7. *The South Beach with a cluster of bathing tents in about 1930; this postcard also shows the amusements on Bray Head in full swing.*

The state of affairs around the railway station improved in the mid 1930s. In 1935 the International Hotel at last came back to life, if only in a humbler capacity as the A.P. Friendship Holiday Association Home. Shortly afterwards the remaining floors of the Marine Hotel were remodelled in an attractive contemporary style and it was reopened as the railway buffet, continuing in business until the early 1970s. There seems to have been a general upswing in tourism at that time and a number of new hotels appeared on Strand Road.

The railway companies had previously taken the main role in promoting Irish resorts such as Bray in Britain, but from the 1920s a new impetus came with the establishment in 1925 of the Irish Tourist Association. Hotels across Ireland were enrolled in the association, funding came from local authorities, and guides and maps were produced for free distribution in Britain, North America and elsewhere. Government funding was provided for the tourism industry from 1939 with the establishment of Bord Cuartaíochta na hÉireann, the first Irish Tourist Board.

Bray continued to grow slowly during the twenties and thirties. The main development was of two kinds: infill on the roads between Main Street and the seafront; council housing in Little Bray and at the south end of the town in the Vevay Road area. There was little development on the sea front except for the addition of houses between Royal Marine Terrace and martello tower no. 2. Much of the infill consisted of bungalows, many of them distinctively orange-roofed. Those lining Florence and Galtrim Roads were relatively substantial; those further away from the town centre on the Meath, Putland and Sidmonton Roads were for the most part of modest dimensions. In many respects they resembled the typical dwellings aimed at the retirement market then being erected in British resorts, although in practice many were rented out in the summer months.

INTERNATIONAL HOTEL: REOPENING

'Yet another cause for rejoicing is the announcement that the International Hotel will be reopened in the summer as a hostel run by the Guest House Association of Hyde Park, London. This hotel, once the most fashionable of all Bray's large hotels, has stood empty since the Great War, and has passed through many vicissitudes in the last twenty years. During the War it was used as a hospital for limbless soldiers, and I have often wondered why it was not taken over by the Hospitals' Trust for a convalescent home — ideally situated, as it is, so near the sea and the promenade. In 1931, when the River Dargle overflowed its banks and numbers of people were left homeless until the water subsided, the owner of the International, Mr. Bethel, generously put the hotel at the disposal of the refugees, who camped out in its spacious rooms, sleeping on borrowed mattresses on the floor. Every Armistice Day the ceremony at the War Memorial is watched from the balcony by Lady Powerscourt, Lady Meath, and members of the Women's section of the British Legion in Bray, but except for this one day in the year the building is lifeless. Now its imposing façade is being painted; its windows shine once more, and through them one catches a glimpse of great activity on the part of painters at work on the interior decoration. The gardens around the hotel have been weeded, the bushes clipped, and now geraniums bloom where once was an unsightly litter of papers. When the redecoration is completed the International will once more take its place among the attractive features of Bray town.

(*The Irish Times* 11 May 1935; reprinted in Times Past, *The Irish Times* 11 May 1995)

The grounds of Galtrim House also gave way to development with the construction of Galtrim Park, also lined with bungalows. A dozen new houses were built on the south side of Herbert Road on either side of the junctions with the present Davitt and Parnell Roads — these two new roads were laid out, though not yet built upon. The Main Street area lost its last major slum with the demolition of Hudson's Terrace in the early 1930s, creating an open space until the houses of Fatima Terrace were built by the council some years later.

Possibly the biggest change in Bray housing in these decades was the number of houses that were built by the local authority. Unlike the new

11.8. *Postcard showing northern part of the Esplanade in about 1930, with the Ladies Baths at the left.*

11.9. *A bungalow typical of those built between Main Street and the sea front between 1918 and 1939. These were rented out, often for the whole summer season.*

bungalows near the sea front, this part of Bray's development had no connection with the town as a seaside resort, it was simply typical urban renewal as the council tackled the necessary clearance of old cottages, some dating back to the eighteenth century.

In Little Bray the houses on Back Street and adjoining areas were finally cleared and replaced by terraced rows of two-storey houses. The first new houses were those of St Patrick's Square, built in 1922 on the open space at the junction of Castle Street and the Upper Dargle Road. Substantial clearance and more building took place in Little Bray from 1935, when the medical officer of health and the town surveyor reported, not for the first time, that a large number of old properties around Back Street and Castle Street were unfit for human habitation. The windows of the new houses in St Columkille's Terrace at first looked across to the modest structure of Little Bray Castle, but that was demolished by the council during road widening on Castle Street in 1937–8. (The demise of the castle was noted in the *Irish Press* of 2 May 1938, which declaimed: 'The demolition of the castle severs a link with the invaders of Ireland'.) The Castle Street/Back Street area was to be again dramatically altered in the 1960s with the construction of the Little Bray Shopping Centre. Many Little Bray residents were moved to the new estate of more than 250 houses off the Vevay Road which included Wolfe Tone Square and O'Byrne Road, a move that, although physically the distance was not great, represented a considerable dislocation for an old-established community.

Those residents who moved, however, at least no longer had their lives blighted by the periodic flooding of the Dargle. Following from the disastrous floods of 1905, the Dargle burst its banks after heavy rain in September 1931 and again in November 1965, both times inundating the houses of the old Bray Commons area to a depth of several feet and forcing their occupants to seek temporary refuge elsewhere, a pattern that was to be repeated in the twentieth century yet again with the Hurricane Charlie floods of 1986.

LITTLE BRAY: BAD HOUSING

'We beg to report that the houses, lanes, courts and alleys described herein … are unfit for habitation owing to bad drainage, lack of proper sanitary accommodation, dilapidation, ill-lighting, and ill-ventilation, and are dangerous to the inhabitants of the areas mentioned …'
(Representation to Bray Urban District Council, 10 April 1935, quoted in Colbert Martin, *A drink from Broderick's Well*, Dublin, 1980, p.137)

Bray in the late 1930s was, then, in good heart; the prospects for tourism were good and many of the old housing eyesores had been cleared. But war was to intervene again with the outbreak of hostilities between Britain and Germany in September 1939, and the town was plunged into the years of 'the Emergency'. The annual influx of visitors from Britain ceased as Irish Sea travel became curtailed. The International Hotel became an army base, as did a large Victorian house, Killarney Wood on Herbert Road, which was otherwise in use as a holiday hostel. The nation-wide Local Security Force, part of which later became the Local Defence Force, began recruiting in Bray in June 1940 and in 1942 another of Bray's large Victorian houses, Rock Brae House on Vevay Road, became its headquarters.

There were allotments in the People's Park. Severe petrol rationing, limitations on the use of domestic gas and electricity, lack of any solid fuel other than turf from the Dublin and Wicklow mountains, and all the other privations of wartime even in a neutral state affected Bray and its visitors. The rail service, its locomotives fuelled by turf and anthracite, became erratic and slow so that the Dublin–Bray journey could take two hours; bicycles became the only certain mode of urban transport. With the greater range of aircraft than in the first world war, proximity to the east coast brought its own risks; the bombing of the North Strand, Dublin, in May 1941 took place not so many miles up the road.

11.10. *Bray visitors in a postcard of* c. *1940.*

The war brought one unexpected bonus to Bray. The Agincourt scenes of Shakespeare's *Henry V* — a film made in wartime Britain as a boost to morale — were shot in Co. Wicklow where the necessary resources for massed crowd scenes with large numbers of horses were available. The filming was spread over two months in the summer of 1943 and Bray's flagging businesses received a welcome tonic. This filming foreshadowed the opening of the Ardmore Film Studios at the edge of the town in 1958.

To some extent Bray's role as a seaside resort continued even in the wartime absence of British and American visitors — it remained a favourite destination for Dubliners and for honeymooners and holiday makers from other parts of Ireland, and acquired some Irish visitors who might otherwise have travelled abroad. Bray was particularly popular, both then and after the war, with Dublin's Jewish community based around Clanbrassil Street and Portobello; with their strong overseas connections they had travelled extensively in Europe prewar and with wartime restrictions turned instead to Bray. The Harcourt Street railway line served them very conveniently, both for day trippers and for families who moved out to Bray for a month, or in many cases for the whole summer, with the menfolk commuting daily into the city. There were also at least two kosher boarding houses, Rubinstein's Kosher Hotel, and perhaps a temporary synagogue. Bray was sometimes jokingly called 'Little Palestine' (equivalent to 'Little Israel' today), and there was apparently even a popular slogan: 'Give us back Bray and we'll give you back Jerusalem'. (Historian Dermot Keogh records an opinion of the late 1940s that the number of Jewish families moving to Bray caused a slump in house prices due to anti-semitism; however *Thom's directory* does not list any noticable number of Jewish surnames among the householders of the time.)

THE JEWISH COMMUNITY IN BRAY

'I think we rented our first bungalow for two months at £40 per month. The owner, a Miss Freestone, needed the extra money to supplement a very small income from her parents' investments. … The letting arrangements between the summer visitors and the bungalow owners were based mainly on trust. No leases were drawn up but I never heard of any disputes. The people renting the bungalows usually looked after them as if they were their own.'
(Nick Harris. *Dublin's Little Jerusalem*. A. & A. Farmar, Dublin, 2002, p. 140)

When Irish Sea travel restrictions were lifted after the war ended in 1945, Bray experienced its last flowering as a resort. It finally came into its own, with large numbers of visitors coming from Britain and Northern Ireland. These visitors, free to take holidays again after the war years, came to southern Ireland as a joyful escape from continuing austerity. While clothes rationing ended in 1949, it was 1954 before food rationing was finally abolished in grey post-war Britain; helpings of meat, butter and other dairy products of the size served in Bray's hotels and cafés had not been seen across the water since 1939. Bray was perceived as 'exotic', offering the inexperienced all the novelties of a foreign holiday without any of the challenges of a unfamiliar language and currency. In this period, too, tight currency restrictions meant that Ireland was one of the very few foreign destinations readily available to British travellers, however much they might have longed for continental holidays.

CROSS-CHANNEL VISITORS: ESCAPE FROM ECONOMIC RESTRICTIONS

> *'To the cross-channel visitor, cigarettes, beer, sweets and entertainments are cheaper here than at home. Food, butter, milk, eggs and meat of all kinds are plentiful. Ireland may not be a land flowing with milk and honey, but who wants milk and honey these days when you can have bacon and eggs, or ham and cabbage or roast beef or in fact anything in the food line you could wish for? The kiddies will just love it. You will just love it yourself.'*
> (*Official guide to Bray*, Dublin, *c.* 1950, pp 100–101)

Many of the post-war visitors to Bray came from Belfast, Glasgow, the English Midlands and the cotton and woollen mill towns of Northern England. These were the people who might equally well spend their week or fortnight of annual holidays, Saturday to Saturday, in other resorts around the Irish Sea. Whole towns and their neighbours went on holiday for the same week — the 'Lancashire week', the 'Yorkshire week' — while the mills were closed. Factory workers from Northern Ireland came to Bray particularly in the 'marching season' around 12 July. The numbers were supplemented by Scottish visitors, followed in late August by Irish holiday makers.

One aspect of a holiday that would seem strange today is that in the days when the 'weekly bath' was customary, boarding houses did not provide their guests with much in the way of washing facilities. A dip in the sea was regarded as sufficient between one Saturday and the next; only the better premises had washbasins in bedrooms and taking a bath often involved an extra charge. Visitors were also expected to be out of the premises during the day except at mealtimes — a source of some discomfort in wet weather given

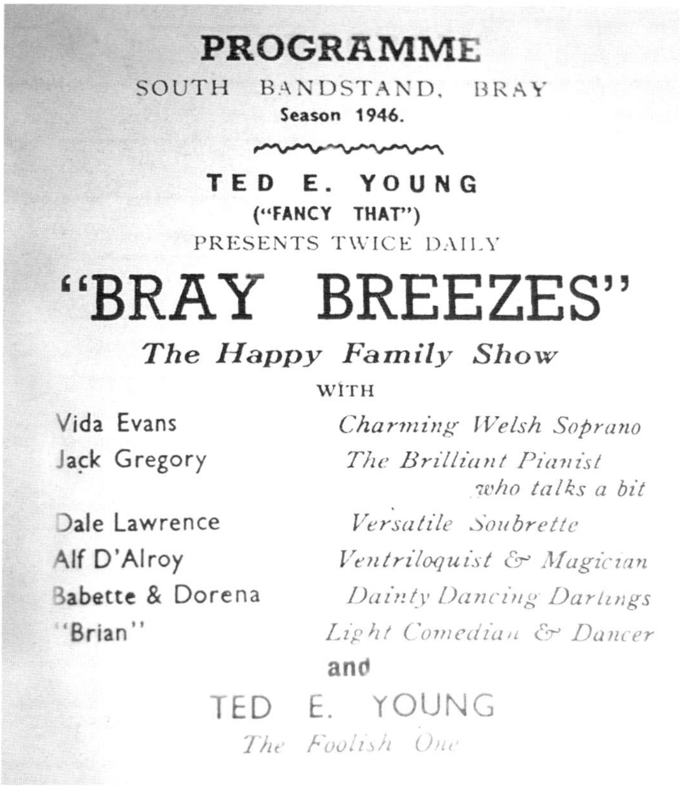

11.11. *'Bray Breezes' poster, 1946*

that Bray's range of indoor entertainments was limited. Holiday makers accepted this as normal; it was only when numbers began to decline that British resorts made a major commitment, not duplicated in Bray, to build substantial indoor recreational facilities.

With this influx of post-war visitors, the International Hotel at last resumed its original role as a major hotel, catering both for the better-off overseas visitors — including the occasional Hollywood film star — and for Dublin families who drove down for Sunday lunch; its post-war advertisements claimed that it had accommodation for 200 guests. But although the International was still the largest hotel in Bray, the three next largest — the Royal, the Esplanade and the Bray Head — all charged slightly more. There were by now a considerable number of hotels on the sea front, offering some two hundred and fifty bedrooms in all, although many were still unlicensed. Walking southwards down the Esplanade in the 1950s the visitor would pass in turn the Fitzwilliam Hotel at nos 2 and 3 Fitzwilliam Terrace, the Edenvale Hotel at no. 10 Brennan's Terrace, the Holyrood Hotel, the Grand Hotel at nos 1 and 2 Wave Crest Terrace, the Rath-na-Seer Hotel next door and the Eagle Hotel occupying the four houses of Montebello Terrace. Three of the houses of Esplanade Terrace were the Kinvara Hotel; the fourth was the Belmont. Next came the Dunallen, Lacy's, the Esplanade, the Strand and the Bray Head Hotels.

The *Official guide to Bray* of *c.* 1950 listed eighteen guest houses in various parts of the town; only five had 'H & C', i.e. a washbasin, in all rooms while eight had no rooms with washbasins. In *Thom's directory* a high proportion of houses on Strand Road were listed under a woman's name — eight out of eleven in Brennan's Terrace, for instance — which reinforces the impression that these were mainly boarding houses.

BRAY HEAD HOTEL

> *'BRAY HEAD HOTEL. This hotel adjoins Bray Head at the south end of a strand much patronized at holiday time. I judged it to possess a certain quality enhanced by its spacious public rooms and their comfortable, modern but restrained appointment. A dance floor ringed by tables in the dining room, lounge bar fitted with wall seats, sun lounge, balconies and some rooms with private baths were duly noted.'*
> (W.G. McMinnies, *Signpost: an independent guide to pleasant ports of call in Ireland.* London, 1951 supplement)

Albert Walk was a busy thoroughfare, with a majority of the terraced houses converted to small shops selling 'Bray rock', ice cream, postcards and souvenirs. It was also one of the areas where visitors could find arcades and 'fun palaces' with games of pongo (bingo) and slot machines. By 1970 there were plentiful cafés on the sea front, including six on Brennan's Terrace. There was a cluster of amusement arcades at the north end, on Fitzwilliam Terrace, in addition to premises close to Bray Head. The amusement park on Bray Head again offered a variety of rides and entertainments.

For three months each year the town was packed to capacity with holiday makers, to the extent that beds were sometimes hard to find. At peak times special late showings were even put on in the cinemas to cater for those who had nowhere else to spend the night. Bray Amusements Committee was reformed; this time its entertainments included sandcastle-building competitions and open-air film shows as well as the more traditional military and pipe band performances and fireworks. It also published a Bray guidebook. There were also events organised every year during An Tóstal

(Ireland at Home), an annual festival held in many Irish cities and towns from 1953 onwards, and which in Bray included art exhibitions, concerts and open-air dances.

The Esplanade still offered Punch and Judy shows, donkey rides, and variety performances in the south bandstand. Rowing boats, paddle boats (propelled by the feet), an amphibious vehicle and several motor boats carried visitors out into the waves. There were swimming galas — a craze inspired by Hollywood films starring the photogenic swimming champion Esther Williams — in Bray Cove Baths, which from 1958 were run by Bray Urban District Council and in the Municipal Baths. Both baths were identified with swimming clubs, the Bray Cove Swimming Club and the Bray Swimming Club respectively; the latter had a reserved area of beach adjoining the Municipal Baths where there was a charge for non-members to swim. Barry's Field, once cultivated by the Belgian refugees and which housed entertainments from the 1930s, was in part transformed into the Fáilte Games Park in 1965; its bowling green catered, as it still does, for visitors who enjoyed a sedate pastime.

An assortment of vehicles ranging from jaunting cars and vis-à-vis to modern coaches took visitors on short or long journeys along the sea front and out into the countryside. The three cinemas were still in business, and shows were put on in the Little Flower Hall, a former boys' school on Herbert Road. The Arcadia Ballroom hosted top British bands and singers, and was a popular venue, the numbers swelled by Dubliners out for a romantic evening

***11.12.** Diving boards behind the Municipal Baths reserved for members of Bray Swimming Club.*

11.13. *Post-war crowds on the Promenade and Esplanade in Bray's last great flowering as a resort.*

on 'dance excursions' that combined ballroom entrance with rail tickets. There was also dancing twice a week in the Braemar Ballroom on the sea front.

For twenty years from 1950 to 1970 Bray had a novel entertainment in the shape of the chairlift that ran part way up Bray Head. Here a new entrepreneur was involved — the grocery-chain owner Eamonn Quinn, who had launched the Red Island Holiday Camp, the first in Ireland, in north County Dublin in 1947 (seaside holiday camps had been introduced to Britain by Billy Butlin in 1937 and were proliferating post-war). He saw possibilities in Bray and bought the large field around Raheenacluig church, together with the Eagle's Nest higher up the Head. The chairlift, with its seven bright yellow pylons and able to carry 350 passengers an hour, was built to link the two; it was unique in Ireland. It proved very popular, but maintenance costs were heavy, and it closed when business began to decline. Much of the field was converted to a pitch-and-putt course, replacing a smaller course nearby.

AERIAL CHAIRLIFT

> *'Bray Head. An Aerial Chairlift Ropeway to the Eagle's Nest, modelled on Swiss lines, is operated during the holiday season from Easter onwards. A small charge is made. All the northern part of the Head is a public park (75 acres). Through it a pathway, 'The Great White Way', has been laid out, leading to the Eagle's Nest, where dancing and refreshments are provided.'*
> (*This is Wicklow; the green guide series*, Dublin, [c. 1960], p. 13)

Dawson's Amusement Arcade on the seafront near Bray Head was to prove more enduring. The family built a substantial concrete building in the 1950s to house a range of diversions such as would be familiar in a British resort: dodgems, a ghost train, the 'super waltzer', hobby horses, a variety of slot machines. The building was to be further enlarged in the 1980s and is still a highly conspicuous feature of the south end of the sea front. There was a major attempt in about 1955 to provide indoor facilities at the north end of the Esplanade 'to attract the monied people', with a proposal to develop Bray Harbour as an amusement centre. The Tourist Traffic Act of 1952, establishing Bord Fáilte (the welcome board), had allocated funding for profit-making schemes, and Bord Fáilte was optimistically asked for the considerable sum of £500,000 to finance building on the old Dock Terrace land, by now the property of the Council. Like the nineteenth-century plans for pavilions, however, funding was not available and the proposal came to nothing.

THE INTERNATIONAL HOTEL IN 1947

> *'We climbed a wide staircase and entered an enormous bedroom which looked out on a blank wall. It was quite dark. There was no hot water. We were told that the hotel had only just been derequisitioned and that they cannot install a hot-water system for some time to come. We are paying ten guineas a week and there's no hot water. ... There is a bleak bare lounge, the door of which will not stay shut. This is unoccupied. There are two bars downstairs. These are so much occupied that it is difficult to force one's way to the counter.'*
> (S.P.B. Mais, *I return to Ireland*, London, 1948, p. 80)

A vivid, if rather uncomplimentary, picture of a stay in Bray in the immediate post-war period is painted by the English writer S.P.B. Mais in *I return to Ireland*, published in 1948. For most of August 1947 he and his family stayed in the newly reopened International Hotel. The entrance was crowded with 'expensive-looking' cars, with visitors basking in armchairs outside the porch — the hotel had no gardens to speak of after the Arcadia Ballroom was built. There was only one telephone in the hotel, a much sought-after one at the reception desk, and there was no hot water in the bedrooms. It is not surprising, considering that the vast building had not functioned as a hotel since 1914, that there were problems. British hotels and resorts were facing similar post-war difficulties, with the greater complication that many British beaches were disfigured by stout anti-invasion pillboxes and barbed wire.

The Mais family found the Esplanade 'black with trippers, most of whom lay in deck-chairs with their backs to the sea and their faces to the sun'. They thought the sea cold for bathing, the sands 'inconsiderable', and were shocked by the litter. Shunting trains at Bray station kept them awake. There were no facilities for entertainment in the hotel, not even a 'ping-pong' table, and their evening amusement was to 'swing on the gates of the level-crossing and watch the succession of trains take the trippers back to Dublin',

11.14. *Amusement arcades offered a range of diversions.*

trippers who minutes before had stood ten-deep on the platform. But they admired the old-fashioned thatched, whitewashed cottages close to Bray Head and the Head itself, where they climbed up to the Eagle's Nest, and Mais's young daughters were pleased with the three cinemas, the jazz bands in the Arcadia Ballroom and the amusement parks.

The family was impressed by the choice of food, with plentiful eggs and bacon for breakfast and a 'wonderful cold buffet' for lunch including salmon and duck. They were surprised at the abundant meat in the butchers' shops, very different from the 'shillingsworth' a week allowed in England, and delighted to find that they could take four pounds of it back with them through customs. They also revelled in the purchase of new clothes, free of the necessity for clothing coupons.

ATTRACTIONS OF BRAY, 1950s

'Bray Head with cliff walk, chair-lift and restaurant. Mile-long promenade, sandy and shingle beach, and amusement centre. Bathing also at Naylor's Cove pool. Rowing-boats and pedalos for hire. Fresh-water and sea-fishing; tennis and croquert; horse-racing at Leopardstown (6 m.) and Dublin tracks; 9-hole golf course near town, 4 others (including internationally-famous Woodbrook) within easy reach; 5 ballrooms; 2 cinemas; 2 theatres.'
(Advertisement for Doon-a-Lawn Hotel, Strand Road, in *This is Wicklow*, Dublin, c. 1955)

'Bray was the special place, a train ride away, in a train made up of small compartments, each window secured in place by a leather strap. Bray, with its chip shops and the amusements, the bumper cars and slot machines, the beach and the esplanade, the deck chairs, the band on the bandstand, the kiosks selling sweets and ice cream and buckets and spades and little propellers on a stick to hold up and watch the breeze make them spin, the chair lift up Bray Head, and at the top of Bray Head the crucifix overlooking it all. The vacuum flask had not yet become commonplace. You brought cups and tea, a teapot, and you bought one of those little triangular cartons of milk. There were houses near the seafront with handwritten signs announcing that you could buy boiling water there. We bought boiling water, we went down to the beach, my mother made tea, and we had a picnic.'
(Gene Kerrigan. *Another country: growing up in '50s Ireland*. Gill & Macmillan Ltd, Dublin, 1998, p. 79)

11.15. *South end of Bray beach in a 1960s postcard.*

11.16. *Naylor's Cove's bathing pools,* c. *1950.*

The entertainments provided in these years and the crowds that patronised them were very different from those originally envisaged for 'the Brighton of Ireland'. The shows and amusements were comparable with those available in Morecambe, Southport and Rhyl, if nowhere on the same scale as those of the outstandingly popular Lancashire resort, Blackpool. While most British visitors thoroughly enjoyed the ambience of post-war Bray, others who expected some resemblance to the grandeur of the 'real' Brighton inevitably suffered disappointment.

11.17. The chairlift operated for twenty years until 1970 (postcard view courtesy John Hinde).

Two dominant features of resorts elsewhere, in North Wales for example, that Bray never acquired were a holiday camp and a summer residential complex of caravans or home-made shacks. The two post-war holiday camps near Dublin, Mosney's and Eamonn Quinn's Red Island, were both north of the city. (Quinn did, however, bring large parties of Red Island campers down to Bray to his enterprises.) Caravan and hut development took place mainly on sand-dune sites, again on the north side and also further south at Brittas Bay. The Bray area perhaps offered no suitable locations for such low-cost and spreading tourist accommodation; the town lost out on business, but was spared the accompanying eyesores.

The post-war resurgence of Bray was only to last for some twenty years. The decline in the numbers of British and Northern Ireland visitors that took place in the years close to 1970 was attributed at the time to the onset of the Northern troubles from early 1969 onwards and, more locally, to conflicts on the sea front between rival gangs of 'mods' and 'rockers' and the murder of a Scottish holidaymaker in 1959. But the change was part of a much more fundamental shift in holiday patterns, both here and abroad.

11.18. *Poster for the chairlift and Eagle's Nest.*

Most importantly, the arrival of reasonably-priced air travel meant that holiday makers could soak up sunshine and acquire a becoming tan on a warm mediterranean beach instead of hoping for the best in an uncertain climate. Moreover the new widely-available package holidays took all the anxiety out of reaching these distant and enticing destinations. In 1961 less than one in eight British holiday makers went out of Britain and Ireland; by 1985 one in three went to the continent, a third of these to Spain and the Balearic Islands. Most resorts were severely affected — Douglas, Isle of Man, for instance, saw the number of hotel and guest-house bedrooms available halved over that same period. In Bray the number of rooms in hotels and guest houses registered with Bord Fáilte fell from over six hundred in 1969 to two hundred in 1985.

At the same time the arrival of the mini car in 1959 had marked the start of universal car ownership — within a few years family cars replaced the host of bicycles and mopeds on the streets of Irish towns. Bed and breakfast

11.19. *Postcard of the sea front in the 1960s; the Eagle's Nest and chair lift are just visible on Bray Head.*

homes catering for the traveller began to appear across Ireland; the holidaymaker was freed from the necessity of travelling by train and remaining in the same spot for an entire week or fortnight's break. Dún Laoghaire noticeably lost business as British visitors brought their own cars over on the ferry and set off further afield before their first night's stop. Bray was affected in the same way; it was both too close to Dublin and Dún Laoghaire and yet not sufficiently central to be used as a base for a visit to the capital. Motor transport also freed both day trippers and holiday makers to seek sandy and uncrowded beaches further from Dublin, in Co. Wexford, for instance. The Saturday spectacle of visitors arriving by train and struggling down the streets carrying heavy suitcases was coming to an end.

In 1970, though, Bray was about to experience a new period of expansion, one as important as that of the 1850s and 60s. By far the largest town in County Wicklow (Arklow, the second largest, was half its size), the town was to reinvent itself yet again. But the impetus that created the new Bray of the last decades of the twentieth century was one that had no connection with the pleasures of sea bathing, seaside amusements, or even buckets and spades.

Postscript

Bray reinvented 1970–2006

12.1. *Victorian Bray today; the last vacant plots have been filled with houses.*

Bray was to survive the end of the resort era better than many comparable seaside towns around the Irish Sea. Much of this was due to its proximity to Dublin, which saved it from the fate of resorts such as Rhyl and Colwyn Bay in North Wales or Morecambe in Lancashire where no alternative roles filled the gap and where the town stagnated for decades, dependent largely upon attracting day trippers from big cities thirty or forty miles away. Bray, on the other hand, has had major new roles as a dormitory town and as a manufacturing centre, as well as other lesser and perhaps more transitory ones. Employment today is year-round, rather than seasonal. At the same time some of Bray's seaside resort atmosphere has remained, to the benefit of both residents and visitors, and the promotion of the town as a destination for day-trippers is part of the official development plan.

Bray's role as a dormitory town for Dublin was not a new one, residents travelled to city businesses even in the nineteenth century — in the 1890s the railway company offered to run an early train 'to accommodate suburban merchants and their assistants' if a hundred passengers could be guaranteed. By the 1950s many workers, mainly white-collar, commuted by train from Bray to Dublin daily, a daily migration only slightly affected by the closure of the Harcourt Street line on 31 December 1958. Already there was the attraction of lower house prices as well as the benefits of clean air and sea views, advantages of living in Bray that have continued to the present day.

The subsequent decline of Bray as a resort coincided neatly with the considerable expansion of Dublin. The city had spread out on the south side as far as Foxrock by the 1960s; by the end of the century the built-up area extended south of Shankill so that today only a narrow green belt separates residential south Dublin from the northern outskirts of Bray. It was inevitable that Bray would take part in this suburban growth — indeed the town's development presaged the kind of commuter-driven expansion that by the new millennium was taking place throughout Leinster. The boundary of Bray Urban District was extended to the south-west in 1979 to reflect the expansion and to enclose a substantial area with potential for development. The population has continued to rise steadily, if not spectacularly, reaching almost 27,000 in 2006.

***12.2.** Bray Railway Station — buses and taxis have replaced the jaunting cars.*

The Charnwood estate, 178 houses built in the 1960s, was one of the first of Bray's new suburban estates. It was followed in subsequent decades by the great spread of family housing between the Killarney and Herbert Roads, extending as far as the Kilmacanogue River and engulfing both green fields and the gardens of large houses such as Ardmore, Fairy Hill and Glen Lucan; in many cases the houses themselves were demolished. Elsewhere much of the remaining open space has been built upon. Little Bray has acquired new private housing estates at Corke Abbey and more recently along Old Connaught Avenue, together with extensive public housing on the north and west sides of the Upper Dargle Road.

The spacious grounds with their choice views that were once the preserve of the Putland family have at last been eroded. George Putland's landscaped grounds and walled garden, safeguarded for over a hundred years by the Loreto nuns, now shelters St Thomas's Community College, together with houses in the walled garden and close to the convent building itself at Sans Souci Wood. At Charles Putland's Bray Head House, converted to the Presentation College for boys in 1921, the grounds have been cut into by the erection of houses and apartment blocks at The Headlands. Within these new developments, however, both of the Bray houses connected with the influential Putland family have survived. Some of Bray's early-nineteenth-century bathing lodges are also still extant, notably Eden View (part of the Marino Centre), Bay View (Novara House) and Arbutus Lodge.

Despite past experience and relying upon drainage and flood protection works carried out on the Dargle after the Hurricane Charlie floods of 1986, houses have been built on the old marshland at Seapoint Court and, as part of a government-sponsored urban renewal scheme, on the site of the mill and brewery at The Maltings; the latter scheme involved the final obliteration of Bray's last surviving early man-made feature — the medieval mill race. Most recently apartment blocks have been sited on part of the flood plain along the Upper Dargle Road, giving the area near the picturesquely named 'Valley of Diamonds' an almost urban ambience.

As a dormitory for Dublin, Bray has the great advantage of being both a settled town of some size and also — crucially — of being served by a rapid rail link. The 1958 closure of the Harcourt Street line and the reduction of services on the coastal route in 1960 was compensated for in 1986 when the coastal line was electrified as far as Bray, so that commuters have use of the speedy, if sometimes overburdened, DART (Dublin Area Rapid Transit). At the station, the Atmospheric Bar serves city workers where once Edward Breslin sustained tourists in his refreshment rooms, and much of the parking

12.3. *Part of the new civic offices complex, with St Cronan's reflected in the facade of the Mermaid Theatre.*

12.4. *Sea front with new pebble sea defences.*

round about is occupied by the cars of commuters. The revitalised railway does, however, also tempt day trippers once again to enjoy the journey out to Bray by train. The Harcourt Street line may yet be reincarnated, at least in spirit, if proposals to extend the Luas line to Bray are realised.

The road network has also undergone changes since 1970. Just as the main road to Wexford was diverted from Main Street in the early 1800s, so a further diversion became necessary by the 1980s, when the volume of traffic between Dublin and the south-east, including the port of Rosslare, along the Upper Dargle Road became intolerable. European Union funding contributed towards the motorway stretch of the M/N11, bypassing Bray in 1991 along a pleasingly scenic route to the west of the town. In 2005 the M11 was connected to the M50 Dublin ring road, making Bray readily accessible from southern, western and northern national routes. The Southern Cross link built between the N11 and the Greystones road in the mid 1990s, slicing across the lands of Killruddery, has prompted further development, residential, commercial and industrial, on the gentle north-facing slopes of the Little Sugar Loaf. Short of swallowing up the Killruddery demesne altogether, expansion directly south of Bray has almost reached its limit.

There was some growth of industry in Bray in the 1930s, with the establishment in Little Bray of industries such as Haughton's ink, gum and polish works, and Solus Teo's light-bulb factory in the grounds of Corke Abbey — white silica sand for the latter was imported through Bray harbour and the factory was for many years Bray's largest employer, adding the manufacture of bakelite and plastic items to its concerns after 1945. Industrial Yarns, opened in 1958, provided more employment nearby. The Dargle & Bray Laundry also in Little Bray alongside the river, was a major employer until its closure in 1972. The oldest industrial site in Bray, the old mill and brewery complex, housed a wallpaper factory in the brewery buildings from the time Bray Electric Works closed in the mid 1930s until the 1980s. But until the last quarter of the twentieth century Bray had few pretensions to being a manufacturing centre. Today the focus has moved from Little Bray to the south side, with extensive manufacturing and business estates, supported by the Industrial Development Agency, off the Boghall and Southern Cross Roads. Ardmore Studios on the south-west, a centre for the production of many major films, adds another dimension.

For some years after 1970 Bray became notable for the range of private nursing homes, opened in large Victorian houses and catering for the elderly of Dublin at prices lower than those in the capital itself. From a peak of twenty or so, the numbers have fallen again to a handful as the houses have returned to private occupancy or office usage. Their closure has accompanied a rise in the demand for both office space and apartment accommodation.

The centre of Bray lost its oldest surviving focal point with the closure of St Paul's Church in 1973 (it was deconsecrated on 1 April 1977 and converted into an organ factory), but the outskirts gained new foci with the building of the Church of Our Lady Queen of Peace on Putland Road as early as 1946 and again in the 1980s with the grouping of the new courthouse and library with St Fergal's Church off the Boghall Road. At the start of the twenty-first century central Bray has undergone significant renewal with the opening in 2003 of the new Civic Offices and the Mermaid Arts Centre in the grounds of St Cronan's.

More major development is promised at two sites, one central, one peripheral. One is the Florentine Centre, a proposed retail and residential complex between Florence and Quinsborough Roads, with its entrance breaking through old properties on Main Street. The second is on a large tract of land in Little Bray freed by the removal, also in 2003, of Bray Golf Club to a new longer course at Ballynamuddagh on the Greystones road. This land, extending in all to some sixty-two acres (twenty-five hectares), is likely to see the construction of a major mixed use development, with plans in for more than 50,000 square metres of retail space, 1,250 apartments and a new bridge across the mouth of the Dargle. The inclusion of buildings on the flood plain below Bray Bridge has caused some controversy, with residents of Little Bray anxious that this area should remain open space to mitigate future floods and Bray retailers concerned that the new shopping centre should be as close as possible to the existing retail area. So far Main Street has retained its vibrancy into the twenty-first century, but its traders will become increasingly hard pressed with the proliferation of this new generation of vast shopping centres, both in Bray and in other areas around Dublin such as the Dundrum centre, twelve kilometres away, opened in 2005.

Problems with damage to the sea wall and flooding along the Esplanade, particularly at the north end, have continued to exercise the minds of Bray's councillors over the years. Hurricane Charlie swamped the sea front as well as Little Bray in 1986. In November 2000 the familiar combination of heavy rainfall and easterly gales yet again left the sea front under several feet of water. By then work had already begun on a controversial coastal protection scheme involving breakwater groynes, beach replenishment by the importation of thousands of tonnes of material from offshore, and repair of the south harbour pier. The appearance of the beach at the north end has been irrevocably changed, with a wide shingle bank to the level of the promenade railings obliterating what once were places for bathing and playing in the sand. But the sea wall and Esplanade have been protected, at least for the foreseeable future.

The completion of the sewage pumping station near the harbour in 1990 caused sufficient improvement in the seawater quality for Bray's beaches to be awarded a European Union 'Blue Flag' in 1991 and again later. But as standards have become more stringent the town's lack of secondary sewage treatment has told against it; recently it failed to acquire the flag although it was 'compliant with EU minimum values'. Bray's beaches remain popular, however, even though bathing in the chilly Irish Sea has lost much of its attraction except for the hardy.

Many of the buildings important to Bray's history as a seaside resort have not survived. The International Hotel was destroyed by fire in 1974 and this major site was vacant for twenty years, just as the hotel had been empty in 1920s and 30s, until the present leisure centre, Bray Bowl, was built. The remaining floors of the Marine Station Hotel have been replaced by an office building; only the terrace survives, its balustrade reinstated, with a public house underneath. The Turkish Baths were demolished in 1980. The wing of the Royal Hotel at the junction of Quinsborough Road, built by John Quin as his new hotel in 1854, was demolished in 1982 and replaced by shops and offices; the hotel, however, still flourishes, with 130 bedrooms and a leisure centre. Lacy's Bray Head Hotel still stands at the south end of the Esplanade,

***12.5.** 1930s kiosks still sell seaside refreshments.*

12.6. *The site of the International Hotel today.*

but as a ghost of its former self. Joseph Kelly's hot and cold baths at the sea edge is a shell and Naylor's Cove baths have all but vanished. The Arcadia Ballroom, a major focus of entertainment, was destroyed by fire in 1962 and its site is now a warehouse. A large number of buildings are now protected structures, however, including the Town Hall and the surviving martello tower. The comprehensive review of Bray's buildings completed by the National Inventory of Architectural Heritage in 2004 highlights the richness of what remains, both in the surviving sea-front hotels and in the many distinctive houses and terraces.

The location of the railway close to the sea front has continued to have repercussions, particularly in the limited access to Strand Road for large commercial vehicles unable to pass under the low bridges and forced to use Quinsborough Road's level crossing. Bray Bridge, on its ancient site, remains under pressure as the only convenient road access to Bray from the north; a proposal in the 1990s to build a second bridge across the west end of the People's Park proved unpopular.

The earls of Meath's interests in the town are much reduced, though not entirely extinguished. Killruddery House is still their family home and tourists flock to the house and the unique seventeenth-century gardens. The Town Hall stands proudly as a monument to their long connection with Bray, and indirectly as a surviving reminder of the medieval manor and its lordship; heavily restored in the 1990s, the upper floor still houses the

12.7. Bray sea front in 2006 — little different from postcard views of a century earlier.

council chamber of Bray Town Council, and the fast-food restaurant on the ground floor may be imagined as the modern equivalent of the former market hall. Another faint echo of medieval life also persists — the surname Byrne, a reminder of the mountain-based clan that once so alarmed the early settlers, is one of the most common in Bray.

The most enduring feature is the Esplanade, giving Bray its inimitable style, one that is still enjoyed by residents and visitors alike. A treasured amenity, various plans have been put forward in recent years for its enhancement and new lighting and paving have been added. At the same time the modern view along the Promenade towards Bray Head is essentially the same as it was a hundred years ago. The surviving amusement arcades at the south end are a reminder of times past and still provide traditional fun. The National Sea Life Centre provides an entertainment point at the northern end. The villas and terraces along Strand Road have seen a resurgence of commercial usage in recent decades and the hotels and bars have been modernised and extended. The area between Main Street and Strand Road has a distinctive quality not affected by development. Bray residents no longer depend upon an annual influx of visitors for their livelihoods, but everyone in Bray can enjoy the surviving ambience of what was for over a hundred years the most important seaside resort in Ireland.

Presbyterian church.

Bray church.

Bibliography

The principal primary sources for the history of Bray are the records of the Meath and Pembroke estates (Killruddery House, Co. Wicklow; National Archives of Ireland), Bray Town Commissioners and Urban District Council records (Wicklow County Library) and the pages of contemporary newspapers, particularly the *Freeman's Journal* (1763–1924) and the *Wicklow Newsletter* (1885–1927) for which researchers are fortunate to have a comprehensive collection of extracts compiled by C.B. Coghlan (Bray Public Library). The various calendars of state papers and statute rolls of the Irish parliament deal with the early period. *Thom's Irish almanac and official directory* (Dublin 1844, etc.) has detailed information on Bray from 1861 onwards and *The Dublin/Irish Builder* founded in 1859 often describes developments. The *Wicklow People* (1904–) and the *Bray People* (1979–) cover the twentieth century. Full citations for many references taken from these sources can be found in K.M. Davies, *Irish historic towns atlas no. 9, Bray*. Dublin, 1998 (reissued in Anngret Simms, H.B. Clarke and Raymond Gillespie (eds), *Irish historic towns atlas volume II*, Dublin, 2005), where factual material on the component parts of Bray is set out in detailed tabular form.

Bray has been well served by the Ordnance Survey, with maps of 1837–8, 1909 (printed 1911), 1937 (printed 1941), and, most particularly, the maps at ten feet to one mile (1:500) that show the town in great detail as it was in 1870 (printed 1871–8); there are also field books and field name books (National Archives of Ireland). Maps and printed tenement valuations for Rathdown Union are also valuable (Valuation Office, Dublin, originals of maps in National Archives of Ireland).

Of the many publications that deal with the history of Bray or some aspects of it, Liam Clare's *Victorian Bray: a town adapts to changing times* (Maynooth Studies in Local History: no. 18, Dublin, 1998) is invaluable. Isolde Moylan did pioneering work with her Trinity College, Dublin, 1972 moderatorship thesis 'The development and growth of Bray, *c.* 1750–1900'.

The book of Bray, edited by John O'Sullivan, Tony Dunne and Séamus Cannon (Blackrock, 1989), contains substantial articles by a number of contributors. Canon G.D. Scott's *The stones of Bray* (Dublin, 1913, reprinted Bray, 1984) remains the most inspirational — if sometimes fanciful — history of early Bray. The web site of the National Inventory of Architectural Heritage (www.buildingsofireland.ie; 2004) describes and illustrates over six hundred individual buildings, an important source illuminating the development of the town's fabric.

The two Bray local history societies have made a significant contribution with their journals *Bray Historical Record: Journal of the Old Bray Society* (nos 1–8, 1986–2000) and *Journal of the Cualann Historical Society* (nos 1–5, 1985–2004). The Old Bray Society has published *A pictorial history of Bray, Co. Wicklow*, in four volumes: *The seafront and environs* (Bray, 2003), *The town and its people* (Bray, 2004), *The town and its people parts two and three* (Bray, 2005, 2006), all by Henry Cairns and Owen Gallagher; Arthur Flynn's *Bray in old photographs* (Dublin, 2004) covers some similar ground. Cyril Dunne's *A history of golf in Bray: Bray Golf Club centenary book* (Bray, 1997) includes several little-known nineteenth-century views.

Bray is included in Brian White's 'Transport, education, religion ... in the towns and villages of County Wicklow, 431 A.D.–2004 A.D.' (privately circulated). In the 1980s James Scannell issued a series of information sheets in conjunction with the Old Bray Society.

The story of seaside resorts outside of Ireland has been well-documented, both in general and for individual resorts. A few general sources drawn on are Alain Corbin, *The lure of the sea: the discovery of the seaside, 1750–1840* (Paris, 1988; English translation, London, 1995); Lena Lencek and Gideon Bosker, *The beach: the history of paradise on earth* (New York, 1998); and John Walton, *The English seaside resort: a social history 1750–1914* (Leicester, 1983).

Other general Bray sources and publications

Brien, Christopher. *In the lands of Brien*. Bray, 1984.

[Cairns, Henry, and Gallagher, Owen]. *A stroll through the historic streets of Bray, etc*. Pamphlet series. Bray, 2006.

Clare, Liam. *Exploring the coast from Killiney to Bray*. Foxrock, 1993.

Davies, K.M. 'For health and pleasure in the British fashion: Bray, Co. Wicklow, as a tourist resort, 1750–1914'. In Barbara O'Connor and Michael Cronin (eds), *Tourism in Ireland: a critical analysis*. Cork, 1993, pp 29–48.

Davies, K.M. 'Bray'. In Anngret Simms and J.H. Andrews (eds), *Irish country towns*. Cork and Dublin, 1994, pp 131–41.

Davies, K. Mary. *Bray, Co. Wicklow; Irish historic towns atlas no. 9*. Insert with *History Ireland*. Bray, 2004.

Dublin Evening Post, 1778–1875.

D[onnelly], N[icholas]. 'A parochial history of Bray', parts 1–[14]. In *Bray Catholic Monitor*, ii (1897); *BCM*, iii (1898). 'Parochial history of Bray and Enniskerry', parts [15]–[31]. In *BCM*, iv (1899); *BCM*, v (1900).

Eaglais Pheadair Naofa, Bré Beag: St Peter's Church, Little Bray, 1837–1987. [Bray, 1987].

Faulkner's Dublin Journal, 1726–1825.

Flynn, Arthur. *History of Bray*. Cork & Dublin, 1986; reprinted with revisions, 2004.

Garner, William. *Bray architectural heritage*. An Foras Forbartha, Dublin, 1980.

Hannigan, Ken and Nolan, William (eds). *Wicklow: history and society*. Dublin, 1994.

Loughrey, Francis. *Old Bray and its neighbourhood; some forgotten stories about the 'Gateway to the Garden of Ireland'*. Bray, 1998.

Mac Aongusa, Brian. *The Harcourt Street Line: back on track*. Blackrock, Co. Dublin, 2003.

Martin, Colbert. *A drink from Broderick's Well*. Dublin, 1980; reprinted 1981.

Martin, Colbert. *The bridge below the town (1940–1980)*. Bray, 1984.

National Inventory of Architectural Heritage. *An introduction to the architectural heritage of County Wicklow*. Bray, 2004.

Ó Cathaoir, Brendan (ed.). *Holy Redeemer Church, 1792–1992: a Bray parish*. Bray, 1991.

Ó Cathaoir, Eva, and Forde, Jason (eds). *A portrait of Bray*. Bray, 1998.

Paine, Derek. *A pictorial history of Greystones, Bray & Enniskerry, 1835–1980*. Greystones, Co. Wicklow, 2001.

[Reid, J.A.] *St Andrew's Presbyterian Church, Bray, 1858–1958*. [Bray, *c*. 1958].

Saunders's Newsletter. 1767–1878.

[Seymour, F. J.]. *A hundred years of Bray and its neighbourhood from 1770 to 1870 by an old inhabitant*. Dublin, 1907; facsimile reprint Blackrock, 1978.

Shepherd, W.E. *The Dublin & South Eastern Railway*. Newton Abbot, 1974.

The way to Bray: celebrating 150 years of railway services, 1854–2004. Iarnród Éireann booklet, [Dublin], 2004.

Tynan, Eddie. *In the shadow of Bray Head: a memoir*. Bray, 2006.

Selected additional sources for individual chapters

Prologue: The scene is set

Corlett, Christiaan, 'The prehistoric ritual landscape of the Great Sugar Loaf'. In *Wicklow Archaeology and History*, i (1998), pp 1–8.

Corlett, Chris[tiaan], 'The Rathdown slabs — Vikings and Christianity'. In *Archaeology Ireland*, xvii, no. 4 (2003), pp 28–30.

Leahy, Daire, 'Burnt mounds and flint scatters — recent finds on the Little Sugar Loaf'. In *Wicklow Archaeology and History*, ii (2002), pp 27–34.

Davies, K.M., 'A note on the location of the Roman burial site at Bray, Co. Wicklow'. In *Archaeology Ireland*, iii, no. 3 (1989), pp 108–109.

Chapters 1 & 2. 'Our manor of Bree': Bray 1173–1311 & 'In continual fear of like mischief': Bray 1311–1666

Brooks, E.StJ. 'The de Ridelesfords'. In *Journal of the Royal Society of Antiquaries of Ireland,* lxxx, (1950), pp 115–38; lxxxii, (1952), pp 45–61

Davies, K.M. 'The castle of Bray'. In *Journal of the Cualann Historical Society,* [no. 2] (1986), pp 22–5.

Dix, E.R. McC. Dix, 'The lesser castles in the Co. Dublin: Little Bray'. In *Irish Builder*, 1.9.1898, p. 133.

Gilbert, J.T. (ed.). *Register of the Abbey of St Thomas, Dublin*. London, 1889.

Map of part of the estate of Messrs Donnellan, Mac Mahon & others situate in the county of Wicklow, to accompany *Rental of lands adjacent to the town of Bray ...to be sold ... 24th day of June, 1858 ...*, scale 50 ft to one inch. Copy in Meath estate papers, 408a.

O'Byrne, Emmett. *War, politics and the Irish of Leinster, 1156–1606*. Dublin, 2003.

O'Keeffe, Tadhg. 'Medieval frontiers and fortification: The Pale and its evolution'. In F.H.A. Aalen and Kevin Whelan (eds), *Dublin city and county: from prehistory to present*. Dublin, 1992.

Pavia, Sara, and Bolton, Jason. 'Solid as a rock? Oldcourt Castle, Co. Wicklow.' In *Archaeology Ireland.*, xiii, no. 2 (1999), pp 15–18.

Price, Liam. 'Powerscourt and the territory of Fercullen.' *Journal of the Royal Society of Antiquaries of Ireland,* lxxxiii, (1953), pp 117–32.

Price, Liam. 'The grant to Walter de Ridelesford of Brien and the land of the sons of Turchil.' *Journal of the Royal Society of Antiquaries of Ireland,* lxxxiv, (1954), pp 72–7.

Price, Liam. 'The Byrnes' country in Co. Wicklow in the 16th century.' *Journal of the Royal Society of Antiquaries of Ireland*, lxvi, (1936), pp 41–66.

Turner, Joseph. 'Old-court Castle, Co. Wicklow, 1799'. Watercolour. Royal Irish Academy SR 3 C 33.

White, N.B. (ed.) *The red book of Ormond*. Dublin, 1932.

Chapter 3. More settled times: Bray 1666–1760

Bushe, Letitia. 'View of the village of Bray, Co. Wicklow, 1736'. Watercolour. National Gallery of Ireland.

Cary, G.S. 'Hearth money roll for Co. Dublin'. In *Journal of the Kildare Archaeological Society*, xi (1930–3), pp 386–466.

Down Survey. 'The barony of half Rathdowne in the county of Dublin', 'The half barony of Rathdowne in the county of Wicklow', [1657], scale 160 Irish perches to an inch. Reproduced Ordnance Survey, Southampton, 1908.

Gurrin, Brian. *A century of struggle in Delgany and Kilcoole ... 1666–1779*. Dublin, 2000.

'Partition of the manor of Great Bray, 1 April 1666'. Meath estate deed 161/Pembroke estate deed 321.

Pender, Séamus (ed.). *A census of Ireland circa 1659*. Dublin, 1939.

Price, Liam. 'The hearth money roll for Co. Wicklow'. In *Journal of the Royal Society of Antiquaries of Ireland*, lxi, (1931), pp 164–78.

Chapter 4. 'A very small town'; Bray in 1760

Barker, Jonathan. 'A map of Great Bray in the county of Wicklow surveyed in 1762 by Jonathan Barker', scale 20 Irish perches to an inch. In 'A book of maps and references to the estate of the right honorable Richard Lord Viscount FitzWilliam ...'. National Archives of Ireland 2011/3/1.

Davies, K.M. 'A newly-discovered reference table to the 1764 map of Bray, Co. Wicklow'. In *Wicklow Archaeology and History*, ii (2002), pp. 83–6.

Nevill, Jacob. *An actual survey of the county of Wicklow by Jacob Nevill, 1760*, scale [1 Irish mile to an inch]. Dublin.

Nevill, Jacob. 'A map of several plots of ground and houses in and about the town of Bray ...', 1764, scale [12 Irish perches to an inch]. Also redrawn copy, lacking Little Bray, by [B.T.] Patterson and [John] Kempster, 1873. Meath estate papers G46.

Rocque, John. *Actual survey of the county of Dublin*, scale 2 ins to the mile. London, 1760.

Taylor, George, and Skinner, Andrew. *Maps of the roads of Ireland, surveyed in 1777*. London and Dublin, 1778.

Chapter 5. 'Sea bathing and goat's whey': Bray 1760–1850

A.B. *Observations made during a short excursion to Dublin, Delganny &c. in 1823*. Liverpool and Dublin, [1823].

Bartlett, W.H. 'Bray', 1842. Engraving. In N.P. Willis and J.S. Coyne, *The scenery and antiquities of Ireland*. i, London, [1842], p. 110.

Brocas, S.M. View of the Dargle mouth, *c*. 1800. National Gallery of Ireland, reproduced in Cyril Dunne, *A history of golf in Bray*, p. 6.

Chart, D.A. (ed.) *The Drennan letters*. Belfast, 1931.

Cowen, William. 'Bray near Dublin, 1825'. Pen and ink drawing. In private ownership.

Corlett, Christiaan and Medlycott, John (eds). *The Ordnance Survey letters: Wicklow*. Roundwood, Co. Wicklow, [2000].

Duncan, William. *Map of the county of Dublin*, scale [2 1/4 inches to 1 mile], Dublin, 1821.

Harbison, Peter (ed.). *Beranger's rambles in Ireland*. Bray, 2004.

Herity, Michael (ed.). *Ordnance Survey letters: Dublin*. Dublin, 2001.

Lucas, Richard. *General directory of the kingdom of Ireland*. ii, Dublin, 1788.

Map of properties east of Main St, Bray, with reference table, 1841, scale [2 ft to the mile]. Meath estate papers G39.

Nattes, J.C. 'The mill at Bray, 1807'. Pen and wash. In private ownership.

Nevill, A.R. *The county of Wicklow … taken from actual surveys*. 1st ed. 1798, reprinted 1814–34.

Nicholl, Andrew. 'Village of Bray, Ireland', [*c*. 1840]. Pencil drawing. In private ownership.

Nimmo, Alexander. Map of the shore at Bray showing proposed piers. [*c*. 1825]. National Library of Ireland 16 J 17(2).

O'Donnell, Ruan. *The rebellion in Wicklow 1798*. Dublin, 1998.

Pigot's national commercial directory of Ireland, 1824. Dublin, 1824.

Pratt, C.V. 'Bray, 1829'. Pencil drawing. In private ownership.

Putland estate maps, Bray Head and neighbouring lands. National Archives of Ireland M 6286/5.

Quin papers. In private ownership.

Rutty, John, *An essay towards a natural history of the county of Dublin*. Dublin, 1772.

Taylor, John. *The environs of Dublin*, scale 2 ins to the mile. Dublin, 1816.

The postchaise companion or traveller's directory. Dublin, 1784.

Wright, G.N. *A guide to the county of Wicklow*. London, 1822.

Chapter 6. 'A favourable bathing place': Bray in 1850

Clare, Liam, 'The Putland family of Dublin and Bray'. In *Dublin Historical Record*, liv, no. 2 (2001), pp 183–209.

'Fisheries: mouth of the Bray River, counties of Dublin and Wicklow'. Declaration by commissioners of public works and fisheries in Ireland, 1853. Copy with Meath estate leases 17.

Fraser, James. *Guide to the county of Wicklow*. Dublin, 1842.

General Valuation of Ireland. Printed tenement valuation, Rathdown Union (Little Bray), 1849; part of Rathdown Union (Bray), 1852. Manuscript town plan, *c.* 1849, scale five ft to the mile (1:1056). Valuation Office, Dublin. Map originals in National Archives of Ireland.

Lewis, Samuel. *A topographical dictionary of Ireland*, London, 1837, vol. i, pp 222–3.

Martello towers: county of Wicklow, 1859, scale 50 ft to an inch. London, 1862.

Vaughan, Edward. 'The estate of William, earl of Meath, in Great & Little Bray, 1853', scale 2 ft to the mile. Meath estate papers G40.

Chapter 7. 'The Brighton of Ireland': Bray 1850–70

Act for the Improvement of the Town and District of Bray, 23 July 1866, 29 & 30 Vict., c. 261.

Adamson, S.M. *Seaside piers*. London, 1977; reprinted 1983.

Bray improvements: plan shewing the extent of proposed township pier and works at Bray. [*c.* 1866], scale 6 inches to the mile. Meath estate deeds 573a.

Bray Gazette, 1861–3.

Clare, Liam. *Enclosing the commons: Dalkey, the Sugar Loaves and Bray (1820–1870)*. Dublin, 2004.

Clare, Liam. 'The enclosure of Bray Commons'. In *Bray Historical Record*, vol. I, no. 7 (2000), pp 28–33.

Davies, K. Mary. 'A lost Victorian treasure — Bray's Turkish Baths'. In *Journal of the Bray Cualann Historical Society*, no. 5 (2004), pp 12–18.

Gaskin, J.J. *Irish varieties*, Dublin, 1869; facsimile reprint Dalkey, 1987.

Godkin, James and Walker, J.A. *The new hand-book of Ireland*. Dublin and London, [*c.* 1870].

Gordon, John. 'Bray strand, 1858', scale 200 ft to an inch. Meath estate papers.

[Heffernan, D.E.] *Heffernan's illustrated plan of Bray*, scale 1 ft to the mile. [*c.* 1870]; facsimile reprint with commentary by K.M. Davies, Bray, 2000.

Holohan, J.R. 'Bray coastguard station'. In *Bray Historical Record*, no. 3 (1989), pp 44–51.

Lease of land near Bray, County Wicklow, 25 October 1860, between John Quin and William Dargan.

Nicol, Erskine. 'The seafront at Bray, Co. Wicklow', 1862. Pencil and watercolour. National Gallery of Ireland, Dublin.

'Plan shewing the disposition of the roads and intended improvements of Bray strand, 1859', scale 60 ft to an inch. Meath estate papers G42.

Plan of the Upper Commons of Bray as laid out in lots for sale, 1860, scale 132 ft to an inch.

Powell, G.R. *The official railway handbook to Bray*, Dublin, 1860.

Riall, Phineas. Diaries. In private ownership.

Shifrin, M.R. *Victorian Turkish baths: their origin, development, and gradual decline*. www.victorianturkishbath.org.

Vaughan, Edward. 'The estate of William, earl of Meath, in Great & Little Bray, 1853', scale 2 ft to the mile. Meath estate papers G40.

Wiseheart, J.S. *The tourist's illustrated guide book to Dublin, Kingstown, Bray, and the County Wicklow*. Dublin, 1865.

Chapter 8. 'All the advantages': Bray in 1870

[Craig]. *A guide to Bray and the picturesque scenery in its vicinity, Co. Wicklow: published by authority of the township commissioners*. Dublin, 1884.

General Valuation of Ireland manuscript revision books. Valuation Office, Dublin.

Martello tower no. 2. Personal communication, the late Colonel T.J. O'Brien.

Rental, map, particulars and conditions of sale of houses and premises in the town of Bray ... to be sold ... 28th day of March, 1922. Land Judge's Office, Dublin, 1922 (estate of Macrory and Coade).

Vestry minutes, Church of Ireland, Bray.

Chapter 9. 'This delightful locality': Bray 1870–1910

'Attorney-General *v*. Bray Township Commissioners and the Bray Pavilion Company (Limited)'. In *Law Reports (Ireland): Chancery Division*, vol. iii, 1879, pp 345–75.

Bray Township Act, 1881 (44 & 45 Vict., c. 143); Bray Township Act, 1890 (53 & 54 Vict., c. 161); Bray Urban District Council (extension of time) Act, 1900 (63 & 64 Vict., c. 115).

'Caretaker's lodge, People's Park, Bray, Co. Wicklow'. Line drawing. In *The Irish Builder* 23.2.1884.

Doran, A.L. *Bray and environs*. Bray, [*c*. 1905]; facsimile reprint, Bray, 1985.

Doyle, John. H.J. *Byrne and Company Limited: 1857–1982*. Bray, 1982.

Findlater, Alex, *Findlaters: the story of a Dublin merchant family 1774–2001*, Dublin, 2001.
Irish Tourist, 1894–
Joyce, Maureen. 'Bray town hall'. B.A. mod. thesis, TCD, 1997.
Martin, Colbert. *The woodcarvers of Bray, 1887–1914*. Bray, 1985.
Pertwee, Bill. *Beside the seaside*. London, 1999.
Prentice, Richard. 'Tourism'. In Robinson, Vaughan, and McCarroll, Danny, (eds), *The Isle of Man: celebrating a sense of place*. Liverpool, 1990, pp 248–67.
Royal commission to inquire into local government and taxation of towns in Ireland, report; mins of evidence; appendices part 1, H.C., 1877, [c 1676], xxxix, 1, pp 19, 211–37, 52.
Scannell, James. 'Two Victorian tram schemes for Bray'. In *Bray Historical Record*, vol. i, no. 7 (2000), pp 82–6.
Sullivan, Lucinda. *An address ... delivered before the British Association for the Advancement of Science, on Thursday, the 22nd August, 1878, being the occasion of their visit to the Cripples' Home, Bray*. Dublin, 1878.

Chapter 10. 'Bray, beautiful Bray': Bray in 1910

'Extract from Dublin fire chief's report for 1916'. In *Bray Historical Record*, no. 1 (1986), p. 39.
Meath, earl of. 'Letter re housing of the working classes'. In Cairns, Henry, and Gallagher, Owen, *A pictorial history of Bray, Co. Wicklow: volume two*, p. 69.
Moore, J.W. 'The rainstorm of August 24–26, 1905, in eastern Ireland'. In *Quarterly Journal of the Royal Meteorological Society*, vol. 32, no. 137, pp 1–10.
O'Riordan, Colum. 'The Dublin Artisans' Dwellings Company'. In *Irish Architectural and Decorative Studies; Journal of the Irish Georgian Society*, vii (2004), pp 156–83.
Porter, Frank. *Porter's post office guide and directory of the County Wicklow, 1910*. Dublin, 1910.
Scrapbook of the flood of 25 August 1905. Bray Public Library.

Chapter 11. Buckets and spades: Bray 1910–70

'Belgian refugees'. In *Bray Parish Quarterly Calendar* [Church of Ireland], spring 1915, p. 3; winter 1915–16, p. 3.
Delap, H.A. 'Recent protection works carried out on the sea wall, Bray'. In *Transactions of the Institute of Civil Engineers of Ireland*, lxxii (1945–6), pp 279–304.

Findlater, Alex, *Findlaters: the story of a Dublin merchant family 1774–2001*. Dublin, 2001.

Harris, Nick. *Dublin's Little Jerusalem*. Dublin, 2002.

Housing records, 1922–*c*. 1950. Garda Síochána archives, Garda Museum, Dublin Castle.

'International Hotel'. Description in *Irish Times*, 11 May 1935, reprinted 11 May 1995.

Ireland: gem of the sea: guide to Dublin & Wicklow section, Great Southern Railways. Dublin, [*c*. 1925].

Keogh, Dermot. *Jews in twentieth-century Ireland*. Cork, 1998.

Letters from St Helen's, Bray, April/May 1916. In private ownership.

Maguire, M.J., *Through the garden of Ireland: an illustrated guide ... issued by the Dublin and South Eastern Railway Co*. Dublin, 1912.

Mais, S.P.B. *I return to Ireland*. London, 1948.

Ní Chuilleanáin, Eiléan (ed.), *'As I was among the captives': Joseph Campbell's prison diary, 1922–1923*. Cork, 2001.

Official guide to Bray; issued by Bray Amusements Committee, Dublin, [*c*. 1950]

Pictorial and descriptive guide to Dublin and its environs, Ward Lock & Co., London, 1935–6.

Rivlin, Ray. *Shalom Ireland: a social history of Jews in modern Ireland*, Dublin, 2003.

'S. MacS.' 'The fight in the Bray area'. In *Dublin's fighting story, 1913–1921*. Tralee, 1947, pp 185–192.

The World's Fair, 1904–.

This is Wicklow; the green guide series. Dublin, [*c*. 1960].

Postscript: Bray reinvented 1970–2006

Annual *Bray Directory*, later *Bray and North Wicklow Directory*, published by the Bray Chamber of Commerce.

Bray development plans; Bray draft development plan, 2005–2011.

www.Braytowncouncil.ie.

www.braywatch.com.

Index

Adelaide Rd, 146, 206
Albert Walk, 295
Alexandra Terrace, 191
amusement arcades, 284, 295, 298, *11.14*
Amusement Park, Bray Head, 284, *11.7*, 295,
Anchor Tavern, 95, *8.1*, *8.2*, 187
Anglo-Irish Treaty, effect on Bray, 278
Anglo-Normans, 20, 29–35, 41
Aravon School, 206
Arbutus Lodge, 86, 136, 269
Arcadia Ballroom, 265, 282, *11.5*, 296–7, 300, 312
Archbishop Alen's Register, 42
Archbold family, 52 57, 72
Ardilaun House (Bray Lodge), 136
Ardmore Film Studios, 292, 309
Assembly Rooms, see Turkish Baths
Back St, 45, 61, 73, 74, *6.15*, 135, 136, 209, 273, 290
Ballymorris, 70
Ballywaltrim, 57, 70
band performances, 171, 172, 213, *9.3*, 242, 274
bandstands, 205, 275, 276, 296, 223, 242, 264, *10.10*, 282
Barker, Jonathan, map of 1762, 32, 46, 64–6, *4.1*, 68
Barrack Lane, 153
barracks, military, 33, *3.4*, *3.5*, 61, 62, *3.6*, *4.1*, *4.2*, 66, 98–9, 106, 112, 113, 187; fever hospital in, 102, 112
barracks, police, 193, *8.1*, 257, 277–8, 280
Barre, William, architect, 198
Barry family, showmen, 284
Barry's Field, 276, 282, 296
Barter, Dr Richard, 156, 157, 158, *7.15*, 196
Barter, Richard, scukptor, 156
Bartlett, W.H., view of 1842, *2.2*, 73, 110, *6.1*
bathing boxes, huts, machines, tents, 88, *5.6*, 93, 95, 128, 169, 170, 202, 220, 223, 233–4, 285, *11.7*
bathing lodges, 84–6, *5.2*, *5.3*, *5.4*, 122, 307
bathing place, men's, on Esplanade, 246
bathing practices and regulations, 79, 83, 84, 93, 170–1, 246–7, *11.2*, 281, 285, 286, 311
baths, see Kelly's, Railway, Municipal, Naylor's Cove, Turkish
battle of 1401, 43–4
Bay View, see Novara House

Beechurst (Rich View), 86
Belgian refugees, 276
Bellevue, 86
Belton Terrace, 136
Benson, Sir John, architect, 156
Black Death, 43
'black rents', 43
Bloody Bank (Sunnybank), 43–4
boat house, customs', 105, 127, 207
boating, see regattas
Boer war, effect on Bray, 210, 216
borough, medieval rural, 34; burgage plots, 36, 38
Brabazon Cottages, 268
Brabazon family, see Meath, earls of
Braemar Ballroom, 297
Bray Amusements (Improvement) Committee, 212–13, 234, 244, 275, 295
Bray Art Furniture Industry, 258, 277
Bray Auxiliary Hospital for Incurables, 268
Bray Bridge, 30–31, *4.1*, *4.2*, 54–5, 60–1, 62, *3.6*, 73, 5.11, 110, *6.1*, *6.14*, *6.18*, 184, 187, 234, 273, 312
Bray Club, *8.8*, 195
Bray Cottage, 117, 188
Bray Cove Baths, see Naylor's Cove
Bray Golf Club, 245, 272–3, 310
Bray Head, see Sans Souci
Bray Head Hotel, see Lacy's Bray Head Hotel
Bray Head House (Newcourt, Presentation College), 68, 84, *5.5*, 119, 142, 151, 175, 191, *8.6*, 307
Bray Head Park, 245, 263, 284
Bray Industrial Exhibition, 245
Bray Laundry, 268
Bray Library, 257–8
Bray Lodge (Ardilaun House), 136
Bray Pavilion Company, proposed concert hall and floral promenade, 213, 215
Bray races, 172, 244–5; see also racecourse
Bray Savings Bank, 136
Bray Township Acts, 179, 221, 229
Bray township commissioners, 174–6, 179, 217, 218, 220–21
Bray Urban District and Town Council, 259, 266, 306, 313
Brennan, John, 146, 159, 162, 191, 203, 211
Brennan's Parade, 146, 203, 253
Brennan's Terrace, 146, *8.13*, 203, 295
Breslin, Edward, 146, 147, 148, 149, 162, 172–3, 175–6, 190, 200, 202, 206, 211, 212, 213, 215, 216, 223, 226, 231, 234, 240, 264–5
Breslin's Royal Marine Hotel (Marine Station Hotel), 147–8, *7.5*, *7.6*, *7.7*, 150, *7.17*, 168, 169, 177, 179, 182, 183, 237, *9.19*, 247, 250, 255, 264–5, 276, 281, *11.6*, 287, 311
brewery, *5.11*, 99, 100, 131, 132, 179, 207–8, *8.16*, 209, 307, 309
Brí Chualann, name change, 280
Brighton, England, 83, 181, 233, 235
'Brighton of Ireland', use of term, 161, 168, 183, 263
Brighton Terrace, 188, *8.5*, 259
Broderick's Well, 74
Bronze Age remains, 20
Bushe, Revd John, 62, 74

Bushe, Letitia, *3.6*, 62
Butler, Theobald, 35
Byrne, Elizabeth, bathing attendant, 88, 128, 223
Byrne, W.H., architect, 229
Caernarvon, lord lieutenant, 221
camp, military, 49
Carlisle Grounds, 71, 130, 145, 163, 173, 183, 195, 199, 213, *9.5*, 217, 232, 234, 240, 277; Bray Aquarium Company, 217; roller-skating rink, 217
Carrickmines, 84
Carrickmines Castle, see Walsh family
Casement, Roger, in Bray, 206
Castle St, 45, *2.2*, *2.3*, 61, *6.15*, *6.16*, 135–6, *8.17*, 209, 272, 273, 290
castle, 'Ten pound', see Little Bray Castle
castles, see Great Bray Castle, Little Bray Castle, Oldcourt Castle, tower houses
chairlift, 284, 297–8, *11.17*, *11.18*
charabancs, 255, 10.4, 274
Charles I, 53, 58
Charnwood estate, 307
Cherry Garden, 59, 71, 130, 207
cholera, in Bray, 112
Christ Church, 153, 164, 190, 258, 275
Church Rd, 153, 190
Church Terrace, 38, 113, *6.3*, *7.10*, 153, 187, 231, 253
cinemas, 265, 274, 281–2, 296
climate, 15
Coach Inn (Sherman's), 137
coal yard, 207
coastal erosion, 17, 273
coastal protection works, *12.4*, 310–11
coastguard boat house, 205
Coastguard station, Putland Rd, 262–3
coastguard station, Strand Rd, 103, 128, 143, 204, 262
Cock Walk or Wake, 59, 71, 128
Coláiste Ráithín, 259
College Close, 70
commons, medieval, 37, 59
commons, sea front, *4.2*, 71
Commons, Upper and Lower, 74, *4.2*, 132–3, 164–5, 166, 266–7, *10.11*, 310
commuters to Dublin, 306
concert troupes, *9.20*, 242–4, 275, 277, 282
Cork Lodge, 137–8
Corke Abbey, 62, *5.5*, 74, 96, 138, 142, 143, 309
council chamber, see Town Hall
courthouse, Main St N. end, *3.3*, 93, *6.7*, 122, *8.1*, *8.2*, 193, 278
courthouse, Main St S. end, *3.2*, 68
Cowen, William, drawing of 1825, 66, 73
Crampe or Crump, Geoffrey, 42, 46
Critchley's Lane, see Pound Lane
cross, Bray Head, 264
cross, early-Christian, 25
Cuthbert, Mr, 127, 209; see also coal yard
cyclists, 234, 241, *9.21*, 248
Dalkey, 34, 41, 42
Dargan Terrace, see Duncairn Terrace
Dargan, William, 145–6, *7.4*, 154, 156, 157, 159, 163–4, 175, 179, 195, 207, 211

Dargle Glen, 80, 82
Dargle River, 17–19, 30, *4.5*, 71, 74, 126–7, 166, 207, 219; watering place, 63; see also dock, fishery, floods/protection works
DART, 307
Dawber, Edward Guy, architect, 227
deer park, 37
Delgany, 80; Fitzsimons Hotel, 149
Derdach, church and cottages of, 25, 36
Devil's Glen, 80
dispensaries, 136, 187
dock, Dargle estuary, 179–80, 207
Dock Terrace, see Harbour Terrace
donkey rides, 244, 285, 296
Donnellan, John, 113–4, 122–3, 135
Donovan, Jeremy, 58, 59
Doran, Alexander, 212, 253, 265
Down Survey, 52, 55, 57, 61
Dublin & South Eastern Railway Co, 273
Dublin Artisans' Dwellings Co. houses, 266–7, *10.12*
Dublin Rd, 209
Dublin, Wicklow, & Wexford Railway Co., 213
Dufresne, Charles, 162, 211, 212, 216, 220, 236
Duncairn (Dargan) Terrace, 93, 163–4, 195
Eagle Hotel, 262
Eagle's Nest café, 284, 297, 300, *11.18*
Eden View, see Prospect Cottage
Edward I, 35
Edward IV, perhaps in Bray, 50
Edwards family, Oldcourt, 57, 68, 118
Eglinton Rd, 198
Eglinton Ville, 23, *8.15*
electricity works/supply, 232, 266, 271, 309
Ellingsworth, Thomas, 54, 57, 59
Enniskerry, 80
Esplanade, 154, *7.12*, 156, 179, 201, 204–5, 218–23, 233–4, 241–2, *9.21*, 244, 247, *10.1*, 275, *11.19*, *12.7*, 313; see also martello tower no. 1, sea wall
Esplanade Hotel, 262, 294
Esplanade Terrace, 204
fair green, 209, 268
fairs, 57, 122, 136, 268
Fairy Hill, Main St, see Galtrim House
famines, medieval, 42; Great Famine, 100–102
Father Healy Nursing Association, 272
Fatima Terrace, 68, 121
fever hospital, see barracks, military
fireworks displays, 213
fishermen, fishermen's cottages, 71–2, 103–4, 127, 128, 132, 204, 220, 223, 233, 263
fishery, Dargle, 36–7, 42, 59, 72, 131–2
FitzWilliam family, 52, 54, 64–6, 70
Fitzwilliam Terrace, 128, 202, 203
floods, Dargle, Little Bray, 73, 135, 167, 269–72, *10.16*, 281, 290, 307
floods, sea front, 201, 202, 218–21, 310; see also Fontenoy Terrace, Martello Terrace
Florence Rd, 150–1, 206, 229, 257, 258

Fontenoy Terrace, 205–6; flooding, 219, *9.7*, *9.17*
footbridge, over Dargle mouth, 207
footpaths, paving of, 177
ford, near Bray Bridge, 23, 30, *1.5*, 61
ford, near weir, 55, *5.1*
forest, submerged, 17
forges, 68, 116, 117
Fox, William, 50
French School, 206–7
Galtrim House (Fairy Hill), 70, *6.8*, 122–3, 199, 266, 288; Hydropathic Establishment, 157–8
Galtrim Rd, 261–2, *10.8*
gas works/supply, 177, 188, 207, 219, 231–2, 266
geology, 15
Gladstone, William, British politician, 190
Glen of the Downs, 15, 80
goat's whey, 79, 84
Goldsmith Terrace, 195–6, *8.9*
Golf Club, Bray, 71
golf course, on seafront commons, 71, 72
Grand Marine Park, see Bray Head Park
Grand Marine Promenade, 221
Great Bray Castle, 32–3, *1.3*, *1.4*, 35–6, *1.5*, 43, 45–8, 54, 55, *3.1*, *4.1*, 66, 112–3; see also Rokelscourt Castle
Green Park, 59, 67, 89
Greystones, 249
Hall's Court, 115, 188
harbour, 125, 127, 179, 223–5, 298
Harbour (Dock) Terrace, 207, 231, 298
Haughton, Dr Edward, 157–8
hearth money rolls, 57
Herbert Rd, 54, *7.10*, 153, 179, 187, 257, 288–9
Herbert, Sidney, 54, 84, 86, 151, 153, 187, 190
Hibernian Bank, 187
Higher Park, see Mount Park
hiring place, Bray Bridge, 273
Hodson, Sir George, of Holybrooke, 70, 100, 101, 119, 162–3, 184, 187
Holy Redeemer Church and its predecessors, *5.9*, 113–4, 188, *8.4*, 229, 258
Holybrooke House, 119, 121
Holyrood House/Hotel, 262
Holywood, 262
Home for Crippled Children, see Sunbeam House
home rule, support for, 275
housing, Little Bray, 136, 273
housing, local authority, 267–8, 287, 289–90, 307
Hudson's Terrace, 121, 191, 231, 289
Hurricane Charlie, 307, 310
Imperial Hotel, 265
industry, 309
influenza epidemic 1918–19, effect on Bray, 277
International Hotel, 159–63, 167–8, 173, 183, 187, 210, 212, 230, 235–7, *9.16*, *9.19*, 245, 247, 250, 255, 265, 276–7, 280–1, *11.6*, 287, 288, 291, 294, 298–300, 311, *12.6*; Princess Patricia Military Hospital, 276–7
jaunting cars, jarveys and vis-à-vis, 149–150, 173, 233, 247, 253, 255, 263

Jewish community, Dublin, links with Bray, 292
Jobber's Lane, 66–7
Joyce, James, in Bray, 201
Keatley family, 58–9, 71, 93
Kelly, Joseph, 201, 221
Kelly's Baths, 169–70, *8.12*, 312
Kilbride, 55, 70
Kilcoole, gun running, effect on Bray, 275
Killarney, lands of, 55, 70
Killarney Rd, 57, 70, 89, 117, 178, 188, 259
Killarney Wood, 291
Killisk House convalescent home, 262
Killruddery, 49, 53, 56, 68–9, *4.4*, 72, 97, 107, 119, 121, 142, 309, 312
Kilmantain Place, *10.6*, 259
King Edward Rd, 259
kiosks, sales, *12.5*, 282
Kirke, George, 53
Lacy's Bray Head Hotel (John Lacy) 183, 205, 218, 219, 237, *9.17*, *9.18*, *9.19*, 255, 263, 294, 295, 311–12
Lacy's Hotel, Strand Rd, 262
Ladies' Baths, see Municipal Baths
landholders, 14th cent., 50, 17th cent., 57, 58, 60
Lawless, Sir Hugh, 42
Lawless, Maurice, 51
lighting, public, 176–7, 232; see also electricity works, gas works
Little Bray Castle, *1.5*, 44–5, *2.1*, *2.2*, *2.3*, 47, *3.1*, 58, 59, *4.3*, 135, 290
Little Flower Hall, 296
livery stables, 255
lord lieutenants and notables, visits by, 94, 96–7
Loreto Convent, 20, 69, *6.4*, 142, 151, 175, 189, 204, 230; convent schools, 189; see also Sans Souci
Lower Dargle Rd, 165, 166
Lucas's directory, 90–91, 127
mail coach routes, 68, 95, 136
Main St, 23, 38, 50, 55, 57, 63, 67–8, *5.7*, 113, 115, 164, 183, *8.3*, 187, 191, 192–3, 121, 225, 227, 234, *9.24*, *10.5*, 275, 310
Mais, S.P.B., opinion of Bray, 298–300
Maltings, The, 131
manor of Bray, 31, 35–40, 42, 52, 53; see also Meath family
Manse, Presbyterian, 198
'march, the', 41, 42, 43, 45
Mareys, Sir Adam de, 50, 52
Marine Station Hotel, see Royal Marine Hotel
Marino Centre, see Prospect Cottage
Marisco, Christiana de, 30, 35
market, weekly, grant of, 35
market house, near Bray Bridge, *3.3*, 121–2
market house, see Town Hall
market place, *3.3*, 35, 57
Martello Terrace, 71, *8.12*, 201; flooding, 219–20, 221
martello tower no. 1, *5.5*, 101, 126, 143, *7.11*, 205, 213, 219, 223
martello tower no. 2, 58, 71, *5.5*, 104, *6.9*, *6.10*, *6.11*, 124, 125, 143, 200, 312
martello tower no. 3, *5.5*, 126, 268
Mathew, Father, in Little Bray, 106

Meath, earls of, Brabazon family, 48, 52–3, 54–6, *3.1*, 58, 61, 65, *4.2*, 72, 100, 112, 119, 122, 124, 131, 132, 133, 172, 175, 179, 190, 191, 203, 225–9, 259, 260, 266, 269, 272, 273, 312; lords of the manor, 53, 132, 164, 213, 215, 225–6, 229, 312
Meath Arms Inn, see Royal Hotel
Meath Hospital Convalescent Home, 269, 272
Meath Industrial School for Girls, see Royal Drummond Institution
Meath Rd, 54, 58, 151, *7.8*, 206
Mermaid Arts Centre, *12.3*, 310
Methodist chapel, Brighton Terrace, *6.3*, 116, 188, 259
Methodist church, 198
milestone, 73–4
mill and brewery, *1.2*, 32, *1.5*, 54, 55, *3.1*, 62, *3.6*, *4.2*, 72–3, *4.6*, *5.12*, 131, 207–8, *8.16*, 307, 309
Mill Lane, *6.14*, 131
Mill or Night Park, 55, *3.1*, 67, 89
Moran, Charles, 60, 67, 72, 91
motor cars, 234–5
motorway, M11, 309
Mount Cashel Arms Inn, 91
Mount Herbert, 187
Mount Park or Higher Park, 58, 124
Municipal Baths (Ladies Baths), 213, 215–6, 223, 245, 247, *11.8*, 296, *11.12*
name plates, street, 233
Naylor's Cove, 245–6, 263, 281, 296, 300, *11.16*, 312
Nevill, Jacob, map of 1764, 65–6, *4.2*, 72
Newcastle Mackinegan, 34, 42
Newcourt, Putland Rd, see Bray Head House
Newcourt, Vevay Rd, see Sans Souci
Newenham Deane & Son, Sir Thomas Manley Deane, architects, 227, 259, 269
Newtown Vevay, 57, 119
Night Park, see Mill Park
Novara Ave, 67, 68, 121, 150, 191
Novara House (Bay View), 68, *5.2*, 86, 121, 191
Novara Terrace, 207
nursing homes, 309–10
obelisk, Bray Head, 264
O'Byrnes, 41–2, 43–5, 313
O'Connell, Daniel, in Bray, 106
O'Kelly, Edmund, 162
Old Connaught Ave, 74
Oldcourt, 68, 70, 119, 175, 191
Oldcourt Castle, *2.4*, 49, 119, 259, 260
Ordnance Survey, maps of Bray, 88, *5.13*, *5.14*, *6.2*, 117, 123, 184, *8.1*, *8.4*, 205, 225, 253, 254
O'Tooles, 41–2
Our Lady Queen of Peace Church, 310
Pale, The, 41, 43
Parochial Hall, 258
Partition of 1666, 54–5, 57, *3.1*
Pembroke, earls of, 54; see also Herbert, Sidney
penny dinners, Little Bray, 273
People's Park, 74, 164–5, 208–9, 269, *10.14*, *10.15*, 291
pier, fishing, proposed, 223
pier, seaside, proposed, *7.23*, 180–2, 216–7, 225
pierrots, see concert troupes

Pigot's directory, 91–2
population and housing figures, 57, 58, 89–90, 102, 119, 210, 306
Porter's directory, 253–5, 273
pound, *3.2*, 68–9, 121, 192, 227
Pound Lane, 117, 188, 189, 231, 259
Powell, G.R., *Railway handbook*, 168, 182, 195
Powerscourt Arms, Enniskerry, 149
Powerscourt estate and waterfall, 34, 79, 80, 82
Powerscourt family, Wingfield, 70, 116–7
Presbyterian chapel, Main St, 116
Presbyterian church, St Andrew's, 196, 198
Presbytery, Herbert Rd, 257
Presentation College, see Bray Head House
Prince of Wales Terrace, *8.7*, *8.8*, 195
Princess Patricia Military Hospital, see International Hotel
Prospect Cottage (Eden View, Marino Centre), *5.3*, *5.4*, 86, *8.1*, 117–8
Purcell's Field, 231
Purcell's Terrace, 188
Putland family, 21–22, *0.6*, 68, 88, 100, 102, 107, 118, 119, 129, 151, 175, 191, 205, 262–3, 307; see also Bray Head House, Sans Souci
Putland Rd, 151, 206, 276
Quin family, 91–4, 101, 113, 121, 122, 128, 144–5, 156, 159, 175–6, 193, 211
Quin's Hotel, see Royal Hotel
Quin's Walk, 93, *5.9*, 95, 122, 123, 144, 145, 195
Quinsborough Rd, 144–5, 150, *7.13*, 164, 178, 193, 195, 198–9, *10.9*, 256
Quinsbray coach service, 93–4, 95, 122
racecourse, Bray commons, 132–5; see also Bray races
Rack Rent House, 272
Raheenacluig, 23–5, *0.7*; well 24–5, 57, 113
Railway Baths, 169
railway, 107, 109, *7.1*, *7.2*, *7.3*, 140–7, 148, 149, 177, 167, 168, 213, 273, 292, 306, 307, 309; station, 124, 144, 146, *7.21*, 177–8, 183, 199, *9.15*, 245, 255, *12.2*, 307, 309
railway, light, Bray–Enniskerry, 218
railway, switchback, proposed, 217
ratepayers' grievances, 230
Rathmichael, 42
Raven's well or Regan's well, 139
Ravenswell House, *3.1*, 58, 59, 63, 71, *5.5*, 138–9, 142, 143, 226, 245, 272
Ravenswell Rd, 74, 166, *7.19*, 226
rebellion, 1798, effect on Bray, 97–100
Red Book of Ormond, 35
regattas, 104, 171–2, 174–5, 212, 244, 274, 278, *11.4*, 284
rental of 1284, 33, 35–7
rental of 1311, 33, 35–8
Riall, Phineas, 182, 190
Rich View (Beechurst), 86
Ridelesford, Sir Walter de, 25, 29–32, 34–5, 38, 53
Ridelesford, Sir Walter de, junr, 30
Rising, Easter 1916, effect on Bray, 277–8

Rock Brae House, 291
Rock of Bray, 20, 68
Rocque, John, map of 1760, 65–6, 73
Rokelscourt Castle, 42–3
roller-skating rinks: Carlisle Grounds, 217, Esplanade, 282; Royal Hotel, 257
Romano-British burials, 20–23
Romantic Movement, 79
Royal Drummond Institution (Meath Industrial School for Girls), 260, *10.7*, 277
Royal Hotel (Quin's Hotel), 60, 67, 91–5, *5.8*, 100, 103, 121, 122, 133, 139, 149, *7.18*, 164, 168, 182, 183, *8.2*, 192, 193, 237, 257, 278, 280, 281, 294, 311; see also Quin family, Quin's Walk
Royal Marine Hotel, Royal Marine Terrace, 281
Royal Marine Hotel, see Breslin's Royal Marine Hotel
Royal Marine Terrace, 200, *8.11*
St Andrew's National School, 257
St Cronan's, *6.6*, 121, *12.3*, 310
St Mary's Convent, Graney, 31, 52
St Paul's Church and predecessors, 25, *1.1*, 32, *1.5*, 50–51, *2.5*, 54, 55, *3.1*, 62, *3.6*, *4.1*, 66, 70, *5.10*, *5.11*, 110–12, 187, 190, 257, 275, 310
St Peter's Church, 106, 137, *6.17*, 272; parish hall, 137
St Peter's presbytery, 272
St Thomas's Abbey, Dublin, 31, 34, 38, 53
Sans Souci (Newcourt, Bray Head), 20, *4.2*, 69, *5.5*, 88, 107, *6.4*, 117, 118–9, 123, 128, 151, 189, 191; see also Loreto Convent
Scalp, The, 15, 79, 82
School Lane, 117
schools, 68, 116–7, 129, 136, 137, 131, 257, 259, 272
Scott, Canon G.D., 66, 22, 253, 259
Scraphall, *4.2*, 67, 91
sea, early opinions of, 82
sea travel, 82–3, 168–9; see also wrecks
sea wall and promenade, 211, *9.1*, 220–23, 225, *9.8*, *9.9*, *9.10*, *12.4*, 310–11; see also coastal erosion, protection works
Seafield House, 84, 191
Seapoint House, 58, 127, 130
Seapoint Rd, 38, 62–3, *3.6*, 70, 71, 130, 145, 151, *7.9*, 178, 207
sewers, 177, 178–9, 231
Seymour, Robert, 127, 130
Seymour's Dock, 127, 130, 179, 207
Shankill, 34, 42
Sharkey, Robert, 71
shelters, sea-front, 223, *9.11*
Sherman's public house (Coach Inn), 137
shipping, 127
Sidmonton Rd, 206
Sidmonton Sq., 206
Sisters of Charity, 272
Slater, William, architect, 190
Slí Chualann, 23
smuggling, 104–5
Southern or Sotheron family, millers, 72, 131, 132, 175
Stones of Bray, see Scott, Canon G.D.
storms, effects of, 127, 128, 225; see also floods
Strand Rd, 145, 153–4, 178, *8.14*, 202–6, 240, 253, 294–5

Strandville, 84
Sun Inn, 60, *4.2*, 67, 91
Sunbeam House (Home for Crippled Children), *10.13*, 268
Sunnybank (Bloody Bank), 43–4
Sunnybank Inn (Wicklow and Wexford Hotel), 136
Swan River, 49, 54, *3.1*
swimming galas, 296
Synge, John Millington, in Bray, 206
Taylor, John, map of 1816, *5.5*, 87–8, 89
technical school, 259
tennis courts, 223, 282
Thompson, Dr, monument to, 255, 257
touring from Bray, 79–81
tower houses, Fassaroe, Killruddery, Old Connaught, 49
Town Hall, 68, 225–9, *9.12*, 245, 312–13; wyvern drinking fountain, 227–8, *9.13*
Trafalgar Private Hotel, 262
tramways, proposed, 218
tuberculosis, 84
Turkish Baths (Assembly Rooms), 156–8, *7.14*, 164, 173, 177, 178, 195, 196, *8.10*, 237, 239–40, 244, 265, 270, 281–2, 311
Turk's Head, see White Lion
Tyrconnell, earl of, 53, 54–6, *3.1*
Uí Briúin Chualann, 22–3, 30
Upper Dargle Rd, 43–4, 74, 95–6, 165, 209
urinals, 223
Vanguard, HMS, off-shore collision, 245
Vevay Rd, 57, 68, 89, 117, 178, 188
vicars of Bray, 50, 52
Victoria Hotel, 262
Vikings, 22, 23
villas, 84, 86, 96
vis-à-vis, see jaunting cars
visitors, post-1945 from Britain and Northern Ireland, 293, 302
visits to Wicklow beauty spots, 173
Waller, Dr, 175
Walsh family, Carrickmines, 41, 43, 48, 49
war of independence, effect on Bray, 277–8
wars, world, effect on Bray, first, 275–7, second, 291–2
water supply, 74–5, 176–8, 230, *9.14*
Weld, Isaac, 101, 139
White Coons, 264, *9.20*
White Lion (Turk's Head), *4.2*, 67–8, 91, 150
Wicklow and Wexford Hotel (Sunnybank Inn), 136
Wicklow county, creation of, 73
Wicklow Mountains, 15, 40, 41, 79
Wilde, Sir William and Oscar, 204
William Henry Elliott Home for Little Children, 272
Woodbine Lodge, 87, 122
wrecks, shipping hazards, 102–3, 105–6
wyvern drinking fountain, see Town Hall